Communication Convergence in Contemporary China

US–CHINA RELATIONS IN THE AGE OF GLOBALIZATION

This series publishes the best, cutting-edge work tackling the opportunities and dilemmas of relations between the United States and China in the age of globalization. Books published in the series encompass both historical studies and contemporary analyses, and include both single-authored monographs and edited collections. Our books are comparative, offering in-depth communication-based analyses of how United States and Chinese officials, scholars, artists, and activists configure each other, portray the relations between the two nations, and depict their shared and competing interests. They are interdisciplinary, featuring scholarship that works in and across communication studies, rhetoric, literary criticism, film studies, cultural studies, international studies, and more. And they are international, situating their analyses at the crossroads of international communication and the nuances, complications, and opportunities of globalization as it has unfolded since World War II.

Communication Convergence in Contemporary China

INTERNATIONAL PERSPECTIVES ON POLITICS, PLATFORMS, AND PARTICIPATION

Edited by Patrick Shaou-Whea Dodge

MICHIGAN STATE UNIVERSITY PRESS | *East Lansing*

♾ The paper used in this publication meets the minimum requirements of
ANSI/NISO Z39.48-1992 (R 1997) (Permanence of Paper).

Michigan State University Press
East Lansing, Michigan 48823-5245

LIBRARY OF CONGRESS CATALOGING-IN-PUBLICATION DATA
Names: Dodge, Patrick Shaou-Whea, editor.
Title: Communication convergence in contemporary China : international perspectives
on politics, platforms, and participation / edited by Patrick Shaou-Whea Dodge.
Description: East Lansing : Michigan State University Press, 2020.
| Series: US-China relations in the age of globalization | Includes bibliographical references and index.
Identifiers: LCCN 2019057351 | ISBN 9781611863765 (paperback)
| ISBN 9781609176501 (PDF) | ISBN 9781628954111 (ePub) | ISBN 9781628964127 (Kindle)
Subjects: LCSH: Communication—Technological innovations—China.
| Cyberspace—Government policy—China. | Telecommunication policy—China.
| Internet and international relations—China. | Internet and international relations—United States.
Classification: LCC P96.T422 C635 2020 | DDC 302.20951—dc23
LC record available at https://lccn.loc.gov/2019057351

Book design and typesetting by Charlie Sharp, Sharp Designs, East Lansing, Michigan
Cover design by Erin Kirk New
Cover art: Secondary school students protesting in the Central District in Hong Kong
on Aug. 22, 2019, photo by Lam Yik Fei, for *The New York Times*,
https://www.nytimes.com/2019/09/01/world/asia/hong-kong-protests-education-china.html.

Michigan State University Press is a member of the Green Press Initiative and is committed to developing
and encouraging ecologically responsible publishing practices. For more information about the Green
Press Initiative and the use of recycled paper in book publishing, please visit www.greenpressinitiative.org.

Visit Michigan State University Press at *www.msupress.org*

ON THE INTERSECTION OF EDGE BALL AND COURTESY:
NOTES ON SCHOLARSHIP IN THE AGE OF GLOBALIZATION

Like America or France or Brazil, China is a nation-state riven with fault-lines along region and race, ethnicity and education, linguistics and libido, gender and more general divisions. The US media tends to portray Chinese society as monolithic—billions of citizens censored into silence, its activists and dissidents fearful of retribution. The "reeducation" camps in Xinjiang, the "black prisons" that dot the landscape, and the Great Firewall prove this belief partially true. At the same time, there are more dissidents on the Chinese web than there are living Americans, and rallies, marches, strikes, and protests unfold in China each week. The nation is seething with action, much of it politically radical. What makes this political action so complicated and so difficult to comprehend is that no one knows how the state will respond on any given day. In his magnificent *Age of Ambition*, Evan Osnos notes that "Divining how far any individual [can] go in Chinese creative life [is] akin to carving a line in the sand at low tide in the dark." His tide metaphor is telling, for throughout Chinese history waves of what Deng Xiaoping called "openness and reform" have given way to repression, which can then swing back to what Chairman Mao once called "letting a hundred flowers bloom"—China thus offers a perpetually changing landscape, in which nothing is certain. For this reason, our Chinese colleagues and collaborators are taking great risks by participating in this book series. Authors in the "west" fear their books and articles will fail to find an audience; authors in China live in fear of a midnight knock at the door.

This series therefore strives to practice what Qingwen Dong calls "edge ball": Getting as close as possible to the boundary of what is sayable without crossing the line into being offensive. The image is borrowed from table tennis and depicts a shot that barely touches the line before ricocheting off the table; it counts as a point and is within the rules, yet the trajectory of the ball makes it almost impossible to hit a return shot. In the realm of scholarship and politics, playing "edge ball" means speaking truth to power while not provoking arrest—this is a murky game full of gray zones, allusions, puns, and sly references. What this means for our series is clear: Our authors do not censor themselves, but they do speak respectfully and cordially, showcasing research-based perspectives from their standpoints and their worldviews, thereby putting multiple vantage points into conversation. As our authors practice "edge ball," we hope our readers will savor these books with a similar sense of sophisticated and international generosity.

—Stephen J. Hartnett

Contents

Communication Convergence and "the Core" for a New Era

F or eight hundred years, Beijing's north-south central axis has served as the backbone of Chinese history, piercing culture and ritual with an ancient energy pushing geopolitical development into the twenty-first century and beyond. Along this central axis run Tiananmen Square, the Forbidden City, the Drum and Bell Towers, and ancient platforms such as the Temple of Heaven, which was used by emperors to ritualistically align the heavens with earth, to renew the rhythms of Chinese synchrony, and to replenish the harmonious balance between people and nature.[1] Since the fall of the Qing Dynasty, the People's Republic of China has used this "energy from the center" to progress on the path of an "alternative modernity."[2] In contemporary times, this central axis revolves around the Communist Party of China (hereafter CPC or Party) guiding national development on "the Path of Socialism with Chinese Characteristics in the New Era." Constituted at the CPC's Nineteenth Party Congress in late October 2017, that phrase now stands as an all-important source of a new kind of "energy," one focused entirely on the Party's political control of communication in China.

In a speech opening the Nineteenth Party Congress, President Xi Jinping proclaimed that "China and the world are in the midst of profound and complex changes."[3] These profound and complex changes foretell the story of the consolidation of power and the triggering of new types of communication convergence between the government, Party, and state media. This period of transformation and consolidation signals the shift to what Xi has called a "New Era," which will be driven by his political slogan and rallying call, the "Chinese Dream." President Xi's objective is national rejuvenation, entailing "an entirely new posture," one driven by the accumulation of power in the name of political stability, national security, and Chinese sovereignty. From the vantage point of the West, achieving rejuvenation and realizing the Chinese Dream entails challenging the United States' global leadership and securing China's regional dominance by 2025 and then global supremacy by 2050.[4] As Xi has celebrated, China's "international standing has risen as never before."[5] And so this new posturing, with China standing taller and firmer than ever before in the age of globalization, brings together China's contemporary march out of its "century of humiliation" and its subsequent revolutionary years down the "road of rejuvenation," all while building upon the legacies of Mao Zedong, Deng Xiaoping, Jiang Zemin, Hu Jintao, and now Xi Jinping.[6]

China's rise as the world's fastest-growing economy also brings with it the rebalancing of the forces of international competition and global rivalry, which has spread international suspicion, especially in America, on issues of military and geopolitical power, ideology, nationalism, fairness, trade, and technology, among others.[7] Whereas Mao closed China's doors to the West, Deng opened up economic ones in 1979. Since then, China's story of communication convergence has gone international, bringing together media platforms with Party politics, ideology, and information flow and containment, thus setting the stage for a new chapter, one where China is set on achieving its "two centenary goals" and where Chinese power could very well re-center itself at the core of a new global world order.[8]

Known as "the core" in China, a status proclaimed in an official communiqué released at the Sixth Plenary Session of the Eighteenth Party Congress, President Xi is now designated as the head of state, Party, and government, with the support of the leadership of the military, economic leaders, the legislature and judiciary, anticorruption forces, and domestic and foreign policy elite.[9] Not since the days of Chairman Mao has there been more power accumulated at the center of Party leadership. At the Great Hall of the People, on December 18, 2018, in a speech marking China's forty-year anniversary of reform and opening up, Xi further cemented the convergence of power at the core, stating "the Party must control all tasks" if China is to continue on with its miracle transformation.[10] Xi's one-and-a-half-hour speech was a double-down decree that with the Party running everything, and with Xi at the core, economic growth, development, and China's overall global standing would continue on their trajectory toward realizing the Chinese Dream. In this sense, any talk of "communication convergence" in contemporary China must begin with President Xi, the nation's new "core" leader, who now controls all levers of power.

As part of this push for political stability via consolidation, with the Party running everything, on February 19, 2016, President Xi made official state visits to the *People's Daily* newspaper, Xinhua News Agency, and China Central Television (CCTV), China's three largest media mouthpieces.[11] Xi ordered all state-run media to strictly follow the Party's leadership, publicly mandating that they "align their ideology, political thinking, and deeds to those of the CPC Central Committee," and "help fashion the Party's theories and policies into conscious action by the general public."[12] The mission of the Party's media, as Xi explained, is to "provide guidance for the public, serve the country's overall interests, unite the general public, instill confidence and pool strength, tell right from wrong, and connect China to the world."[13] Accordingly, the role of the media is now more prevalent than ever in cultivating the Party's image at home and disseminating it abroad. Further building on this mission, Xi explained that the Party's media have six basic responsibilities: (1) upholding socialism and guiding public opinion, (2) focusing on the Party's major task and serving the interests of the country, (3) uniting the people and boosting morale, (4) fostering social morality and forging cohesion among the people, (5) refuting mistaken ideas and discerning between truth and falsehood, and (6) connecting the country with the outside world.[14] As these mandates indicate, under President Xi's new model of socialism with Chinese characteristics, all communication platforms are now meant to serve nationalist interests, to stifle dissent, and to push forward the "China Dream." Under these conditions, communication "convergence" amounts to enhanced and unquestionable Party domination, with Xi as the paramount "core."

In his speech delivered after touring China's "Big 3" leading news providers, Xi reiterated that state media must serve the CPC and that "publicity through media is an important responsibility of the CPC."[15] Furthermore, all news and media outlets from that point forward must support China's "great rejuvenation" and work toward realizing the Chinese Dream by avoiding all criticism of the Party.[16] The top-down directive impacting all communication in China was reiterated during the Nineteenth Party Congress, thus launching China into new territory, where communication in the world's most populous country is now more prevalent than ever, yet also less free.[17] As Xi's visit to state media indicates, as the Party media's mission and responsibilities in his speech laid out, and as the Party's communiqué mandates, the role of Party and politics, media, and ideology are converging in new, centralized ways, refiguring China's entire communication platform to its core.

Shortly after President Xi's announcements about Party control of state media, in June 2016, scholars from over ten countries convened in Beijing to address notions of democracy, nationalism, citizenship, human rights, environmental priorities, and public health.[18] The international conference, cohosted by the Communication University of China (CUC) and the US-based National Communication Association (NCA), addressed these broad issues as questions about communication: about how China and the United States envision each other and how our interlinked imaginaries create both opportunities and obstacles for greater understanding and strengthened relations. Throughout the conference, scholars asked if the convergence of new media technologies, Party control, and emerging notions of netizenship in China would lead to a new age of opening and reform, greater political domination by the Party, or perhaps some new and intriguing combination of repression and freedom. The chapters that comprise this book are a compilation of some of those essays from the conference threaded by the guiding themes of communication convergence and politics, platforms, and participation, offering various international perspectives from, about, and how the United States and China are coming together and moving apart in ways that could impact future relations. As the United States and China increasingly come together, and while convergence is bringing together communication technologies, people, and platforms in new ways, it also raises key questions in terms of information flows, control, and regulation—and hence the future of US–China relations. The case studies that comprise this book document the ongoing changes, challenges, and transformations within these processes, offering readers informative snapshots of how US–Chinese relations are changing on the ground, in the lived realities of our daily communication habits.

Convergence

In the opening chapter of this book, Stephen Hartnett observes that convergence is "a new social reality where different platforms of communication—TV, radio, print news, entertainment, and the internet in all its variations—come crashing together. Whereas scholars once hoped this moment of convergence would facilitate new forms of enlightened conversation and citizen participation, it now appears that the age of convergence might be turning into a nightmare populated by misinformation, niche consumerism, and slander." As Hu Zhengrong foregrounds in his response, technology and science are driving the processes of convergence, as it is happening in China, where new platforms and modes of communication are born and evolve. As they come crashing together, they alter the need to innovate systems of distribution and the reception of information, thereby transforming the communication supply chain. What makes the flows of convergence so complicated in China is the wide new range of institutional configurations along a central axis of power, with media producers, technology experts, and business leaders rallying around the Party, with Xi at the core. According to Klaus Bruhn Jensen in *Media Convergence*, media convergence is about the "migration of communicative practices across diverse material technologies and social institutions."[19] As Henry Jenkins argues in *Convergence Culture*, this phenomenon is also about "the flow of content across multiple media platforms, the cooperation between multiple media industries, and the migratory behavior of media audiences who will go almost anywhere in search of the kinds of entertainment experiences they want."[20] For both Jensen and Jenkins, communication convergence entails the bringing together of people, politics, and media institutions in new configurations, on new platforms, for new purposes, leading to new forms of participatory culture, community, and "the redistribution of symbolic power—the capacity to speak, to create, to argue and persuade."[21] This convergent media environment is thus, in these ideal formulations, one of ongoing transformation, contestation, and ever-expanding user participation, with different cultures responding in different ways[22]—yet the key question remains of how such processes function in China, where "the core" now seeks to control all aspects of communication.

In international contexts, convergence is a social and technological pattern as well as a cultural and political phenomenon. At a fundamental level, it deals with the changes, transitions, and transformations of mediums and platforms as well as those happening in and through the processes of communication. While this coming together on social and mobile platforms of participation has led to new engagements, new communities, and new voices, it has also given rise to new forms of regulation, repression, and control.[23] In the United States, for example, while convergence is happening between and among platforms—where freedom of speech, expression, and the press are highly valued—it has also given rise to the simultaneous fragmentation of media and political voices, such as in the ongoing contention among and between a wide array of US political parties, subcultures, and fringe elements.[24] In the Chinese context, and through the dialectics of power and resistance, political domination in China can shape forms of contention, but cannot altogether prevent it. Thus, politics shapes and is shaped by new modes of participation and online citizen activism.[25] I have argued elsewhere that while less aggressive modes of contention are oftentimes more effective, to realize its rejuvenation to greatness, China will have to incorporate a diversity of perspectives and a plurality of voices in its national narratives.[26] Although the rise of Weibo brought with it a strong wave of online activism, there have also been growing government efforts to contain it.[27] As Powers and Jablonski posit in *The Real Cyber War*, this suggests not political upheavals or revolutions in China, but rather a stronger sense of authoritarian adaptation on the part of the Party.[28]

In the shift from legacy media to electronic modes of communication, the distribution mechanism, as Ithiel de Sola Pool conceived it, goes through a period of prolonged change and transition, where collisions happen over a period of time, where media systems compete and collaborate, where convergence is dynamic and not necessarily stable or unified but rather dynamic and ever in flux. Old technologies die and transform while new ones evolve at the same time.[29] As Jun Xiao and Helin Li have explained, "The main focus of media convergence researches both in China and the West is on the reform of communication practice brought about by technological renovations. The reform will influence many aspects of media such as the adjusting of industry strategies, consumer choices, and the modes for news production."[30] Both the United States and China are immersed in this period of prolonged change, with increasing access to information and resources domestically, but also crashing together most recently in global politics, trade, technology, and ideology. In this prolonged period of change and transition—marked by collisions, cooperation, and competition—technological renovations and clashing perceptions continue to escalate tensions surrounding fair practice, intellectual property, human rights, and fundamental values. These clashes highlight the need to transform relations between the United States and China.

Indeed, as the CPC and United States continue to update modern information technologies, netizens have increasing access to information, greater chances for participation, and additional opportunities for international engagements. Chinese developers have expanding access to this big data with relatively fewer restraints than in the United States, raising concerns for those fighting the artificial intelligence race. Moreover, as the United States advocates for "internet freedom" with more open communication systems and access to connected networks and platforms, ongoing cases of the spread of disinformation, rampant fake news, Twitter bots, and echo chambers continue to wreak havoc throughout democratic systems (as in the case of Facebook, Cambridge Analytica, and other data-marketing companies influencing the 2016 US presidential election).[31] These ongoing cases further fuel Chinese arguments that the US system is fraught with inadequacies and that the best way forward is to continue on its current path of sanitizing China's web platforms of "vulgar and illegal content," or threatening dissidents that subvert state power—all under the guise of protecting internet security—thus building what Human Rights Watch has called a digital totalitarian state.[32] Modern information technologies also serve as justification for the United States to push back on China's repressive state apparatus due in part to the fear of big-data analysis systems like the national "Social Credit System," which monitors and then rewards or punishes citizens based on social behavior; the "Police Cloud," which monitors and tracks categories of people; and the "Integrated Joint Operations Platform," which detects deviations from "normalcy," connecting behaviors to political untrustworthiness.[33] In this way, competing tensions, clashing values, and worldviews proliferate; as Evan Osnos has indicated: "The national narrative, once an ensemble performance, is splintering into a billion stories—stories of flesh and blood, of idiosyncrasies and solitary struggles. It is a time when the ties between the world's two most powerful countries, China and the United States, can be tested by the aspirations of a lone peasant lawyer."[34] Thus the paradox of simultaneous convergence and fragmentation between the United States and China continues, ever entangled, wobbling toward a future not yet set.

Convergence and Fragmentation in US–China Contexts

Over eight hundred million Chinese are now connected to the internet, according to a June 2018 estimate in a report released by the China Internet Network Information Centre.[35] Compare that with the 89 percent of households in the United States in 2016 that had a computer, and an estimated 274 million Americans connected to the internet in 2018.[36] In managing the world's largest online community, the question used to be whether the Party would be able to keep up with the pace and adapt to the sheer size of change in a rapidly connected China. Still, China has come a long way since it first connected to the global internet in 1994.[37] Through the late 1990s and early 2000s, the Chinese internet and civil society had "an interdependent relationship," with the internet contributing to the growth of civil society and "fostering public debate and communication, while civil society [has] facilitated the diffusion of the Internet by providing the necessary social basis for communication and interaction."[38] The early internet days saw shifts in agenda-setting power from traditional and legacy media outlets to internet blogs, instant messaging, bulletin board services, social networking sites, and search engine aggregate tools. As Xiao Qiang notes, the Chinese internet is not only a contested space but also brings with it the catalyst for social and political transformation, among them changes in netizen rights like the right to know, the right to express, and the right to monitor the government.[39]

Over the last twenty-five years of domestic development, there are some key points of communication convergence and fragmentation worth noting between China and the United States. For instance, March 8, 2000, has proven to be a crossroads between US and Chinese imaginaries in terms of the future of the global internet. US president Bill Clinton, speaking on the United States' signing of the agreement to bring China into the World Trade Organization (WTO), quipped, "We know how much the Internet has changed America, and we are already an open society. Imagine how much it could change China. Now there's no question China has been trying to crack down on the Internet. Good luck! That's sort of like trying to nail Jell-O to the wall."[40] Clinton's speech appealed to American audiences to support China joining the WTO, for he believed it would usher in a new era of economic liberalization and a future of greater openness and freedom for the people of China. By accelerating China's progress toward economic freedom, he hoped for reform of political and human rights as well as for the opening up of the Chinese internet. Nineteen years later, we see Clinton was wrong, as China has been able to "dismantle the three bulwarks of the Internet's power: anonymity, virality, and impunity."[41] This point of fragmentation is indicative of the incongruities in the United States' notion of "internet freedom," China's notion of "internet sovereignty," and clashing global perspectives over what Powers and Jablonski call the real cyber war.[42]

Consider another juncture point between the United States and China. In 2005, the internet freedom-sovereignty dilemma that technology companies faced put Yahoo and Jerry Yang, Yahoo's chief executive, in the spotlight. Yahoo had provided information to Chinese officials that helped "convict a Chinese journalist for leaking state secrets to a foreign Web site."[43] Shi Tao, the journalist, had shared an email from Chinese authorities detailing restrictions placed on journalists and any coverage ahead of the fifteenth anniversary of Tiananmen.[44] As US tech companies increasingly looked to expand in China, this dilemma fueled debate on the impending perils of clashing US–China values, restrictions on speech and expression, and national security, as well as the future of information flows and interconnected networks in cyberspace. In 2005 Yahoo sold its China operations to Alibaba, and in turn bought 40 percent of Alibaba. At a US congressional hearing two years later, the committee chairman, Tom Lantos, told Jerry Yang and Yahoo's general counsel, Michael Callahan, "Much of this testimony reveals that while technologically and financially you are giants, morally you are pygmies."[45] As these stories indicate, many American observers have begun to worry that increasing convergence between the markets in China and the United States carry a series of complicated ethical challenges.

Or consider the lead-up to the 2008 Beijing Olympics, which offers an example of both convergences and fragmentation in this age of global communication. As part of its bid to host the games, Beijing relaxed internet restrictions via a promise to the International Olympic Committee that journalists would have the same internet access in the 2008 Beijing Olympics as they had had in previous games.[46] However, during the Olympics some journalists reported restrictions in terms of accessing information about the Falun Gong, Chinese dissidents, the Tibetan government in exile, and the 1989 Tiananmen Square massacre; at the same time, Chinese internet users reported additional restrictions.[47] After the Olympic Games ended, even more robust internet restrictions were instituted. Sites like Facebook, YouTube, Google, and Twitter experienced what Eric Schmidt and Jared Cohen describe as the "blatant filtering" of information and the blocking of entire platforms popular in other parts of the world. Nonetheless, the 2008 Olympics were hailed as a triumph for Beijing. As this example suggests, by implementing censorship, government regulation, "astroturfing" by hundreds of thousands of paid posters in support of the Party—what have been termed China's "Wu Mao Dang," or 50 Cent Party—monitoring, self-regulation, and the Great Firewall, China has been highly effective in controlling both domestic and international public opinion, in part by controlling the flow of information on its internet, thus keeping its netizens away from foreign applications and content.[48]

With the growing prominence of the Chinese internet and increased connectivity to international systems, the Chinese government released a 2010 white paper in English, stating that the Chinese government "guarantees the citizens' freedom of speech on the Internet as well as the public's right to know, to participate, to be heard, and to oversee in accordance with the law."[49] At the same time, the white paper stipulates that "no organization or individual may produce, duplicate, announce, or disseminate information having the following content: being against the cardinal principles set forth in the Constitution; endangering state security, divulging state secrets, subverting state power and jeopardizing national unification; damaging state honor and interests," and so on. Among fifteen other stipulations, the key line declares that "Chinese citizens, foreign citizens, and all other legal persons and organizations within the territory of China must obey."[50] As this order makes clear, state security, Party interests, and internet "sovereignty" all trump the freedom of speech and expression in Chinese cyberspace. Indeed, in a 2018 *Global Times* article about new rules that would expel CPC members who express support for bourgeois liberalization online, Professor Su Wei's sentiment captures the essence that the Party fully backs tightened regulations even further: "Cyberspace has become the major battlefield of ideology construction . . . the revised regulations aim to tighten the management of Party members, whose Party spirit was loose previously. . . . The rules are needed. Along with the rapid development of the Internet, the Party's management of its members' views should also extend to the new platform."[51] Su's argument and the Party controls it supports indicate a particular version of convergence in which nationalism, obedience, and communication control coalesce. In this model, communication convergence is synonymous with Party control.

The same year that "The Internet in China" white paper was released, Google pulled out of China, announcing it would no longer censor searches from the Google.cn site. Google redirected traffic from its China site to Hong Kong based in part upon the realization that Chinese hacking attacks had targeted them and other US tech companies in an attempt to acquire information on dissidents and spies. US secretary of state Hillary Clinton mentioned the case in a 2010 speech at the Newseum in Washington, DC, stating, "The most recent situation involving Google has attracted a great deal of interest. And we look to the Chinese authorities to conduct a thorough review of the cyber intrusion that led Google to make its announcement." Linking to the US stance on internet freedom and arguing against the fragmentation of the global internet, she explained that "ultimately, this issue isn't just about information freedom; it is about what kind of world we want and what kind of world we will inhabit. It's about whether we live on a planet with one Internet, one global community, and a common body of knowledge that benefits and unites us all, or a fragmented planet in which access to information and opportunity is dependent on where you live and the whims of censors."[52] If Su's arguments pointed to a Chinese version of communication convergence where social media and the internet are controlled by the CPC, Clinton's comments point to a different version of communication convergence, one driven by international human rights and US-led notions of global citizenship and open access.

In unpacking what he called "Google and the Twisted Cyber Spy Affair," Stephen Hartnett has argued that the episode represents a version of the United States' rhetoric of "belligerent humanitarianism," in which Americans belligerently tell others how to live while invoking universal norms regarding human rights and humanitarian values—the position is both aggressive and high-minded at the same time.[53] Additionally, Hartnett notes how the hard-right purveyors of the United States' rhetoric of "warhawk hysteria" and the CPC's rhetoric of "traumatized nationalism" were used to justify extreme responses to the incident, which as he explained, built up patterns of misunderstanding and crisis escalation. Ultimately, Hartnett argues for better US–Chinese relationships and the need for a more equitable version of globalization. He suggests that the United States and China need to do so through the "re-envisioning of rhetorical habits," thus changing the way the United States and China talk about and to each other. What is at stake for the future, and how we as "communication scholars can help our leaders, both in China and the United States, handle such rhetorical occasions," he maintains, rests on our ability to move "from anger to prudence, from arrogance to humility, from a slavish devotion to wealth to fulfilling human needs, and from nationalistic myth making to cosmopolitan dialogue."[54] From this perspective we see yet a third variation of communication convergence, one tethered neither to Party control nor to US leadership, instead pointing to a cosmopolitan sense of citizenship that transcends national affiliation.

Back in China, the Party responded with the need for increased internet security. Thus, as Guobin Yang has noted, "The tightening and expansion of Internet control that started with Weibo in 2010 accelerated after Xi Jinping became China's supreme leader in 2013."[55] As Yang explains, in the "pre-Weibo" era there were just as many cases of online protest as later happened on Weibo between 2010 and 2012; however, these earlier incidents happened on other available platforms, like bulletin board systems and blogs."[56] Since the advent of Weibo and other such platforms, however, Jesper Slæger and Min Jiang have argued that official microblogging on Weibo by local governments in China has become an extension of e-government efforts at social management and extensions of the larger context of Chinese administrative and social management. By pointing out how local governments use Weibo, they maintain, we are better able to explain "the persistence of State power despite waves of contentious digital politics in contemporary China."[57] These comments indicate how the Party, in the face of fragmenting communication networks in China, has sought to reimpose a sense of control, illustrating again the convergence-fragmentation dialectic.

Recently, Weibo was reprimanded by the Cyberspace Administration of China in January 2018, when the site was forced to shut down its "Hot News" feature, where many netizens had gone for the latest trending news. As the administration explained, "Sina Weibo has violated the relevant Internet laws and regulations and spread illegal information. It has a serious problem in promoting the wrong values and has had an adverse influence on the Internet environment."[58] Weeks later, Weibo reopened its "Hot News" feature, but it was newly updated, showcasing state propaganda articles over other trending news, and included a new section called "New Era," referencing the political ideology of "Xi Jinping Thought."[59] This recent blending and mainstreaming of Party ideology on Weibo is one more example of the interplay between politics, platforms, participation, and the ongoing pulse of the Chinese internet, where the Party is updating and adjusting to new communication technologies. When new voices on new platforms for new movements emerge, CPC regulations and restraints are mandated so that the flows of information and communication are within the parameters of what Xi laid out in the Party media's mission and responsibilities.

In addition to domestic efforts such as the one with Weibo, we see the Party ramping up its efforts to cultivate and disseminate the spread of positive news internationally. For example, in September 2018, President Xi called for the building of a new Chinese mainstream media, "the China Media Group" (CMG), one that oversees films, books, television, magazines, and newspapers. Xi called on the CMG, comprising China Central Television, China National Radio, and China Radio International, to "integrate radio and television, domestic publicity and international communication, and traditional and new media, as well as improve their international communication capabilities."[60] As Xi explained, this new convergent media group is to be the "Voice of China"—offering a clear echo of the United States' Cold War efforts via its Voice of America programming—and its mission is to focus on "external propaganda work," targeting overseas Chinese and foreigners.[61] As the tools of communication technology become increasingly sophisticated, and as the United States and China continue to crash together, we will no doubt see more efforts by both sides to innovate and develop their respective content and delivery mechanisms, hence plugging into and transforming the global communication supply chain.

My attempts here have been to position some of the previous examples of internet freedom and sovereignty in US–Chinese context. In doing so, my goal has been to help situate the chapters that comprise this book. Accordingly, the chapters address the question of what happens when competing aspirations, foundational differences, cultural values, historical struggles, ongoing cyber-spatial (re)configurations, and future global imaginings all come crashing together—when our systems simultaneously converge and fragment.

The aim, then, of this book is to dive into the processes of convergence and fragmentation as they are happening within China and oftentimes between the United States and China, and the contentious relationships between politics, platforms, and participation that are transforming US–China relations. By looking to Chinese and US examples, we engage an opportunity of comparative value. At play in all this are the competing US and Chinese notions of internet freedom and sovereignty, access to social and mobile platforms, regulation and control, the role of governments, and the participation that fuels the pulse of change and transformation. As the United States and China both make further efforts toward rejuvenation, in the struggle to make American great again, as well as in the struggle to make China great again, competing and contrasting values offer new opportunities for insight into the pressing need for more research that engages questions of communication convergence in intercultural and international contexts, as well as new opportunities for transcultural imaginings and understandings that foster peaceful futures.[62] This book is an attempt to do so.

Chapter Outline

The chapters in this book offer case studies that showcase international perspectives on the ongoing trends of convergence and fragmentation. Overall, they provide a glimpse into what happens (and what will continue to happen) as the United States and China interact. And so the chapters in this book are organized into three parts. The first set of chapters deals with communication and fragmentation in the "New Era." Past NCA president Stephen Hartnett steers the conversation in the first chapter with past CUC president Zhengrong Hu and colleagues. Driven by an international and comparative approach, they discuss the evolution of US–China relations with a focus on the paradox of simultaneous communication convergence and fragmentation in the age of globalization. Hartnett, Hu, and colleagues are hopeful that international conversations like these help build trust, collegiality, and facilitate the type of understanding that is needed so that the United States and China move together toward peaceful futures.

Andrew Gilmore tackles the ongoing struggles in the process of mainlandization as playing out in Hong Kong. Gilmore argues that rather than directing sole blame for the Umbrella Revolution on Party politics, we should note that the combination of the city's unique mix of plutocratization (the city is now ruled by the rich) and the Party's ongoing amplification of the mainlandization of Hong Kong (by imposing its political systems, education, culture, and media upon Hong Kong) laid the grounds for the overwhelming pushback of political participation that made the Umbrella Revolution so exciting. This complex mix of factors, rounded with the fragmentation of a hybrid Hong Kong identity—and CY Leung as scapegoat and synecdochical proxy for Party blame—led to a charged situation. As a case study, then, Gilmore's analysis spotlights the paradox of convergence and fragmentation in the plutocratization of Hong Kong, the Party's controversial mainlandization efforts, and how debates over the governance of Hong Kong offer telling case studies for the future of both local democracies and global relations.

Zhi Li and Xi Wang turn to fragmentation and convergence in the constructions of national imaginaries in US and Chinese documentaries. They show how the Party's outdated machinery of direct-effects propaganda, such as in the documentary *The Road to Rejuvenation*, has been ineffective in building positive national imagery. In contrast, they examine the discursive techniques of the documentary *America: The Story of Us* and highlight its diversity of fragmented and contrasting perspectives, including hidden and subjugated subject positions that shine the spotlight on America's legacies of racism, oppression, inequality, and sexism, among others. Via this comparison, they flag a deep contrast: on the one hand, national image construction in China that deals with the propaganda techniques of one coherent, grand narrative, such as in *The Road to Rejuvenation*; on the other hand, the complex layering of contrasting voices and images that represent American life in *America*. Their reading is a hopeful one, turning to *A Bite of China* as an example of a more sophisticated Chinese text that moves the viewer away from forced propaganda techniques toward more local portrayals—the move from a forced convergence to the celebration of fragments—all intersecting within larger narratives. Ultimately, Li and Wang argue that as China's contemporary documentaries play catchup with American documentaries, they are more successful when they veer from Party-driven propaganda. They call for Chinese filmmakers to highlight the internal contradictions in contemporary Chinese life and call for a new era of international collaboration and cooperation between American and Chinese documentary makers, hoping that by working together, they might enhance understanding within the US–China relationship.

The second group of chapters deals with communication, convergence, and crisis. Michelle Murray Yang and Da Wang show us the shots fired by the United States with the 2014 indictments of five People's Liberation Army officers for engaging in cyberattacks against US companies. They show us the shots fired back in the *People's Daily*, where President Obama was represented as a hypocritical American leader with a chokehold on the world, at the head of the United States' cyber surveillance program. Murray Yang and Wang perform a comparative news framing analysis of US and Chinese representations, arguing that the dispute and dueling narratives further fuel distrust between the United States and China. Indeed, Chinese leaders routinely cast US leaders as hypocritical, while the United States is increasingly frustrated with China for not abiding by the distinction between cyberespionage conducted for economic advantages and cyberwar-like actions that threaten national security. They argue that despite the challenges and setbacks, the United States and China must continue efforts to find ways to deliberate, negotiate, and compromise.

Jufei Wan and Bryan R. Reckard turn our attention to Meng Wanzhou, Huawei, and the 2019 cybersecurity crisis. In a comparative rhetorical analysis they show how US discourse revolving around international trade and cybersecurity is based on threat construction, "the rhetoric of warhawk hysteria," and an "imperial rhetorical style," collectively working to generate anxiety and build support for uncompromising trade policies.[63] In contrast to the United States' uncompromising stance and global anti-Huawei campaign, they turn to Huawei founder Ren Zhengfei, who gave a series of interviews and testimonies in Chinese state media. Wan and Reckard argue that Ren and Huawei adopted a tit-for-tat rhetorical strategy to denounce the United States' anti-Huawei global campaign while, ironically, raising concerns about the United States' actions as threatening to global free markets and human rights. They also detail Huawei's deployment of a systematic PR plan to reform its global image and reputation by using the rhetorical tactics of denial, dissociation, avoidance, and redirection. Ultimately, they make the argument that the detention of Meng Wanzhou, the Trump administration's anti-Huawei campaign, and the ongoing rhetorical battle are examples of souring US–China relations, inching ever closer to geopolitical rivalry marked by competition and conflict.

Jack Kangjie Liu and Dan Wang show us evolving citizen engagement and communication convergence trends in the flows of information from legacy media websites to new social media platforms. Focusing on the 2016 Baidu and Ctrip crises, Liu and Wang track "hot" issue spikes in convergence across platforms namely in convergence periods where information and traffic moved from internet reports and websites to Weibo and WeChat. These crises allowed for political commentary on daily life in China, sometimes in scathing testimony voicing netizen anger at companies and the government, generating debate around issues of trust, accountability, and ethical behavior. They argue that enterprises must do the hard work of adhering to ethical business practices, that the government needs to hold such entities accountable for unethical practices, and that the netizens' responses reflect their longing for access to reliable medical information and open participatory platforms.

The third set of chapters deals with case studies of the changing mediascape in China and abroad. Whereas Liu and Wang's chapter examines communication convergence spikes between legacy and new social media platforms, Lisa B. Keränen and Yimeng Li focus on the 2015 Tianjin explosion as a case study in postcrisis media convergence. They examine how renewal discourses were mobilized in official government, media, and citizens' social media discussion of the Tianjin port explosion. They found that renewal discourses were modestly present in Weibo posts but nearly absent in the English-language news coverage in *China Daily*, a missed opportunity, they argue, for national identity work. Overall, their findings confirm the government's PR function of a command style of communication that works to project strength and control in times of crisis.

Todd L. Sandel and Peimin Qiu turn to Macao and the rise of a creatively mixed vernacular among young adults connected on WeChat—a Canto-English-Mandarin code mixing, code switching, emoji-fused, online message-sharing system. In their analysis of WeChat screenshots and interviews with the creators of those messages, they locate new convergences and fragmentations as playing out in and through the flows of language games and identity expressions. Their study shows us how languages come together and fragment at the same time, how China is both complexly unified and diverse, and how identity is continually evolving within and across mediated platforms. They suggest that with the ongoing rise of WeChat and other social media platforms, we may very well see some form of this mixed-vernacular, code-mixing, code-switching pattern of convergence in the communication practices of youth across greater China.

David R. Gruber turns to US and UK framings of China's new thirst for fine wine coupled with soft-power aspirations. Using metaphoric criticism, he shines a spotlight on how American and British media rhetorically position China in comparison with and against Western wine cultures. Unpacking "red dawn," "gold rush," "stampede," and "red planet" metaphors, he confirms the presence of politically suppressive representations that reproduce colonial Western narratives, thus showing how even wine discourse indicates geopolitical anxiety and economic worries about China's rise. Ultimately, he argues that to reclaim terroir—"a terroir with Chinese characteristics"—requires the (re)presentation of an original combination of Chinese soil and palate that works to propel new rhetorical inventions regarding what makes a fine wine "fine" in China. This move, he argues, would allow Chinese farmers and consumers to have a say in production, which entails healthy cooperation between state and Party agendas, business leaders, and industry experts, among other voices.

Recently, an article in *The Economist*, speaking of the ways US president Donald Trump's "America First" nationalism has hampered US–China political and economic integration, declared that "convergence is dead."[64] Despite that negative outlook, as China and the United States grapple with increasingly intertwined futures, the chapters herein comprise a collection of examples showcasing the notion that the paradox of convergence and fragmentation is not dead, but rather is alive and continues to transform both daily life and the US–China relationship. Indeed, as these chapters indicate, whether it is an explosion in a Chinese port city, or globally circulating talk about wine, or protest marches in Hong Kong, or contrasting documentary film styles, our hypermediated world means that what happens in China matters in America, and what happens in America matters in China—we are inescapably bound together in a web of converging media threads, information flows, evolving markets, and clashing national imaginaries.

NOTES

1. See UNESCO's "The Central Axis of Beijing" for more on "the ideal city plan in traditional Chinese culture," the "value of the center in traditional Chinese culture," and Beijing

being "exactly at the center of heaven and earth." The UNESCO site cites neo-Confucianism master Zhu Xi during the Southern Song Dynasty: http://whc.unesco.org/en/tentativelists/5802/.

2. Dilip Parameshwar Gaonkar, "On Alternative Modernities," *Public Culture* 11 (1999): 1–18. See also Stephen J. Hartnett, "Alternative Modernities, Postcolonial Colonialism, and Contested Imagining in and of Tibet," in *Imagining China: Rhetorics of Nationalism in an Age of Globalization*, ed. Stephen J. Hartnett, Lisa B. Keränen, and Donovan Conley (East Lansing: Michigan State University Press, 2017), 91–137.

3. Xi Jinping, "Secure a Decisive Victory in Building a Moderately Prosperous Society in All Respects and Strive for the Great Success of Socialism with Chinese Characteristics for a New Era" (full text of Xi Jinping's report delivered at the Nineteenth National Congress of the Communist Party of China, Beijing, October 18, 2017), translated by Xinhua News, http://news.xinhuanet.com/english/special/2017-11/03/c_136725942.htm.

4. See Elaine Chan, "Made in China 2025: Is Beijing's Plan for Hi-Tech Dominance as Big a Threat as the West Thinks It Is?," *South China Morning Post*, September 10, 2018. For Xi Jinping's China Dream speech see Xi Jinping, "Achieving Rejuvenation Is the Dream of the Chinese People," in *The Governance of China*, vol. 1 (Beijing: Foreign Languages Press, 2014), 37–39. In the same collection of speeches, see also Xi's "The Chinese Dream Will Benefit Not Only the People of China, but Also of Other Countries," 61–62.

5. Xi Jinping, "Secure a Decisive Victory."

6. See Rana Mitter, *Modern China* (New York: Oxford University Press, 2008); Xing Lu, "The Little Book Lives On: Mao's Rhetorical Legacies in Contemporary Chinese Imaginings," in Hartnett, Keränen, and Conley, *Imagining China*, 11–45; Li Junru, *The Chinese Path and the Chinese Dream* (Beijing: Foreign Languages Press, 2014); and *The Road of Rejuvenation* exhibition at the National Museum of China.

7. For example, see Bill Gertz, *The China Threat: How the People's Republic Targets America* (Washington, DC: Regnery Publishing, 2000). For a Chinese perspective, see Liu Mingfu, *The China Dream: Great Power Thinking and Strategic Posture in the Post-American Era* (New York: CN Times Books, 2015).

8. See Zhao Tianyang, *The Tianxia System: An Introduction to the Philosophy of World Institution* (Beijing: Renmin University Press, 2011); and Zhao Tianyang, "A Political World Philosophy in Terms of All-under-Heaven (Tianxia)," *Diogenes* 221 (2009): 5–18. For more on the two centenary goals, see Li Junru, *In Pursuit of the Chinese Dream* (Beijing: Foreign Languages Press, 2015), especially 24–26, "The Task Is to Achieve the Two Centenary Goals," and President Xi's speech at the Boao Forum for Asia on April 7, 2013.

9. At the Sixth Plenary Session of the Eighteenth Communist Party of China Central

Committee, the Party released a communiqué calling on members to closely unite around Xi Jinping as the core leader. See, "Xi's Core Status Is Consensus of CPC: Official," *Xinhua News*, October 28, 2016; and, Chris Buckley, "Xi Jinping Is China's 'Core' Leader: Here's What It Means," *New York Times*, October 30, 2016.

10. The United States and China, in a joint communiqué released on December 16, 1978, announced they would establish diplomatic relations on January 1 of the next year. The forty-year anniversary marked China's reform and opening up. See Chris Buckley and Steven Lee Myers, "China's Leader Says Party Must Control 'All Tasks,' and Asian Markets Slump," *New York Times*, December 18, 2018. For more on China's "miracle transformation," see Justin Yifu Lin, Fang Cai, and Zhou Li, *The China Miracle: Development Strategy and Economic Reform*, rev. ed. (Hong Kong: China University Press, 2003).

11. The CCTV Tower, or the "Pants Building," as it is known to Beijingers, stands firmly as synecdoche for communication convergence in contemporary China. CCTV (the part) stands in for the process of media convergence (the whole). For more on synechdoche in Chinese contexts see Stephen J. Hartnett, Lisa B. Keränen, and Donovan Conley, "Introduction: A Gathering Storm or a New Chapter?," in Hartnett, Keränen, and Conley, *Imagining China*, ix–xlv; see also Michelle Murray Yang, "Chen Guangcheng and the Rhetorical Politics of Dissent: Imagining Human Rights in U.S.-Sino Relations," in Hartnett, Keränen, and Conley, *Imagining China*, 47–89.

12. See *Xinhua News*, "China's Xi Underscores CPC's Leadership in News Reporting," http://news.xinhuanet.com/english/2016-02/19/c_135114305.htm.

13. Ibid.

14. Xi Jinping, *The Governance of China*, vol. 2 (Beijing: Foreign Languages Press, 2017), 360. Speech delivered on February 19, 2016, "Improve All Aspects of Party Media Leadership."

15. Ibid.

16. Xi has termed China's great rejuvenation "the Chinese Dream," a label introduced during a November 2012 speech on the steps of the National History Museum of China overlooking Tiananmen Square. For full text of the speech see Xi Jinping, "Achieving Rejuvenation." Xi delivered the speech on November 29, 2012, when visiting the National Museum of China's exhibition *The Road of Rejuvenation*.

17. "Xi Jinping Thought of Socialism with Chinese Characteristics in a New Era," released shortly after the Nineteenth Party Congress, was written into the Chinese constitution. "Xi Jinping theory" thus joins "Mao Zedong theory" in China's constitution.

18. The First Biennial Conference on Communication, Media, and Governance in an Age of Globalization, 2016, Beijing.

19. Klaus Bruhn Jensen, *Media Convergence: The Three Degrees of Network, Mass, and Interpersonal Communication* (New York: Routledge, 2010), 15.

20. Henry Jenkins, *Convergence Culture: Where Old and New Media Collide* (New York: New York University Press, 2006), 2.

21. Graham Meikle and Sherman Young, *Networked Digital Media in Everyday Life* (New York: Palgrave Macmillan, 2012), 200.

22. There is much research on convergence in various cultural contexts. For Japanese contexts see Patrick W. Galbraith and Jason G. Karlin, eds., *Media Convergence in Japan* (n.p.: Kinema Club, 2016). For Romanian contexts see Georgeta Drula, "Forms of Media Convergence and Multimedia Content—a Romanian Perspective," *Comunicar* 22, no. 44 (2015): 131–140. For Basque contexts: A. Larrondo, J. Larranago-Zubizaretta, K. Meso, and I. Agirreazkuenaga, "Media Convergence and the Newsrooms: The Case of the Basque Public Radio and Television (EITB)," *Profesional de la Information* 21, no. 4 (2012): 347–353. For a Canadian context: David Pritchard and Marc-Francois Bernier, "Media Convergence and Changes in Quebec Journalists' Professional Values," *Canadian Journal of Communication* 35, no. 4 (2010): 595–607. For Austria, Spain, and Germany: Jose A. Garcia Aviles, Klaus Meier, Andy Kalenbrunner, Migues Caravajal, and Daniela Kraus, "Newsroom Integration in Austria, Spain, and Germany: Models of Media Convergence," *Journalism Practice* 3, no. 3 (2009): 285–303. And, for a study on the politics of convergence, hierarchies of difference, and social media activism and "on the ground" activism triggering national debate across America, see Mia Fischer's "#Free_CeCe: The Material Convergence of Social Media Activism," *Feminist Media Studies* 16, no. 5 (2016): 755–771.

23. Here I hear echoes of Guobin Yang saying that it is "as much about technology as it is about people. Power exerts itself through codes, but the codes are designed and implemented by people." See "The Politics of Digital Contention," in *The Power of the Internet in China: Citizen Activism Online* (New York: Columbia University Press, 2011), 44–63.

24. For example, see Gaby Hinsliff, "Trash Talk: How Twitter Is Shaping the New Politics," *The Guardian*, July 31, 2016, https://www.theguardian.com/technology/2016/jul/31/trash-talk-how-twitter-is-shaping-the-new-politics; and Lois Beckett, "Facebook to Ban White Nationalism and Separatism Content," *The Guardian*, March 27, 2019, https://www.theguardian.com/technology/2019/mar/27/facebook-white-nationalism-hate-speech-ban.

25. Yang, *Power of the Internet*, 12–13.

26. Patrick Shaou-Whea Dodge, "Imagining Dissent: Contesting the Façade of Harmony

through Art and the Internet in China," in Hartnett, Keränen, and Conley, *Imagining China*, 311–338.

27. Guobin Yang, ed., *China's Contested Internet* (Copenhagen: NIAS Press, 2015), 3.

28. Shawn M. Powers and Michael Jablonski, *The Real Cyber War: The Political Economy of Internet Freedom* (Urbana: University of Illinois Press, 2015), 168–172.

29. Ithiel de Sola Pool, *Technologies of Freedom: On Free Speech in an Electronic Age* (Cambridge: Belknap Press, 1983).

30. Jun Xiao and Helin Li, "Online Discussion of Sharon Stone's Karma Comment on China Earthquake: The Intercultural Communication of Media Events in the Age of Media Convergence," *China Media Research* 8, no. 1 (2012): 25–39.

31. See Nicholas Confessore, "Cambridge Analytica and Facebook: The Scandal and the Fallout So Far," *New York Times*, April 4, 2018, https://www.nytimes.com/2018/04/04/us/politics/cambridge-analytica-scandal-fallout.html.

32. On the sanitization of China's social media platforms, see Qian Zhecheng, "For China's Web Platforms, the Future Is Sanitized," *Sixth Tone*, December 26, 2018, http://www.sixthtone.com.

33. See Maya Wang, "Cambridge Analytica, Big Data and China," Human Rights Watch, April 18, 2018; for more on the Police Cloud, see "China: Police 'Big Data' Systems Violate Privacy, Target Dissent"; and for the Joint Operations Platform, see "China: Big Data Fuels Crackdown in Minority Region: Predictive Policing Program Flags Individuals for Investigations, Detentions." All of these articles are accessible at https://www.hrw.org.

34. Evan Osnos, *Age of Ambition: Chasing Fortune, Truth, and Faith in the New China* (New York: Farrar, Straus and Giroux, 2014), 5. For more on the "lone peasant lawyer," see Yang, "Chen Guangcheng."

35. See "China Focus: China Has 802 Million Internet Users," *Xinhua News*, August 21, 2018; and, "Chinese Internet Users Surge to 802 Million in Test of Government's Ability to Manage World's Biggest Online Community," *South China Morning Post*, August 21, 2018.

36. The 89 percent estimate of connected American households in 2016 includes computers and smartphones. Eighty-one percent of those households had a broadband internet subscription. You can find these statistics and other estimates here: Camille Ryan, "Computer and Internet Use in the United States: 2016," *American Community Survey Reports*, ACS-39 (Washington, DC: US Census Bureau, 2017). The estimate of 274 million Americans connected to the internet comes from *Statistica*: https://www.statista.com/statistics/325645/usa-number-of-internet-users/.

37. Yang, *China's Contested Internet*. See the introduction for a brief history of the Chinese internet. For more on the historical development of Chinese internet culture see Bei Ju,

Todd Sandel, and Richard Fitzgerald, "Understanding Chinese Internet and Social Media: The Innovative and Creative Affordances of Technology, Language and Culture," in *Se mettre en scène en ligne: La communication digitale,* ed. Marcel Burger, vol. 2 (Lausanne, Switzerland: UNIL, University of Lausanne, 2019), 161–177.

38. Jacques deLisle, Avery Goldstein, and Guobin Yang, eds., *The Internet, Social Media, and a Changing China* (Philadelphia: University of Pennsylvania Press, 2016), 5.

39. Xiao Qiang, "The Battle for the Chinese Internet," *Journal of Democracy* 22, no. 2 (2011): 47–61.

40. President Clinton delivered the speech on March 8, 2000, at Johns Hopkins University. For the full text of Clinton's speech, see "Full Text of Clinton's Speech on China Trade Bill," *New York Times*, March 9, 2000, https://archive.nytimes.com/www.nytimes.com/library/world/asia/030900clinton-china-text.html.

41. See Bethany Allen-Erbrahimian, "The Man Who Nailed Jello to the Wall," *Foreign Policy: Tea Leaf Nation*, June 29, 2016. On the three bulwarks of Internet power, China's past internet czar and minister of cyberspace affairs administration, Lu Wei, dismantled (1) anonymity, with requirements for real name registration; (2) virality, with the contracting of censorship work to internet companies that hired small armies to flag, remove, and report sensitive comments in real time; and, (3) impunity, with the 2013–2015 campaign against online rumors that used celebrity arrests and nationally televised apologies and shaming as examples to threaten others into self-censorship.

42. Powers and Jablonski, *The Real Cyber War.*

43. Joseph Kahn, "Yahoo Helped Chinese to Prosecute Journalist," *New York Times*, September 8, 2005.

44. See "Chinese Journalist Shi Tao, Jailed for Eight Years after Yahoo Gave Up His Identity, Gets Early Release," *South China Morning Post*, September 9, 2013. *China Digital Times*, an online media organization dedicated to "revealing the hidden mechanisms of state censorship by collecting and translating filtered keywords, propaganda directives, and official rhetoric," among other functions, now regularly releases a weekly post translating censorship instructions issued to the media by government authorities, "Directives from the Ministry of Truth." You can access those posts here: https://chinadigitaltimes.net/china/directives-from-the-ministry-of-truth/.

45. "Yahoo Chief Apologizes to Chinese Dissidents' Relatives," *New York Times*, November 7, 2007.

46. Richard Spenser, "Beijing Olympics: China Lifts Internet Restrictions but Warns Foreign Media," *The Telegraph*, August 1, 2008.

47. Tania Branigan, "China Relaxes Internet Censorship For Olympics," *The Guardian*, August 1, 2008.

48. Eric Schmidt and Jared Cohen, *The New Digital Age: Reshaping the Future of People, Nations and Business* (New York: Alfred A. Knopf, 2013). For more on the "Wu Mao Dang," see "50 Cent Party," listed in *China Digital Times*' "Grass-Mud Horse Lexicon": https://chinadigitaltimes.net/space/Fifty_Cent_Party. See also Nicholas Confessore, Gabriel J. X. Dance, Richard Harris, and Mark Hansen, "The Follower Factory," *New York Times*, January 27, 2018, for more on paid postings and social media's black market.

49. See "The Internet in China," *White Papers of the Chinese Government*, released by the Information Office of the State Council of the People's Republic of China (Beijing: Foreign Languages Press, 2012), 227–247.

50. Ibid., 243.

51. Cao Siqi, "New CPC Rules to Expel Members Who Express Support for Bourgeois Liberalization Online," *Xinhua*, September 25, 2018.

52. See Hillary Rodham Clinton, "Remarks on Internet Freedom," speech delivered at the Newseum, Washington, DC, January 21, 2010, Department of State, https://2009-2017.state.gov/secretary/20092013clinton/rm/2010/01/135519.htm. See also Hillary Rodham Clinton, "Internet Rights and Wrongs: Choices and Challenges in a Networked World," speech delivered at George Washington University, February 15, 2011, Department of State: https://2009-2017.state.gov/secretary/20092013clinton/rm/2011/02/156619.htm.

53. See Stephen Hartnett, "Google and the 'Twisted Cyber Spy' Affair: US-Chinese Communication in an Age of Globalization," *Quarterly Journal of Speech* 97, no. 4 (2011): 411–434.

54. Ibid., 430.

55. Yang, *China's Contested Internet*, 4.

56. Ibid., 3. See also Yang's mention of the following iconic cases of online protests in the pre-Weibo era: the Sun Zhigang case in 2003, the BMW incident in 2004, the "black kiln" and the "South China tiger" cases in 2007, and the Deng Yujiao incident in 2009.

57. Jesper Schlæger and Min Jiang, "Official Microblogging and Social Management by Local Governments in China," in Yang, *China's Contested Internet*, 192–226.

58. Zhuang Pinghui, "Weibo Falls Foul of China's Internet Watchdog for Failing to Censor Content: Social Media Platform Told to Shut Down Popular Services for a Week," *South China Morning Post*, January 28, 2018.

59. Karen Chiu and Xinmei Shen, "Microblogging Site Weibo Reveals Big Changes after Government Rebuke," from ABC News: https://www.abacusnews.com/digital-life/microblogging-site-weibo-reveals-big-changes-after-government-rebuke/article/2132078.

60. See "Xi Calls for Building World-Class New Mainstream Media," *Xinhua*, September 26, 2018.

61. For more on the "Voice of China" see Chis Buckley's "China Gives Communist Party More Control over Policy and Media," *New York Times*, March 21, 2018. See also Julia Bowie and David Gitter, "Abroad or at Home, China Puts Party First," *Foreign Policy*, December 5, 2018.

62. See Evan Osnos, "Making China Great Again," *New Yorker*, January 1, 2018, https://www.newyorker.com/magazine/2018/01/08/making-china-great-again.

63. For more on the "rhetoric of warhawk hysteria," see Hartnett, "Google." For more on "an imperial rhetorical style," see Stephen J. Hartnett, "Democracy in Decline, as Chaos, and as Hope; or, U.S.-China Relations in an Age of Unraveling," *Rhetoric & Public Affairs* 19, no. 4 (2016): 626–678.

64. See "China v. America," *The Economist*, October 20, 2018, 11.

PART 1

Convergence and Fragmentation in the "New Era"

On the Paradox of Convergence and Fragmentation in the Age of Globalization

Stephen J. Hartnett, Zhengrong Hu, Qingwen Dong,
Zhi Li, and Patrick Shaou-Whea Dodge

T he essays collected in this book began as presentations before the 2016 version of the biennial conference "Communication, Media, and Governance in the Age of Globalization," which was jointly hosted by the US-based National Communication Association (NCA), the Beijing-based Communication University of China (CUC), and the Journalism and Communication Disciplinary Supervisory Committee of China (JCDS).[1] Held in the state-of-the-art convention center at CUC's leafy campus on the east side of Beijing, the conference offered a remarkable opportunity for scholars committed to international issues to come together across national boundaries in the interest of building bridges of understanding, collaboration, and friendship. To help frame the big questions that drive this book, this first chapter offers a conversation wherein the architects of the conference discuss the evolution of US–China relations by focusing on the paradox of simultaneous communication convergence and fragmentation in the age of globalization.

We began our work with a long, in-person conversation at CUC in May 2017, and then connected electronically throughout the summer and fall of 2017 to polish these contents into publishable form; then we did some more polishing throughout 2018, hence arriving at this text. Then NCA president Stephen J.

Hartnett drives the conversation by posing questions to then CUC president Zhengrong Hu, and subsequently brings Professor Qingwen Dong, Professor Zhi Li, and Associate Professor Clinical Teaching Track Patrick Shaou-Whea Dodge into the conversation.

Stephen J. Hartnett: Good afternoon President Hu, and thank you for that terrific lunch! It is always a delight to be on your campus. I want to ask you three questions about communication: one about convergence, one about new media, and one about governance. As we work our way through these topics, we will also speak about the status of US–China relations, which I think our partnership here embodies in delightful ways. So, convergence: in the United States, we are talking about "convergence" as a new social reality where different platforms of communication—TV, radio, print news, entertainment, and the internet in all its variations—come crashing together. Whereas scholars once hoped this moment of convergence would facilitate new forms of enlightened conversation and citizen participation, it now appears that the age of convergence might be turning into a nightmare populated by misinformation, niche consumerism, and slander. In this scenario, the old "gatekeepers" of journalism are dying and the old forms of entertainment are changing, thus leaving many of us confused about the roles new media plays in our nations. Please talk with me about what "convergence" looks like in China, and what you think it means for the health of civil society in China.

Zhengrong Hu: Thank you, Stephen, for that question, and for visiting my campus again. It is always a pleasure to work with you and our friends in the NCA.

The first thing I will say is that convergence needs to be understood as a new world of *technological significance*. We communication scholars tend to look at the messaging side of things, but it is important to remember that the technology here is immensely complicated and largely beyond the range of our expertise. We won't go into too much detail about this issue today, but I think it is important to foreground the key role of technology and the sciences fueling convergence.

The second thing I will say touches upon *the communication supply chain*. With this phrase, I want to point to how the traditional media is struggling to innovate their supply chain to try to enable their messages to reach new audiences. Think about how newspapers are now all online, or how advertising hits the apps on your phone, or how television is now streaming on various platforms—these are all transformations in how communication is delivered to users. If my first point addresses the technological aspects making communication convergence possible, then my second point leads to the economics and business models of communication driving convergence.

The third key point is to think about how the age of convergence in communication entails a wide new range of *institutional configurations*. Here in China, for example, everyone knows that the Communist Party [hereafter CPC or Party] controls the mainstream media, so convergence entails media producers, technology experts, and business leaders working in conjunction with the CPC—so we have this vast institutional interface. And in China, which I think is true in America as well, we are finding that our existing institutional structures have little idea how to manage or regulate all the aspects of convergence. We have industrial-age institutions trying to make sense of information-age communication technologies and this, obviously, poses a complicated set of problems.

Hartnett: So I am hearing you point to technological issues, supply chain/delivery issues, and institutional configuration/regulation issues, which, when combined in this new stage of convergence, amount to a kind of matrix of communication opportunities and dilemmas. I will confess to being entirely ignorant about the technological aspect of our age of convergence, so let me follow up on the second of your points, about supply chains. In America, the majority of our media content comes through a small number of providers: Yahoo, YouTube, Facebook, Twitter, Google, Amazon, and so on. Many observers are wondering, then, if convergence is just another word for corporate consolidation. We seem to be living in an ironic situation wherein consumers feel they have more choices, and hence more freedom, but at the institutional level a small number of immense corporations function as what amount to old-fashioned monopolies. As you survey this situation from Beijing, are you worried that this accumulation of institutional power could lead to a dangerous consolidation of political power? And could such consolidations of power in turn have negative impacts on our communication environments?

Hu: Oh yes, yes to both points. And that is exactly what is happening in China already, as the central government is encouraging precisely this kind of conglomeration of forces. The big difference between China and America, of course, is that in China, since 1949, the Party has controlled our media environment. But you know, Stephen, historically, this tight linkage between the Party and communication meant many people did not really trust the government-controlled media. I am sure you have heard the old joke about *People's Daily*, where folks would say, "The only true thing it prints is the date." In response to this long-standing skepticism about Party-controlled mouthpieces, now you see CCTV spinning off all kinds of new channels—kid channels, animal channels, sports channels, you name it—in an effort to reach more viewers with a fresh look, yet still all within parameters controlled by the CPC. They are trying to diversify their supply chain, yet within the regulatory control of the Party; in this sense, our communication environment is very tightly controlled. But, on the other hand, we have this explosion of grass-roots-driven new media offering all kinds of new voices. So the Chinese people are kind of split between evolving, but still old-fashioned and Party-controlled, offerings and emerging, innovative, new-media offerings. The question is whether the Party can learn to tolerate other voices. Will it try to incorporate them in its platform, or will it just repress them?

Hartnett: I think in the United States we have learned that government-led repression usually backfires, which is why we love the First Amendment. But, on the other hand, when so much free speech meets new social media technologies, especially with no new regulatory controls in place, then some really strange things can happen. And so it feels, in America, that even as we worry about the corporate consolidation of the supply chain, we are witnessing a simultaneous fragmentation of media: right-wing blogs, separatist websites, nationalist zines, niche podcasts, neo-Nazis, you name it. It seems like the old world of professional journalism is under siege, perhaps getting replaced by what we once happily called "citizen journalism" or "backpack journalism," but which is now appearing more sinister. I think this new, noncorporate, nonprofessional media landscape had a lot to do with how we ended up with Donald Trump as president—folks just tuned out the damaging news from the *New York Times* and *Washington Post*, and tuned in to their local radio screamers or their favorite websites, where Trump was portrayed as a populist rebel. And so, even while that notion of convergence is circulating, people are simultaneously calling this the age of fragmentation or niche consumerism, where we no longer have any common discourse or norms of deliberation. Now, President Hu, you have pointed to how the Party controls the mainstream media in China, yet surely your country is also experiencing this kind of media fragmentation. So, can you please talk to me about how this consolidation/fragmentation process is unfolding in China?

Hu: I imagine that your American media portrays the Chinese media as monolithic, but that really isn't the case at all. The Party controls the established media—the TV and radio and newspapers—but our new social media platforms are evolving much like yours. And China is not only experiencing what you are calling fragmentation, but we are doing so with what some observers have said is as many as seven hundred million internet users—that's two internet users in China for every living American. So the reality is that Chinese society is also being torn up and fragmented because of explosive social polarization, which both drives and is driven by new social media forms from the grassroots.

Hartnett: Wow, seven hundred million internet users! So let me ask you just to clarify that last point, because I think in America there's a very strong perception that China is a one-party state, that the government controls everything, that the Party represses the media, and so on, yet you are describing a much more fluid and complicated situation—is that right?

Hu: Yes, exactly. I think Americans need to understand that we now have had almost forty years of what the Party has called "opening and reform." This has entailed both massive domestic economic reform *and* China opening up to the outside world, not just economically and diplomatically, but culturally and in an interpersonal sense as well. So the Chinese people are becoming more like middle-class people elsewhere. And our new urban lifestyles rotate around values that include more consumer choices, a greater sense of personal freedom, more openness to the outside world, and so on, just like we see happening in Hong Kong, Singapore, South Korea, and so on. And just like in America and these other places, this new lifestyle is totally wired. You've seen our streets and subways: everyone is on their mobile phone! Now, along with that new world of wired convenience and openness, we are also experiencing a terrible wave of cyberbullying. Every day we see more examples of what we Chinese call "language violence," meaning people using new technology and new media to injure others. I think it may be even rougher here in China than in the United States. And then you have the new-media messages coming from separatists in Xinjiang, or from parties arguing about Tibet, or Taiwan, and so on—really, Stephen, the Chinese internet is so incredibly complicated, and sometimes frightening.

Hartnett: I think our American readers are going to be very interested in this idea, because you're portraying a much more complicated China than is imagined by most Americans. In this China, it sounds like the interweaving of new technologies and new supply chains has yet to be matched by any functional oversight from the Party, so that beneath what looks like Party control of the traditional media you find an internet just seething with grievances, causes, rumors, and scandals.

Hu: It seems that both of our nations need to figure this out, for this is precisely where communication and convergence impact governance. Hopefully, China will do so before we experience something like your Trump phenomenon.

Hartnett: Ouch. Had to twist that knife. You couldn't resist, could you? . . . But seriously, on that note, let me turn here to Qingwen Dong to pursue this thread. So, Qingwen, I believe that you hold the distinction of being the first ever Chinese-born chair of a Department of Communication in America—congratulations to you! Because of that position, you're uniquely situated not only as a scholar of new media and communication in an international frame, but also as a cultural ambassador between China and the United States. So, can you please follow President Hu's comments and talk to us about this idea of how China, especially in this age of communication convergence/fragmentation, is in fact a culture that is incredibly complicated and politically fractured?

Qingwen Dong: I would add, Stephen, that any sense of political fragmentation, or of new media technologies driving new communication patterns, needs to address the fundamental question of unequal resource allocation. Both in America and in China, we have vast differences among people in access to information and participation. Some people have a lot of resources, but many others do not. So the kind of internet that people even think about, and the kind of relations people create via new online platforms, is in large part a reflection of other factors. Rural farmers, for example, who feel shut out of the political processes driving China's urbanization plans, have been incredibly active on the internet, yet it is not clear if they are able to transform their new media presence into actual political power. In America, on the other hand, we have seen how Steve Bannon has managed to turn a fringe website (Breitbart) into a platform that is now read daily in the White House. So a key question, I think, is trying to figure out how fringe elements from the web manage, or not, to make the leap into political power. It is a question, then, of figuring out the relationships between participating in new media platforms and making the move into more traditional forms of political participation. That question is as important for China as it is for America, and I think that asking that question will encourage us to think more deeply about the allocation of resources.

Hartnett: Thank you, Qingwen. That is a key reminder to always think about the ways our communication on and about new social media reflects issues of resource allocation—good. You know, we could talk about these questions all day, but I do want to turn to my friend Zhi Li, one of the hardest-working and brightest young men I've had the joy to meet in China, and, I should add, a professor who seems to always be working with teams of students. So I wanted to make sure we talk at least a little about pedagogy. And so I want to ask you, Zhi Li, to please describe how you try to teach your students to navigate the kinds of big questions we are discussing here.

Zhi Li: Well, Stephen, as you and President Hu and Qingwen have said, it's an age of simultaneous consolidation and fragmentation, and it's pretty hard to wrap your head around that kind of contradictory yet complimentary arrangement, right? So one thing we are really trying to do here at CUC is emphasize the importance of being ethical citizens. It's almost like the more things change in terms of technology, or supply chains, or regulation, the more we need to teach our students the foundational concepts of trust, and honesty, and integrity. As you know, though, I also think it is important to meet students where they are, and that can involve some humor and using lots of teaching examples taken from new media. Finally, I would add that here at CUC we are trying to do our best to make sure that our students not only are smart consumers of communication and good critics of it, but also have the production skills to make their own media. Making blogs and websites, shooting good video, and knowing how to edit—these are just basic skills that all communication students should know.

Hartnett: Indeed, Zhi Li, that's a great point. You know, every time I come to your campus, I am so impressed by your facilities and by how your students are all walking around with cameras and microphones and fancy laptops—they're all wired up and ready to go! Which makes me want to share with President Hu the fact that when I am joking around with Patrick, I call him a cyborg, because he knows more about new media technology than anyone I know. He doesn't just look at his computer, he opens six different windows at the same time and is accessing multiple screens, all while listening to audio files, sending texts, answering his phone, and tracking satellites on radar. No, really, it's like he's a one-man intelligence outfit, half human and half machine. So Patrick, following on Zhi Li's point about ethics and production skills in our age of convergence/fragmentation, how is it that you—as a cyborg and all—navigate these complexities?

Patrick Shaou-Whea Dodge: Come on, Stephen, you are starting to sound like my grandpa! This is how we live nowadays. What you call being a cyborg I call being plugged in! But seriously, I want to add to Li's notion of ethics by talking about voice. Students are getting inundated with messages all day every day, and as we've said here, they come from government sources, corporate sources, grassroots sources, and also some pretty dangerous sources—and it is sometimes hard to distinguish between them. It's even harder, within this deluge of information and noise, to answer the questions "Who am I?" and "What do I have to say?"—what is my "voice" in all of this? Now, within that question, I love new media platforms, because they are open-sourced and user-driven, and that means our students can participate on them and perhaps build their own voice. I especially love how these new media platforms cross national boundaries, so my students in Beijing can work with my students in Denver, or potentially in India or Tibet, or wherever, and this means we have a new generation of communicators with immense new power over what they consume, what they produce, and who they work with.

Hartnett: That feels to me, Patrick, like the hopeful, cyborg-style answer, that new media technologies are in fact enabling a new kind of global freedom. I think all of us here love that notion and wish it were so. But what would you say, Patrick, to what we know are the Party's efforts to block that kind of international solidarity and information flow? Yesterday, from a café in Beijing, I tried to go to the *New York Times* and couldn't get there. Then I tried to go to the *Washington Post* and I couldn't get there. As a scholar living in China, I know you struggle with these "Great Firewall" issues every day. So how do you have multiple perspectives fueling international solidarity when so many perspectives are blocked?

Dodge: This is where we go back to President Hu's point about the relationships between technology, communication, regulation, and governance. What's happening here in China is that with every step of communication regulation coming down from the Party, there are ten forms of resistance popping up. In this case, everyone in China with a certain level of resources knows that you just use VPNs to scale the Great Firewall. I have a handful on my laptop at any given time, so if one is blocked, then I use another—we all do this. We heard from our friends in the Party that they do this too. From this perspective, what the government calls regulation in the name of governance crashes into what I would call a larger sense of ethics, for if we agree that having access to information and being able to participate are keys to a healthy civil society, then using VPNs to get around the Great Firewall isn't so much rebellion and resistance as it is ethical and necessary.

Li: And we should remember that using those VPNs is in itself a marker of resource allocation. Not everyone has them or even knows what they are. Jumping the Great Firewall in China is a very middle-class kind of thing. This does not happen in the countryside or poor neighborhoods.

Dong: And just as that ability to deploy VPNs in the interest of joining larger conversations about civil society is a classed activity, so the Party here in China is also engaging in selective centralization, in the sense that they are marshaling their own technologies of surveillance against dissident intellectuals, human rights lawyers, and provocative artists. It really is a cat-and-mouse game, kind of a censorship/resistance dialectic, with all parties using new media technologies to serve their interests.

Hartnett: I like that metaphor of a game of hide-and-seek, or of cat-and-mouse, wherein citizens on new media platforms are in this constant dance with the authorities, building new spaces of communication as fast as they can. For me, that image summarizes how governance and resistance go hand in hand, how censorship and freedom are intertwined, and how new media technologies are being deployed by all sides in those equations.

With that image in mind, let me pivot now to the question of US–China relations. So, we're doing this interview as part of a book, and the book has come out of a series of conferences cohosted by the NCA, CUC, and JCDS, and all that work together has meant, over many years now, that we've all moved from being collaborators to becoming friends. So, first, thanks to all of you for your tremendous work. Second, do you see our conferences and this book as instances of how building opportunities for communication can lead to intercultural collegiality? And, third, thinking in terms of the big picture of US–China relations, does this notion of collegiality offer some hope for how our two nations might build better understanding between us?

Hu: Oh yes, in my view, our conferences have been very successful. What has made them so interesting, I think, is that we can come together around a shared set of concerns, say about communication, or convergence, or fragmentation, yet our national contexts are different, meaning our conversations have all had a strong element of comparative evaluation—there has been lots of listening across cultures and learning from each other. That combination of listening and learning is the foundation of collaboration and, I think, the first step toward a sense of intercultural understanding. Certainly, then, I would like to think that what we are trying to do with our conferences is to create platforms where such collaborations and collegiality can flourish. If you think that is a symbol of our nations learning to work together, then I am flattered.

Dong: I think that is what we are trying to do with these conferences, yes. And I would add that as we deepen these international pathways of collaboration and collegiality, we are seeing more and more Chinese graduate students coming to study in America. So, hopefully, our American colleagues can help to support this movement. At the University of the Pacific, we also now offer summer institutes, these weeklong intensive seminars where American and Chinese scholars work and learn with each other. We've seen that these seminars lead to all kinds of collaborative research projects, and so that's another avenue of building pathways of friendship between our two nations.

Li: And, I would add that we are pursuing similar partnerships here at CUC, including our Visiting Fellows Program with the NCA. It's important, I think, to make sure that what we are calling these pathways toward collegiality are embedded in recurring events, like conferences, or fellowships, so that we can build momentum over time, ideally institutionalizing the communication patterns that will fuel better relations between the United States and China.

Hartnett: You are all so right: I think that's really our task here, to try to create enduring platforms for Chinese and American scholars to learn together, to work together, and hopefully to become the kinds of friends and colleagues who can both advocate for and embody better communication between our nations.

So let me pivot again, for even as we try to build these bridges of collaboration and collegiality, the same new media communication forces we have discussed above are also driving an international wave of extremism. In Britain, a new nationalist populism has taken the form of folks voting to leave the European Union, the so-called Brexit. And of course Trump in America has been stoking this wave of xenophobia and white nationalism—it is very alarming, in both cases. So while we do our best to build platforms for international collaboration and collegiality, it seems other forces are dividing the world into little fiefdoms of anger. Is that happening in China as well?

Hu: You know, Stephen, what is interesting is that in both Britain and America it seems like that new populism, that new nationalism, is directed outward against others. You seem to spend a lot of time being afraid of things outside your borders. But in China, our populism, if you can call it that, is being driven by mostly domestic grievances. The incredible pace of our urbanization means we have tremendous conflicts between different social groups. This goes back to our discussion about fragmentation, as I see the biggest threats to China not coming from outside the nation but from within it. We need to do a much better job of *modernizing with justice*, of building a new China that includes everyone, not just the new, wired, urban elites.

Dodge: Yes, yes, and that notion of modernizing with justice points to a key concern, which is finding a way to merge our new media technologies, our new communication supply chains, and our new forms of regulation in the interests of healthy civic debate. Where both China and America get into trouble, I think, is when large sections of the population feel excluded from the conversation, right? That was the essence of Trump's victory: he tapped into this seething mass of unhappy, rural voters who felt abandoned by globalization. The farmers in China feel the same way. The urban poor in China feel the same way. Their political anger begins from a sense of exclusion, from their sense that all the things we're talking about today do not include them.

Li: Yeah, I think that's right on: the web has managed to open up new spaces of production and participation, but it has also exacerbated class divisions. I know you probably don't see this from America, but we have just as many social fractures in China as you do, maybe more, and many of them go back to this question of resource allocation—who is enjoying the benefits of "reform and opening," and who is feeling left behind?

Dong: And remember that those political divisions—whether we call them class, or rural versus urban, or ethnic and cultural, or regional—are all in some sense indications of how folks relate to new media technologies. Who has access to Wi-Fi? Who has the training to build websites? Who has the cultural capital to do the networking needed to convert their social media concerns into mainstream political actions?

Hartnett: That's why in the United States some of the groups I really respect are trying to do things like make sure everyone has equal access to Wi-Fi. They argue that the conversation cannot be democratic without full participation, so equal access to Wi-Fi becomes a baseline for healthy communication. The problem with this position, of course, is that by looking so hard at the question of access to technology, we can forget to think about questions of content—I am not so sure America benefits when more Klansmen have Wi-Fi! Still, as someone trained in a certain set of American values, I am inclined to think our First Amendment teaches us that more communication will, in the end, sort itself out—we like to believe that open discussion leads to good decisions and all that which comes after.

Li: And this is why the question of the governance of information is so important in China, for we tend to have a different sense of how healthy communication takes place. We don't have your First Amendment, and we don't have your traditions of open deliberation. And, you know, in America that is often portrayed as a bad thing, as if China is the land of repression. But then, we don't have Trump in power, do we? So the really tricky question is finding a balance between celebrating open deliberation, ideally fueled by new media technologies, yet also making sure that the governance of the nation is mature and credible. We have 1.5 billion people in China, we can't get this wrong, there is too much at stake.

Dong: This is why, I think, the Party is learning to tolerate, and maybe even respect, the voices of the people on all kinds of issues, just as long as they don't question the legitimacy of the Party itself. It feels, then, like the Party is trying to figure out how to utilize all these new forms of communication technology to help build a more inclusive and transparent political process, yet at the same time it can't go as far as the United States down that road of free speech. So along with the paradoxes of convergence and fragmentation, I think we're at a key historical point for the Party, as it tries to modernize and pursue more "opening and reform," albeit slowly and carefully.

Hartnett: And, you know, Qingwen, I think that those of us who work and travel and study in China eventually all come to see that there is a certain logic in that sense of a more controlled version of governance. We Americans are wedded to our First Amendment; it's almost like a religion to us. Yet as the Trump victory indicates, many, many Americans now believe that their federal government is dysfunctional. In comparison, every time I come to China I'm struck by the fact that the Party clearly works in many senses: China has these beautiful highways, beautiful airports, the best public parks I've ever seen. There's no homeless people on the streets, and your colleges and universities are bursting with bright young students eager to serve the nation. There is a sense that China has it going on, China is hot, China is doing some things very well, better even than the United States. So I think we have to admire how the Party has managed that wave of progress.

Dodge: With all of that tremendous energy, of course, wrapped up in potential ecological disaster—what we are calling the "airpocalypse" in Beijing—are imprisoned dissidents, tea talks, and tight control of the internet. But still, yes, the vision of the Communist Party for the past forty years has rested on this notion that if it can improve people's living standards, then they will happily sacrifice some political liberties. So instead of the religion of free speech and expression, President Xi Jinping is pushing his notion of "the China Dream," wherein everyone can expect a better house, or a better car, or a better job. And, in that dream you don't need free speech, you just need a sense of national harmony of everyone pulling together to rejuvenate China, to help make China great again.

Hartnett: Oh wow, Patrick, so you're saying Trump's "Make America Great Again" and Xi's "China Dream" are in fact very similar, sort of nostalgic pleas for some lost national greatness, for which everyone needs to pull together against the hostile world. Talk about convergence . . .

Dodge: Yeah, you bet. As we've seen at the National Museum where *The Road of Rejuvenation* is the central exhibit, the Party is now pushing this idea that China was, for centuries, the center of civilization. It was "the Middle Kingdom" that ruled the world. And President Xi is telling people that China can fulfill that role again, that it should fulfill that role like it is some national destiny. But my sense is that the people of China are less concerned about being the new "Middle Kingdom" than simply having a better life. Folks would like to be able to breathe without face masks, you know? Folks would like their water to not make them sick. Folks would like to be able to afford housing that doesn't force them to live in anonymous high-rises on the outskirts of town. In this sense, I think the Party in China, not unlike the government in America, is facing a real legitimacy crisis: they need to deliver on their promises, they need to show the people that the "China Dream" is not just empty talk.

Hu: Well, yes, and of course the Party knows this: they know both that they have to deliver the daily goods and innovate their governance structures. And this means, of course, that our conversation about how to harness new media technologies for better communication will really become one of the key tasks of the day.

Hartnett: That's exciting news, President Hu. And you know, Patrick and I have been meeting with the Party as well, talking about these same issues, and our friends at the International Department of the CPC say the same thing: that the "China Dream" is slowly but surely going to encompass a more open sense of citizen participation, both in traditional and in online forums. I'd like to believe that by having these kinds of conversations—at our conferences, in this talk today, across all kinds of international forums—we are doing our part to help build the sense of interpersonal and cross-institutional collegiality that will help facilitate the understandings that we need to make these processes more fruitful. In that sense, I'd like to thank you gentlemen for your contributions to all of our efforts. In closing, I'd like to think that we are doing our small part to help China and America learn to work together for a better future.

Epilogue

The conversations recorded here were infused with a sense of hope and forward momentum, yet by the spring of 2018 it appeared that US–China relations were heading for rough waters. President Trump announced an array of tariffs against

China, triggering alarm bells about a possible "trade war"; China's President Xi maneuvered the People's Congress into abolishing presidential term limits, meaning he can stay in office indefinitely. The hardening of Trump's anger toward China, and the hardening of undisputed one-party and even one-man rule in China, left observers wondering if the two great nations were digging in on their respective nationalisms, hence girding for conflict. We have no crystal ball for predicting where any of this will lead, yet the energies from this conversation seem now, in retrospect, even more urgent, for if US–China relations are to improve, then surely better communication habits and institutions will be a key ingredient of that possible success.

NOTE

1. Additional support was provided by the University of Colorado Denver's International College of Beijing, with special thanks to Pam Jansma, the Dean of the College of Liberal Arts and Sciences, and to the University of Colorado Denver's Center for International Business, Education, and Research, with special thanks to Manuel Serapio.

Convergence and Fragmentation in the Umbrella Revolution

A Rhetorical Analysis of the Mainlandization of Hong Kong

Andrew Gilmore

n the summer of 2014 Hong Kong captured the world's attention as its citizens collectively mobilized, descending throughout the streets of their city to express frustration at the Chinese Communist Party's (hereafter CPC or Party) "political suppression" of Hong Kong.[1] The Standing Committee of the National People's Congress had announced that Hong Kongers would not be allowed to choose candidates for the 2017 Hong Kong election. The Umbrella Resvolution, symbolically named after protesters used umbrellas to represent their calls for genuine universal suffrage and, at the same time, protect themselves from the police's use of tear gas and water cannons, was one of the largest and most prolonged on-street occupations ever witnessed. In acts described as "illegal occupation activities" by then chief executive CY Leung, Hong Kong's busiest areas were forced to a standstill for nearly three months as ephemeral campsites sprang up across the city.[2]

Although most Western and local news coverage of the Umbrella Revolution focused on Hong Kong's desire for democracy and genuine universal suffrage, a return trip I took to Hong Kong (where I had previously lived for three years) six months after the end of the occupation of city streets revealed that, for some, electoral restrictions are, in fact, not the main root of dissatisfaction in Hong Kong. Rather, as will be explored throughout this chapter, the combination of rising rent prices,

CPC controls on free speech, a widespread clampdown on universities, runaway consumerism fueled by Chinese shoppers from the mainland, concerns over health care, and more, have led to deep anger, frustration, and resentment among the city's seven million residents. Throughout this chapter, I refer to these complicated and overlapping causes for political anger under the notion of "mainlandization," which suggests that Hong Kong's long-standing sense of itself as an independent entity is now threated by encroachments from China.

Indeed, after 150 years of British colonial rule, and since Hong Kong's return to the People's Republic of China (the PRC) in 1997, the Party's governance of the city has been a contentious issue.[3] Take, for instance, the signing of the Sino-British Joint Declaration that set out a number of specific terms to which the Party agreed in relation to Hong Kong's return to China from the United Kingdom (UK). Despite the Declaration, because of the Party's actions, Hong Kongers feel their unique identity has increasingly eroded amid reunification with the mainland occurring at a rate that is much quicker than the fifty-year term outlined in the Declaration. The Party's approach to the governance of Hong Kong has been a contentious issue for Hong Kongers, ultimately resulting in hundreds of thousands flooding the streets and bringing their city to a standstill during "Occupy Central Through Love and Peace," the formal title of the protests that morphed into the Umbrella Revolution. From this perspective, the Umbrella Revolution was the culmination and outpouring of over fifteen years of fear, anger, and frustration that spilled onto the streets of Hong Kong and, in turn, presented the Party with a number of hurdles in its governance of the city. The issue, as locals saw it, was that the Party's governance of the city had diluted their language, identity, culture, tradition, and history. The longtime British colony was fearful, in short, that it was being recolonized, albeit this time by the CPC. As a case study in communication, then, the Umbrella Revolution shows us Hong Kongers fearing their forced convergence with the mainland, while we find the Party fearing the rebellion as foreshadowing of the possible fragmenting of the nation.

My conversations with a number of activists, bloggers, humanitarians, and journalists highlight the effects of China's ever-increasing influence over Hong Kong—often referred to as the *mainlandization, sinification*, or *Chinafication* of the city—as the real source of discontent. Described by journalist Alex Lai as the "erosion of the city's freedoms following the 1997 handover," the notion of mainlandization has led to many Hong Kong citizens feeling the uniqueness of their city has slowly ebbed away.[4] As a result of Hong Kong's position as a quasi-independent territory of China, and in response to the perceived erosion of the city's distinctive way of life, this chapter seeks to address the different tenets of the Party's governance of Hong Kong and to explore how the Party's influence is seeping into and affecting the daily-lived experience of Hong Kongers. These questions are fundamentally about *communication*, about how the CPC envisions its rule over Hong Kong, and how each expression of that new authority seems to send the Hong Kongers into paroxysms of protest, which are then covered by local and international media, hence creating the sense of a wave of political protest. Moreover, given the flow of information in the age of convergence, the news from Hong Kong was beamed to viewers around the world, meaning the local disturbances soon became a global phenomenon.

To provide context for these claims, I begin this chapter by exploring the increasing social and political pressures that have resulted from the mainlandization of Hong Kong. I discuss how the mainlandization of the city has influenced and affected a number of government policies, including education, housing, and media policies.[5] I argue that instead of directing sole blame for Hong Kong's current predicament toward Party politics and the city's electoral restrictions, interviewees describe the *plutocratization* of Hong Kong—in which the city is becoming ruled by the rich—as the real threat to the democratic future of Hong Kong. My interviewees argued that this process of mainlandization has raised housing prices, infiltrated the city's sense of a free press, and driven the identity of Hong Kongers even further away from their mainland counterparts. Instead of a convergence between the Chinese and Hong Kong ways of life that was sought as a result of Hong Kong's return to China in 1997, the notions of mainlandization and plutocratization have led toward a sense of growing fragmentation, hence illustrating what Hartnett and Hu, in the first chapter, highlight as one of the possible dangers of the age of convergence.

Next, I turn attention to CY Leung, Hong Kong's chief executive from 2012 to 2017. After his controversial election victory in 2012, many Hong Kongers feared the mainlandization process would accelerate as Leung symbolically represented the "catalyst for and champion of China's escalating moves to control Hong Kong."[6] Scholars, China-watchers, interviewees, and other people I spoke with believe that Leung encapsulates many of the tenets of the mainlandization and plutocratization of Hong Kong, and, I argue, at the same time, acts as a proxy for Beijing by being positioned as a scapegoat for Hong Kong's dissatisfaction, unrest, and resentment toward the Party. In terms of communication, then, Leung serves as a symbolic node for the debates discussed herein, standing as both the Party's proxy in Hong Kong and therefore as the target of the wrath of Hong Kongers. Indeed, Leung's position as what David Gruber has called the "synecdochical embodiment of the [Chinese] nation," and his acceptance and compliance to bow to the will of the Party, makes him a divisive and unpopular figure among Hong Kongers.[7] Throughout his time in office, Leung served as an important buffer and gatekeeper by enabling the Party to tighten its grip over the governance of Hong Kong. To this end, I make the argument that through all the historical twists and turns leading Hong Kong to its current predicament, Leung became a figurehead who was ridiculed by those frustrated, angry, and unhappy with the Party; however, at the same time, Leung also "saved face" for the Party by redirecting some of Hong Kong's anger and criticism away from President Xi Jinping and toward himself.

Finally, because the Umbrella Revolution encapsulates what many in the West anticipate as China's inevitable future—in which the now empowered and wired masses force the Party to open up and move toward democracy—it served as a remarkably powerful site of debate in US sources about politics and communication in China. At the same time, many observers in China saw the Umbrella Revolution as the work of imperial Western forces seeking to destabilize China. As this volume seeks to address how communication influences relations in and between the United States and China, so the Umbrella Revolution stands as a fruitful case study for how the two nations envision each other, seeing in the Umbrella Revolution a wide range of hopes and fears about the opportunities and dilemmas of convergence and fragmentation.

The Mainlandization of Hong Kong: Convergence, Fragmentation, and Fear

Since Hong Kong was handed over to China in 1997, the citizens of Hong Kong have increasingly felt the effects of the mainlandization of the city. To be more specific, Cheong defines the term as indicating "the erosion of freedom, plurality, tolerance, respect for human rights and the rule of law."[8] Gruber simply characterizes mainlandization as the "encroaching influence" of mainland China.[9] Scholars and China-watchers contend that the erosion of the city's sense of autonomy and unique characteristics is becoming more visible with each passing day.[10] One interviewee I spoke with summed up her feelings quite clearly, telling me that Hong Kong is "going down the toilet completely. Every day I spend in Hong Kong, I feel a little bit less in love with it."[11] From this perspective, mainlandization is synonymous with the forced convergence of Hong Kong with the mainland, amounting to nothing less than annexation or colonization.

A number of policies implemented by the Party, including handing down revised and Party-favoring education standards and media manipulation, are contributing factors to the mainlandization of Hong Kong. As I discuss later on in this chapter, many of these policies are inextricably linked to the plutocratization of the city as the social class lines in and between Hong Kong and the mainland blur, leading to further tension and unrest. Despite the fact that it will be another thirty years before Hong Kong's full reunification is finalized with the mainland, the process of unification is happening more quickly than many Hong Kong citizens would like. In turn, this acceleration of the reintegration process is leading to "increasing social and political pressures on [Hong Kong] society."[12] How events will unfold when the fifty-year term of the Joint Declaration expires in 2047 is still unclear.

Since the handover in 1997, evidence points to numerous attempts by the Party to strip Hong Kong of its "special administrative region" title.[13] One such endeavor occurred in 2009, when the Chinese State Council announced plans to transform Shanghai into a global financial and shipping center by 2020. Hong Kong business leaders were astonished by the possibility of their city falling behind Shanghai as China's leading financial and commerce hub.[14] Instances like this, when interpreted as attempts "to downgrade Hong Kong's importance," highlight the sense that what was once described as the "invisible hand" of the Party is becoming more prominent to Hong Kongers with each passing day.[15]

Before I turn to explore a number of Party decisions and policies that have contributed to the mainlandization of Hong Kong, I will address another of the major facets of the crisis: the Party's insistence on heavily influencing who leads Hong Kong and how its Legislative Council functions. Indeed, the Party's insistence on both preselecting the pool of candidates for whom Hong Kongers can vote and then determining their norms of deliberations provides overwhelming confirmation that the Party is seeking to control Hong Kong's daily governance. To this end, Leung was already seen as a Party sympathizer before he was elected as Hong Kong's chief executive in March 2012. As I will highlight throughout this chapter, during his time in office, Leung made a number of statements that reinforced his allegiance to the Party and, more often than not, can be construed as rhetoric that was sent directly from the Party, supporting Gruber's claim that Leung was a "party appointed stooge."[16] By delivering Party rhetoric to Hong Kongers, Leung attempted to take the brunt of criticism and outrage, and, in doing so, deflected anger and resentment away from the Party. In essence, Leung was the public face behind the CPC's mainlandization efforts, amounting to a convergence symbol for the debates swirling around the Umbrella Revolution.

Mainlandization as Culture Clash

The "dirtier" side of the mainlandization of Hong Kong is visible in a variety of forms, including the great "social, identity, and cultural tensions" that exist between Hong Kong citizens and residents from the mainland.[17] The attitude toward mainlandization, at least as argued by my Hong Kong interviewees, sees mainlanders "spit, litter, jaywalk and cut in line . . . they talk too loudly, eat on the subway and otherwise flout Hong Kong's more refined standards of public behavior."[18] Wealthy mainland visitors to Hong Kong are "dismissed as loutish boors who constantly flaunt their newfound wealth with newfound arrogance. . . . To the people of Hong Kong, the rich shoppers are *wong chung*—locusts—who buy whatever they can."[19] Hong Kongers disdain for "mainland parents allowing their children to urinate or even defecate in public" demonstrates just "how far apart culturally Hong Kong and mainland China are."[20] This notion of mainlanders using public areas as a bathroom is sometimes perceived as an urban myth around the city, but evidence does exist.[21] As one interviewee told me, "I used to say I can't believe that, but I've actually seen it a couple of times now, and at first, I kept thinking, God, this has got to be staged . . . but no, I've actually seen it."[22] As these examples demonstrate, many in Hong Kong perceive mainlandization as a culture clash between the urbane locals and Chinese interlopers who behave poorly.

As their city converges with the mainland, Hong Kongers feel they are losing the fight against mainlandization, and so stories that draw attention to the flaring tensions between Hong Kongers and mainlanders are commonplace across Hong Kong and Western media.[23] The rift between Hong Kongers and mainlanders, however, is evident on both sides. For example, Kong Qingdong, a Peking University professor, used an appearance on a Beijing talk show to air his disdain for the expectation from Hong Kongers that mainlanders should speak Cantonese when in the city. Kong was firm that mainlanders "don't have the responsibility to speak [the Hong Kong] dialect"—a linguistic reminder of ongoing cultural fragmentation—arguing instead that "everyone has the responsibility to speak Mandarin," the Party's preferred language of national convergence. But Kong did not end his comments there, instead adding a mean-spirited twist, noting that whereas in the past, Hong Kongers "were British running dogs, now they are just dogs."[24] For this nationalist Chinese scholar, the linguistic questions of speaking Cantonese or Mandarin are wrapped in a mainlander's contempt for the ways Hong Kong has been entwined historically with Western powers and culture.

The issue of the boorish behavior of mainland tourists is not limited to Hong Kong. There are increasing reports of Chinese tourists defacing centuries-old Egyptian sculptures or urinating on German highways as record numbers of Chinese tourists with "piles of cash but also mountains of problems" expand their horizons and travel the globe.[25] As China has become open in its bid to converge with the rest of the world, the China National Tourism Association has gone to great lengths to attempt to educate China's world travelers with the publication of a sixty-four-page illustrated *Guidebook for Civilised Tourism*.[26] With Chinese tourists overtaking Americans and Germans as the world's top-spending tourists, Chinese president Xi Jinping has even attempted to improve the habits of his nation's travelers, telling them, "Do not leave water bottles everywhere. Do not damage coral reefs. Eat less instant noodles and more local seafood."[27] Hong Kong, then, is not the only place chaffing at the hand of mainland visitors.

Mainlandizing Hong Kong's Political System

Despite the many dimensions of mainlandization, perhaps the most pressing concern is the mainlandization of Hong Kong's political system. As a result, Hong Kongers are "embroiled in fervent debates" regarding the issue of democracy and the "ominous erosion of civil liberties."[28] Human rights scholar Xiao Shu believes the corruption of the city's politics is "messing Hong Kong up" and that the Liaison Office of the Central People's Government in Hong Kong is at the heart of this corruption. Through the sale of Congress and National Committee seats at banquets and the offer of "power-for-money deals," the Liaison Office has "drowned in the ocean of corruption," Xiao alleges, thus impacting Hong Kong's integrity.[29] Here again, then, we see a Hong Konger arguing that China's mainlandization program amounts to a cultural assault, the imposition of values (supposedly) foreign to the locals.

Beijing's refusal to allow genuine universal suffrage was among the major causes—although, as I highlighted in my introduction, not the main root of Hong Kongers' dissatisfaction—leading to the outbreak of the Umbrella Revolution. The CPC's insistence on only allowing Hong Kongers to vote from a carefully selected Party-approved pool of candidates is a clear indication of the mainlandization of Hong Kong. Although the rigid sovereign voting rights were not overturned by Hong Kong's prolonged on-street occupation, when a number of Hong Kongers under the age of forty, including Nathan Law—a major figurehead of the Umbrella Revolution—won seats on Hong Kong's seventy-member Legislative Council (LegCo) in 2016, a triumph over the pro-Beijing opposition.[30]

Despite the Party still exerting power and influence over the makeup of LegCo and the governance of the city—registered Hong Kong voters elect only 50 percent of the seventy seats—one of the successful candidates, Sonny Shiu-Hing Lo, has described the 2016 election as representing a "generational change in the pro-democracy movement." For Nathan Law, the youngest person to ever be elected to LegCo, his success was a self-confessed "miracle."[31] Whatever progress was made, however, was expeditiously shattered when six of the newly elected prodemocracy advocates of LegCo, including Nathan Law, were disqualified from taking their seats due to what the Party deemed "improper oath-taking."[32]

Leung's assertion that "oath-taking must be done strictly by the book with no additions or deviations" in order to demonstrate that the electee "sincerely and truly believe[s] in the pledges under the oath that he or she is taking"—further evidence of Leung's status as a proxy for maintaining Chinese law in Hong Kong—was flouted by each of the disqualified candidates, acts described by opposition lawmakers as a "declaration of war."[33] Reports suggest that after quoting Mahatma Gandhi—"You can chain me, you can torture me, you can even destroy this body, but you will never imprison my mind"—Law's tone of delivery changed, as if he was asking a question, when it came to stating that he would "swear allegiance to . . . the People's Republic of China."[34] Despite the seemingly great advances made by leaders of the democracy movement, Hong Kong is still firmly governed by the Party. This suggestion was not lost on one of the disqualified electees, Leung Kwok-hung, who was outraged: "This can't happen in any place with true democracy."[35] In terms of communication patterns, then, it is interesting to watch as Hong Kongers portray their city as a well-run and corruption-free democracy suffering at the hands of Party-controlled hacks imposing Communist-style control.

The Mainlandization of Education

Since Hong Kong's handover in 1997, the education of the city's youth has been a hotly debated subject.[36] The proposed implementation of "moral and national education" in Hong Kong schools was a major strategy adopted by the Party to help foster a dominant and united Chinese identity across Hong Kong. The proposed education policy included "lessons on Chinese government bodies and the correct etiquette for raising the national flag."[37] Visual and emotive tools, such as flag raising and the singing of national anthems, are used in an attempt by governments to create "symbolic glue" that encourages individuals to bond and build a sense of togetherness.[38] For the Party, Thomas Kwan-choi Tse posits that the goal of such strategies is to encourage Hong Kong citizens "to show loyalty to the central government and to solve the crisis of legitimacy and governance."[39] As has been true globally as well, then, Hong Kongers are debating the roles of public education as a chief means of cultivating a sense of allegiance to the nation-state, with Party-imposed curriculum striking many as a prelude to forced convergence with the mainland.

The sharing of the Chinese national anthem is another contentious issue that has recently reared its head in Hong Kong.[40] The jeering at "March of the Volunteers" at sporting events across the city was not received well by the Party, and suggestions that the recent implementation of the National Anthem Law in the mainland, which punishes people who "disrespect" the anthem by up to fifteen days in jail, could be extended to Hong Kong, has led to further concerns about the increasing mainlandization of the city.[41] In both of these cases of forced educational curricula and the forced singing of China's national anthem, we see Hong Kongers retreating to a sense of local autonomy and freedom—*fragmentation* in the eyes of the Party—as a response to what they perceive as the CPC's crass efforts to impose convergence.

For some, education is used "deliberately to regulate and normalize Hong Kong people as Chinese" through "heavy doses of patriotism." The goal of the education policy is to promote a sense of a shared identity to students who "are taught to be positive about the mainland, learn to appraise its achievements, strengths, and future prospects, and accommodate any differences with Hong Kong."[42] Of course, scholars have drawn attention to the many criticisms of the "brainwashing propaganda" of the National Education Policy that "subtly manipulates a Chinese identity" for students.[43] As the Party targets Hong Kong's youth to encourage and strengthen a kinship with the mainland through the city's education system, Hong Kong's students are not the only group affected, as the city's teachers are required to promote and teach a Chinese ideology. In this way, they are both complicit with the Party's governance of Hong Kong and, at the same time, also victims of mainlandization. Indeed, teachers complain about their academic freedoms being surreptitiously eroded. According to Denise Y. Ho, assistant professor in the Department of History at Yale University, Hong Kong scholars are under surveillance and their classrooms are no long free from outside interference and scrutiny. "What are the implications of the stranger who appears in the audience of your lecture course, who appears again in the talk you've organized on China's Cultural Revolution?" asks Ho.[44]

Many commentators believe that the Party's interference in Hong Kong's education system was laid bare when, in 2015, Hong Kong University voted to reject the promotion of Johannes Chan. Despite recommendations for Chan from countless faculty and students, half of the official committee—all of whom were either appointed by CY Leung or had deep ties to the Party as delegates to the National People's Congress—voted to reject Chan for promotion. According to Ho Fung-Hung, Chan's rejection marked "the death of academic freedom in Hong Kong." Chan's supporters believe that his area of expertise—constitutional law—in concert with his friendship with prodemocracy leader Benny Tai, led to a decision "orchestrated by Beijing." The Chan debacle, I argue, provides clear evidence of the mainlandization of Hong Kong's education system.[45]

Hong Kong resistance to the proposed national education policy resulted in the legislature temporarily shelving the education bill. Leung revisited the bill in 2012, but Hong Kongers, again, were not in favor of the Party-driven and mainland-focused education policy that proposed implementation of pro-China "patriotic lessons" in schools.[46] Despite the fact that Leung's proposed bill was later vetoed, reports suggest that Hong Kong classrooms, nevertheless, are being infiltrated by mainlandization. In 2014 and 2015, advocacy groups suggested that 70 percent of the city's primary schools and 40 percent of its secondary schools use *putonghua* (Mandarin) over Cantonese for Chinese-language lessons.[47] University of Hong Kong lecturer Lau Chaak-ming believes that the gradual elimination of Hong Kong's mother tongue from the city's classrooms provides yet further evidence of how the Party's governance of and influence over Hong Kong is leading to the waning of the city's sense of local identity and culture.[48]

The Mainlandization of Hong Kong's Media

As the Party attempts to limit the use of Cantonese in classrooms, Hong Kong is not the only region where greater Party influence is exerted. Guangdong province (Canton), a two-hour train ride north from Hong Kong, is another Cantonese-speaking region where the CPC has attempted to impose language policies.[49] For instance, the governance of Cantonese spread to a Guangdong TV station when, in 2014, it announced plans to broadcast the majority of its programs in *putonghua*, or standard Chinese.[50] Although local television stations in Hong Kong are still able to broadcast in Cantonese, the increasing influence, power, and control over Hong Kong's media is a growing concern for the city's residents and provides further evidence of the mainlandization of a city that has traditionally been renowned as a place that embraces press freedom.

The rights and freedoms of the city's press were specifically highlighted in the Joint Declaration that was agreed upon prior to Hong Kong's return to the PRC in 1997.[51] Since the handover, however, the mainlandization of the city's press has been a much-explored and debated subject. The editorial independence of Hong Kong's most popular English-language newspaper, the *South China Morning Post* (*SCMP*), was questioned after the publication was purchased by Jack Ma, one of China's wealthiest tycoons and owner of Chinese e-commerce giant Alibaba.[52] Assertions by Alibaba that it purchased the *SCMP* in in order to "promote wider views of China's rise as a global economic power" did nothing to quell the fears of commentators and Hong Kongers alike.[53]

Rumors that the *SCMP* had morphed into a Party mouthpiece were compounded when the publication ran a controversial interview with a recently released Chinese activist who wished to express remorse for her actions against her country.[54] After Wang Yu claimed in the *SCMP* interview, "I am a Chinese and I only accept the Chinese government's leadership," Hong Kong media analyst David Bandurski spoke of how the interview was eerily similar to the type of forced confessions broadcast on Chinese state media that have become commonplace since President Xi took control of the Party in 2012. Incidents like this add credence to journalist Zheping Huang's assessment that as the suppression of Hong Kong media outlets increases, the city's mainstream media take on new meanings as extensions of Chinese state media.[55] In other words, as mainlandization overtakes Hong Kong's mainstream media outlets, news agencies can no longer be fully trusted, as they are pressured into discrediting CPC critics and portraying the Party in a more favorable light.[56] In this instance, communication convergence can feel close to censorship of opposing views and forced complicity with the Party's preferred positions.

The purchase of Hong Kong's oldest and most respected English-language newspaper by a wealthy mainland tycoon is an important development with regards to the mainlandization and plutocratization of Hong Kong and, in turn, indicates the Party's growing governance of the city through its media outlets. Immense corporations such as Alibaba, functioning as what Harnett terms "old-fashioned monopolies," in the first chapter of this book, has led to what many fear is a "dangerous consolidation of political power" that has infiltrated many facets of Hong Kong life. Indeed—the ongoing culture clash, the mainlandization of the political and education systems, the gradual erosion of a free press, the ever-increasing cost of living, and, more worryingly, the visibility of a growing wealth disparity across the city—all lead to concerns that Hong Kong has become a plutocracy controlled by wealthy mainlanders with deep ties to the Party.[57]

The Plutocratization of Hong Kong: A City Ruled by the Rich

As Hong Kong's gap between rich and poor becomes greater than that in mainland China, vast amounts of money spent and invested by elite classes in Hong Kong are leading to the plutocratization of the city.[58] Defined as a society that is governed by the wealthy, elite, or a ruling class of people whose power derives from their wealth, *plutocracy* was a word used habitually by my interviewees in Hong Kong. Indeed, people I had conversations with generally spoke of the success and upward mobility of mainlanders in Hong Kong leading to the fragmentation and disparity of wealth in the city and, hence, to a spiral of downward mobility for locals across Hong Kong.

Within debates about plutocratization, a key source of contention is how mainlanders accumulate wealth—what one observer calls their "ill-gotten gains"—in Hong Kong.[59] For example, the bulk purchasing of apartments, according to one interviewee I spoke with, is a way of laundering money out of China in a bid to circumvent a mainland law that limits the amount of money that Chinese citizens can exchange overseas. This exodus of money from China was highlighted in the 2016 Panama Papers, which reported that Hong Kong's innumerable exchange shops are aiding in the flow of money from the mainland at an "unprecedented rate."[60] Moreover, the leaked documents revealed that at least seven current and former Chinese leaders, including President Xi, and their families were among the biggest perpetrators of these laundering acts. To this end, Chinese leaders can be viewed among the leading plutocrats driving the mainlandization of Hong Kong.

The growing notion of the plutocratization of Hong Kong is reinforced by *The Economist*'s crony-capitalism index. Published on an annual basis, the index is designed to measure and compare countries based on their main sources of wealth, and then to count the number of *crony businesses*, which the publication defines as industries that are "vulnerable to monopoly, or that involve licensing or heavy state involvement."[61] These industries are "more prone to graft" according to the bribery rankings produced by Transparency International, an anticorruption watchdog. The article, which uses *Forbes* data to rank billionaire wealth as a percentage of a country's—or, in the case of Hong Kong, a city's—wealth, ranks the places where government-connected businesses are most likely to prosper. With almost sixty "crony" business sectors versus twenty-two "non-crony" sectors, Hong Kong ranks number one in the world for crony sector wealth. Russia, with less than twenty "crony" business sectors, ranks number two, while the United States was sandwiched between Thailand and Poland in seventeenth place.[62] Interestingly, the locals I spoke with noted that, across the city, this disparity of wealth is the real issue disrupting the daily lives of Hong Kongers and driving their anger toward the Party. In this sense, the Hong Kongers I spoke to are not much different from those Americans who feel that wealth disparities in the United States point to an economy that is fundamentally unfair. In both contexts, the sense of economic injustice fuels a rising tide of political frustration.

Indeed, as in Paris and New York and Beijing, Hong Kong has become a city of extremes. Providing home to the sixth highest number of billionaires in the world, the city now ranges from obscene wealth to desperate poverty.[63] In 2017, the *SCMP* reported that the richest 10 percent of households in Hong Kong earn around forty-four times that of the poorest families.[64] Despite attempts by the Hong Kong government to address the city's wealth disparity, CY Leung made a statement during the height of the Umbrella Revolution explaining that the reason genuine universal suffrage in Hong Kong would not be successful was because "you would be talking to half of the people in Hong Kong who earn less than HK$1,800 a month. Then you would end up with those kind of politics and policies."[65] Leung's statement is indicative of the Party's (radically *not* Communist) stance, in which the post-Communist plutocracy is wary of giving too much power, voice, and political agency to Hong Kong's poorer populations. Put simply, by continuing to refuse genuine democracy, the Party and the Hong Kong government ensure that the rich continue accumulating wealth while the poor continue their struggle to survive in the world's most densely populated city. And so the Party's governance of Hong Kong ensures that the plutocracy is maintained. Nowhere is the notion of the plutocratization of Hong Kong more visible than in the city's unsustainable housing market.

Housing

With a median housing price of US$631,026 and a median income of only US$37,020, 2015 saw Hong Kong ranked at the top of a global list of unaffordable housing for the fifth consecutive year.[66] Because of this imbalance, Hong Kongers have been pushed to the outlying areas of their city. Hong Kong journalist and author Joyce Man expresses the sentiment, "I resent that being a homeowner in Hong Kong means saving for over a decade to buy a miserable hovel in the boondocks."[67] The Tuen Mun suburb is one example of the far-flung areas of Hong Kong where mainlandization is taking hold to the detriment of Hong Kongers. Nestled away in Hong Kong's New Territories, Tuen Mun is a two-hour commute to the city's Central district. With a square footage that is only "slightly larger than the average American kitchen," and a price tag of 2.9 million Hong Kong dollars (about US$375,000), even the cheapest Tuen Mun apartment is out of reach for a frustrated generation "increasingly unable to afford the lives their parents had."[68] Large swaths of Hong Kongers can simply no longer afford to reside in their own city. In this case, China's forced convergence of Hong Kong with wealthy mainland investors has led to a dramatic sense of fragmentation within the city, as large swaths of the population are forced to move out of heavily populated and history-rich neighborhoods into the city's new, far-flung suburbs.

Hong Kong is not exceptional in this sense, as gentrification across the globe is leading to the displacement of local residents who can no longer afford to live in neighborhoods where they have spent their entire lives.[69] The concept of gentrification is often associated with its Anglo-American and Western heartland, but one has only to look at the vanishing of Beijing's heritage through the declining number of hutongs to see that gentrification is spreading to Asia.[70] Indeed, scholars argue that despite a lack of research into gentrification in Hong Kong, the concept is evident across the city.[71] One employee of a Hong Kong community alliance believes that the gentrification of Tin Shui Wai—one of Hong Kong's poorest suburbs—underlines how the city is being "plagued" by the wealth gap that is increasingly polarizing the rich and the poor.[72] Evidence suggests that Hong Kong, then, is undergoing wrenching transformations similar to those seismic real-estate shifts hitting London, Berlin, Denver, and Shanghai. In each of these booming metropolises, families are being forced to move further from the center of the city.[73] In more severe cases, some Hong Kongers are reduced to residing in "wire mesh cages resembling rabbit hutches" in dilapidated Kowloon buildings, rooftop shanty towns, and "coffin homes" that are too small for inhabitants to fully stretch out their legs.[74] Gentrification and mainlandization are also leading to the vanishing of local family-run businesses.[75] Street-side cobblers who mend shoes in a matter of minutes are forced to abandon their rickety tin huts. Locals who have peddled dumplings and egg waffles for generations are being forced to close their doors. Their replacements are yet more lustrous apartment developments unobtainable to the average Hong Konger.

As a result, research suggests that more people than ever are leaving the city as Hong Kongers and expats are increasingly questioning their future in the city.[76] In a heartfelt op-ed for the *SCMP*, for example, Joyce Man echoes the sadness of many Hong Kongers as they contemplate leaving their home city. "It feels like desertion and betrayal," she writes. Hong Kongers are leaving "not because they do not love Hong Kong, but because they can't bear to see the home they love slip away."[77]

Fragmented Identities in an Age of Convergence: Hong Kong, Not China

The unease or, in some case, fear that Hong Kong citizens feel toward the mainland has gradually come to fruition over the past twenty years. Long-standing tensions directed at the mainland and Party were, in fact, initiated by Hong Kongers who risked their lives by migrating from the mainland in the 1950s in order to escape what has been described as "the chaos of the Chinese civil war and Maoist repression."[78] Seeking refuge from the mainland, a large majority of the migrants settled in Hong Kong to raise families.[79] People went to Hong Kong to "seek protection and build a life that was separate from the mainland," and to escape the hard labor, assaults, and repression of Communist China.[80] "Everyone here is a refugee. They came and they knuckled down, they worked really hard and they saved everything that they had, gave their kids a better life, to go to university, and they made it."[81] Over the course of the following fifty years, trepidation toward the mainland was ingrained in the children and grandchildren of Hong Kong's Chinese migrants as the fears, experiences, and prejudices of older generations were shared with younger Hong Kongers.

And so, over time, older-generation Hong Kong families disassociated from their mainland roots and, despite moving to the relative safe haven of Hong Kong, felt that "China was always too close for comfort." Younger family members grew up "know[ing] nothing other than Hong Kong."[82] This experience and mind-set has led to the emergence of fragmented and hybrid identities that merge a sense of being Chinese (in a civilizational sense), Western (in a consumer and freedoms sense), yet mostly Hong Kongese in a unique sense—hence the chants during the Umbrella Revolution and other high-profile events: "We are Hong Kong," "End one-party dictatorship," and "Reject the deterioration of Hong Kong."[83]

Thus, Hong Kong identity and the notion of being Hong Kong-ese has been adopted by citizens who do not "want to be ruled by a country that massacres its own people."[84] When negotiations regarding Hong Kong's sovereignty began in 1982, for example, the Hong Kong public quickly became aware that the city's return to China could become a reality. The Chinese citizens who had fled to Hong Kong were shocked; the nation that they had risked their lives to escape was about to return and take them back. For these Chinese migrants, reunification with the PRC would "defeat their entire life projects" of escaping the clutches of Communist China.[85] As these comments indicate, many Hong Kongers base their sense of self on the premise of *fragmentation from China*; this is why mainlandization strikes them as so dangerous, for it amounts to the forced convergence with the same Communist Party they fled generations ago.

This also explains why differing views about challenging the Party's power appear to be one significant element in the deeply divided mind-sets of different generations of Hong Kongers. While many older Hong Kong citizens believe in a united China, they do not want Communist Party rule. This was reflected in the sentiment of one Hong Konger I spoke to: "I really look for a united China. But they must be unified by the means of democracy, freedom of rule of law, respect of human rights and equality."[86] Speaking with different generations of city residents reveals clear divides between different mind-sets. Much of this stems from the fact that older Hong Kongers have firsthand experiences with the extreme efforts the CPC will deploy to support its totalitarian rule. These experiences have led to older generations that value stability over radical political change, a mind-set that, no doubt, appeases the Party. The maintenance and promotion of a Hong Kong identity, however, is an element of the city's existence that continues to antagonize the Party.

For these reasons, the notion of identity is a delicate issue in Hong Kong.[87] Around 95 percent of Hong Kong's population is Chinese-born, yet, despite being "proudly Chinese," Hong Kongers are deeply "steeped in Western ways," as a result of 150 years of British colonial rule.[88] Accordingly, in Hong Kong "an entire generation act on their sense of alienation from China and its values," resulting in the hybrid and distinct identities discussed above. Thus, Hong Kongers are disconnected from the mainland, "never sure how they fit into the People's Republic."[89] A study carried out by Hong Kong University reveals the disparity in the city's contested and ambiguous sense of identity. In late 2016, 45 percent of the 1,001 people surveyed identified as "Hong Konger," while 47 percent identified as having a mixed identity. Only 16 percent identified as being "Chinese."[90] Maintaining Chinese heritage, culture, and history while, at the same time, upholding the liberties and rule of law that distinguish Hong Kong from the rest of China is a delicate balancing act that forms a major part of everyday lived experience.[91] Indeed, many Hong Kongers draw a clear distinction between China as a nation and China as a Communist regime. For example, one commentator suggested that while Hong Kongers "[do] not wholly repudiate the notion of being Chinese . . . a love of China does not necessarily entail the love of the CPC."[92] Chinese scholar J. F. Tsai similarly notes this incongruity, observing that "in the past one hundred years, Hong Kong people politically identified China as their motherland and yet at the same time held a negative view of the government."[93]

Mainlanders, too, feel a sense of detachment from Hong Kongers. Journalist Sergey Radchenko believes that despite the various elements linking Hong Kong to the mainland, for mainlanders, "Hong Kong is effectively a foreign country."[94] Mainlanders feel patriotic toward Hong Kong, but little is actually known about the city, and the issues and struggles faced by Hong Kongers do not resonate with the mainland. To many mainlanders, Hong Kong is "an attractive but hopelessly remote world of Cantonese pop singers and Jackie Chans"—these cultural divisions make it "virtually impossible to bring the two mind-sets together."[95]

These cultural and communicative divisions stem in large part from the fact that young Hong Kongers have only experienced Hong Kong as a fairly free society separate from the mainland; as a consequence, they had not—prior to the Umbrella Revolution—witnessed Party brutality and its heavy forms of governance firsthand. This youthful exuberance, which could be construed as naivete, led to the sometimes-violent confrontations between Hong Kongers and the police that were witnessed during the Umbrella Revolution. Instead of stability, young Hong Kongers want real change, a life that is not dictated by the CPC, and they are not afraid to stand up to and question the government. Many young Hong Kongers therefore believe in the "one country, two systems" policy "to the absolute max," as they "are saying, 'You [China] stay out of our business and we'll [Hong Kong] stay out of yours.'"[96] It makes sense, then, that the seemingly contradictory and ambiguous sense of national identification that has steadily grown in Hong Kong is viewed by the Party as a threat to its governance. David Gruber explains that Hong Kongers see themselves as "citizens of the world, with strong ties stretching back to England."[97] The Party, however, is unable to accept this notion, as it derails the plans for the "reunification" of Hong Kong with the mainland. Here again we see that the Hong Kongers' desire for a local sense of autonomy, for being fragmented off from the mainland, stands in stark opposition to the Party's goal of national convergence.

CY Leung: Agent of and Symbol of Convergence

Often referred to as "689," a sarcastic reference to the number of votes he needed to secure to preside over a city of over seven million people, CY Leung was sworn in as the chief executive of Hong Kong in July 2012.[98] Leung's tenure as the city's leader was not without controversy. Within seconds of being sworn into his newly acquired role, Leung proceeded to dismay Hong Kongers by presenting his inauguration speech in *putonghua*, as opposed to the Cantonese dialect favored by a large majority of Hong Kong's Chinese residents.[99] Throughout his four-year tenure, Leung was viewed by many as an obedient Beijing lackey, a "Party appointed stooge," a cunning wolf in sheep's clothing.[100] Leung faced a string of controversies during his time as chief executive, including, but not limited to, the HK $400 million Karolinska Institute donation scandal, the discovery of six "illegal structures" at his multi-million-dollar Hong Kong mansion, his daughter working as an underage intern at JP Morgan, and accusations of failing to declare income from a 2011 HK$50 million deal with an Australian engineering firm.[101] Controversy and unrest followed Leung and continued to plague his term in office, culminating, of course, with his handling of the 2014 Umbrella Revolution.

A Hong Konger from a humble upbringing in an immigrant family, Leung was raised in the city's low-income government housing complexes. His past is relatable to the many Hong Kongers stuck within the spiral of downward mobility that cripples the city. Like many families at the time, Leung moved to Hong Kong to seek refuge from political turmoil in the mainland. In the buildup to the 2012 election, Leung went to great lengths to present himself as somebody from the grassroots of Hong Kong, without links to the tycoons who are stifling the city.[102] Revered by his supporters, Leung was a working-class hero, a man of the people who, today, still uses the same briefcase that he used as a student.[103] The view of Leung's supporters, however, is in stark contrast to that of his detractors. Despite his Hong Kong roots, Leung is often despised as a figure that local media have branded an untrustworthy wolf, a closet Communist, and "a very obedient cadre," who has been carefully trained by the Party to carry out its orders.[104] Leung's immense wealth, gained as a result of his successful career in the real estate sector, coupled with his speedy rise through the political ranks, has led to his being referred to as the "emperor of the working class."[105]

Despite the negativity and anger directed at Leung by a large majority of Hong Kong's population, during his tenure as chief executive, Leung was credited with successfully combating some of the issues that drive mainlandization, including banning mainland women from traveling to Hong Kong to give birth, stopping the parallel trading of baby milk powder, and increasing public housing supplies.[106] These successes were not enough to boost his popularity, however, and in 2016, shockwaves rippled across Hong Kong when Leung announced that he would be the first chief executive in the city's history to not seek a second term.

A leader with few sympathizers—to the extent that rolls of toilet paper carrying images of his face were sold—many Hong Kongers were happy to learn of Leung's planned departure; he "had it coming," quipped one observer.[107] Commentators spoke of Leung's "confrontational and belligerent style of governance," which had divided and polarized Hong Kong during his four-year term as the city's leader.[108] Throughout his tenure, marked with multiple controversies and moderate successes, the main issue facing Leung was the fact that Hong Kong citizens did not choose him as their leader. The main obstacle Leung was unable to navigate was his unwillingness and, importantly, his inability to provide Hong Kongers with their desired goal of universal suffrage. Journalist Harriet Alexander asks if Leung was "a cunning wolf or simply a diligent servant of the Party who obediently carried out its instructions." This distinction between Leung's unwillingness or inability to gain the trust and support of Hong Kongers is what made him such a divisive, untrusted, and reviled figure.[109]

Leung may have been born in Hong Kong and may have raised his children in the city, but like many wealthy Chinese families, his children were educated abroad. As the owner of at least five properties around the world, including a multi-million-dollar home on the Peak (Victoria Peak), Leung lives a life that is far beyond the means of the citizens he is supposed to represent. As one interviewee suggested, "The fact that many wealthy Chinese are not investing their vast fortunes back into the country does not demonstrate a belief in Xi Jinping's Chinese Dream; rather, it indicates that wealthy tycoons have an insurance policy" against the collapse of China. "Where do they educate their kids? Where do they buy all of their property? Where's all their money stashed? In very up-market parts of London," claimed one interviewee when asked about Party loyalists in Hong Kong. Leung's reluctance—and that of other Party supporters—to provide his children with a local Hong Kong education and invest in the city appear to provide further evidence of his disinterest in the future of Hong Kong as an autonomous region of China and, as a result, his embodiment of mainlandization.[110] This is a major irony, then, as Leung was the politician tasked with enforcing China's mainlandization policies in Hong Kong, in part by revising the city's convergence-favoring educational programs, even as he sent his children abroad for their own education.

From a communication perspective, Leung's position as a scapegoat for Beijing's attempts to control Hong Kong functioned in a number of ways. First, despite the notion that Beijing should have been the main focus of Hong Kong's dissatisfaction during the Umbrella Revolution, it was caricatures of Leung that appeared on protesters' posters and placards. In the colorful protest signs and street art displayed during the Umbrella Revolution, Leung was depicted as Chairman Mao (a Communist), Pinocchio (a liar), a wolf (a predatory oppressor), a zombie (the living dead that prays on the living), and a vampire (sucking the life out of Hong Kong).[111] Leung's acting as a scapegoat for the Party meant that resistance to its attempts to dominate Hong Kong's governance structures were diffused and directed away from the Party.

Most of the warnings issued to protesters throughout the Umbrella Revolution, including the announcement that the chances of winning concessions from Beijing was "almost zero," were delivered not by the Party, but by Leung. This resulted in Leung taking the brunt of the blame and shielding the Party from criticism.[112] After all, throughout his tenure as the city's leader, Leung was pelted with various objects, including eggs, a glass, Ikea plush toys, and even "hell money," not to mention a constant barrage of verbal abuse each time he was in public.[113] As a leader who was parodied in a Pac-Man-style computer game, which became a hit among Hong Kongers, and who had an abandoned bus decorated and labeled as "CY Leung's coffin"—destination "Hell"—suffice it to say that Leung "lost face" on countless occasions during his tenure as Hong Kong's chief executive, albeit while dutifully protecting the Party.[114]

But Leung was not the only individual targeted. The CPC and its leader, President Xi Jinping, were not let off the hook completely and were—and are still—caricatured in memes and parodies by Hong Kongers.[115] However, throughout the duration of the Umbrella Revolution, President Xi did not feature as prominently on placards and artwork. Instead, Leung's face—often with added fangs—was splashed across banners, shirts, and toilet paper. Moreover, the Party did not have to deal with the "inconvenience" of protests in Beijing, Shanghai, Shenzhen, or any other mainland city. Instead, Leung was left to fend for himself and deal with the wrath of Hong Kongers during a seventy-nine-day protest and, for that matter, his entire four-year reign as Hong Kong's chief executive, while the Party continued to rule over the rest of the nation that is—mostly—obedient and loyal to its Party and leaders.

There is little doubt that challenging a single individual rather than the entire totalitarian regime is easier. An argument can be made that by directing anger and frustration at Leung, Hong Kongers felt that they had more chance of achieving their perceived goal of universal suffrage. After all, attempts to take on the CPC have historically not ended well. Editorials in the *People's Daily*—an official mouthpiece of the Party—warned Hong Kongers of the "unimaginable consequences" that would result from the continued occupation of the city's streets.[116] This also meant that directing anger toward the Party would not have been a wise move, due to the striking similarities between the *People's Daily* editorial published during the Umbrella Revolution and the notorious editorial from the same publication during the 1989 Tiananmen Square protests. Indeed, China-watchers, including Al Pessin, who was expelled from Beijing for his coverage of the Tiananmen Square protests, were quick to draw parallels between the Party rhetoric of 1989 and 2014. For Pessin, the use of the word "chaos" on the front page of the *People's Daily* to describe the acts of Hong Kong protesters was worryingly reminiscent of 1989. As "a significant term in Chinese Communist Party ideology," explains Pessin, *chaos* suggested that Hong Kongers' actions had the potential to "threaten the Party's hold on power."[117] When the word was used in 1989 to describe Tiananmen protesters, the military quickly acted to curb the dissent. When coupled with the sight of Hong Kong police donning military-like uniforms and implementing the use of tear gas and rubber bullets in an attempt to disperse protesters—another vision of Tiananmen—parallels, however faint, could be drawn between Tiananmen and the Umbrella Revolution.[118] Additional threats, such as President Xi's direct warning that any attempt made by Hong Kongers to challenge the Party's authority would be "an act that crosses the red line, and is absolutely impermissible," provided a stark reminder to Hong Kongers that their actions should be well thought through and the possible consequences considered before taking a stand against the Party.[119] We might speculate, then, that targeting Leung was a safer route of political protest than attacking the Party; if this is true, then Leung served as a condensation symbol, a catchall figure encapsulating protesters' anger while deflecting threats against the Party.

The polarizing nature of CY Leung was perhaps best typified in a 2015 address to welcome in the Lunar New Year of the sheep—the first Chinese New Year after the Umbrella Revolution. Leung urged Hong Kongers to "take inspiration from the sheep's character and pull together in an accommodating manner to work for Hong Kong's future."[120] The irony of his appeal appears to have been lost on both Leung and the Party. First, the phrase carries a negative connotation by way of the fact that sheep are commonly viewed as docile animals that follow instructions and do not act independently: a role that Hong Kongers are unwilling to fulfill. Second, by advising Hong Kongers to toe the Party line, Leung is outing himself as a Party loyalist—a role that has been alleged by his detractors and opponents, and that is contrary to his supposed character as a humble Hong Konger. Moreover, if Leung was continuing to portray himself as a Hong Konger, he was also inadvertently admitting to also being a sheep: essentially admitting his status as a Party lackey. Finally, Leung's common depiction as a wolf—a predator of sheep—portrays him as an enemy of Hong Kong and, hence, a key protagonist of mainlandization.

Conclusion

After focusing on the outbreak of Hong Kong's Umbrella Revolution, this chapter set out to explore the perceived notion of the mainlandization of Hong Kong and to address how mainlandization has seeped into and affected the everyday lives of Hong Kongers. Mainlandization is visible through a number of Party-influenced policies including housing, education, and the media, all of which have had a destabilizing effect on Hong Kongers. To this end, I posit that the Party's governance of Hong Kong is a leading, if not *the* principle contributing factor to the mainlandization of Hong Kong. After addressing how mainlandization has been a major factor in the plutocratization of Hong Kong and how this interacted with the long-standing hybrid identities that threaten Party power, I turned to an individual whom I consider to be the chief protagonists of the mainlandization and plutocratization of Hong Kong, the city's former chief executive, CY Leung. I argued that Leung is the ultimate embodiment of mainlandization. Despite portraying himself as a humble Hong Konger, Leung's tenure as chief Executive was plagued by controversy and accusations of shady business dealings, illicit wealth, and Party roots. Finally, I claimed that throughout his time in office, Leung acted as a proxy for Beijing by being positioned as a scapegoat for Hong Kong's dissatisfaction and unrest. Thus, within the dialectic of convergence and fragmentation, Leung was the central figure and key symbol, the literal face of mainlandization and, hence, target of the Umbrella Revolution.

I argue that Leung's role as a scapegoat worked in the Party's favor. Leung's position ensured that, throughout the Umbrella Revolution, he shielded the Party from the bulk of criticism and dissatisfaction by taking the brunt of the blame, which was directed toward him instead of Beijing. Leung lost a great deal of face during his tenure. He was forced to withstand a barrage of verbal abuse, was pelted with eggs, was parodied through cartoon characters and animals, and was even villainized through the memorialization of his pseudo-death.[121] By acting as a scapegoat for the Party, resistance to its attempts to dominate Hong Kong's governance structures were diffused, directed away from the Party and, instead, toward Leung. Thus, while he was ridiculed by protesters, he also protected the reputation and maintained the face of the Party.

And it all worked out in his favor. For all the sacrifices Leung made, despite losing face throughout his tenure as Hong Kong's chief executive—especially throughout the Umbrella Revolution—his loyalty to the Party was rewarded. In 2017, Leung was elevated to vice-chairman of the Chinese People's Political Consultative Conference, the PRC's political advisory body. He received overwhelming support for election as a result of his "firm stance against pro-independence advocacy and the Occupy Central protests."[122] Leung, it would appear, has been heavily rewarded for following Party orders throughout the Umbrella Revolution. Perhaps Leung played a long game and, despite personal tribulation, obediently followed Party lines in order to secure his long-term future.

NOTES

1. Alan Wong, "Ruling Threatens Hong Kong's Independence from China," *New York Times*, December 22, 2017.

2. "Police Clear Final Hong Kong Protest Site at Causeway Bay," *BBC News*, December 15, 2014.

3. See Raquel Carvalho, "Growing Tensions between Hongkongers and Mainland Chinese Sparked by Government's Decisions, Says Activist Priest Father Franco Mella," *South China Morning Post*, January 31, 2016; Bill Chou, "New Bottle, Old Wine: China's Governance of Hong Kong in View of Its Policies in the Restive Borderlands," *Journal of Current Chinese Affairs* 44, no. 4 (January 20, 2016): 177–209; David R. Gruber, "A Beijing Wolf in Hong Kong: Lufsig and Imagining Communities of Political Resistance to Chinese Unification," in *Imagining China: Rhetorics of Nationalism in an Age of Globalization*, ed. Stephen J. Hartnett, Lisa B. Keränen, and Donovan Conley (East Lansing: Michigan State University Press, 2017), 371–394; Ng Kang-chung, "Hong Kong Leader Leung Chun-Ying: Cunning Wolf or Loyal Government Servant?," *South China Morning Post*, December 9, 2016.

4. Alex Lai, "Thousands Protest Hong Kong's China-Fication," *CNN*, July 2, 2012.

5. Daniel Garrett, "Visualizing Protest Culture in China's Hong Kong: Recent Tensions over Integration," *Visual Communication* 12, no. 1 (February 1, 2013): 55–70.

6. Gruber, "Beijing Wolf," 372.

7. Ibid.

8. C. Cheong, "Hong Kong Fears Mainlandization," *China Post*, September 9, 2011, https://www.pressreader.com.

9. David R. Gruber, "The (Digital) Majesty of All Under Heaven: Affective Constitutive Rhetoric at the Hong Kong Museum of History's Multi-Media Exhibition of Terracotta Warriors," *Rhetoric Society Quarterly* 44, no. 2 (March 15, 2014): 149, doi:10.1080/02773945.2014.888462.

10. See Zarina Banu, "Erosion of Hong Kong's Core Values," *Al Jazeera*, September 2, 2014; "Marchers Take to Streets of Hong Kong to Protest Eroding Autonomy," *All Things Considered* (National Public Radio), accessed May 20, 2018; Lally Weymouth, "Hong Kong's Laws 'Are Being Eroded,'" *Washington Post*, April 9, 2015.

11. Interview with the author, June 8, 2015, in Hong Kong; note that to protect them from possible reprisal, all interview subjects are quoted herein anonymously; all interviews used herein were conducted according to Colorado Multiple Institution Review Board Protocol 15-0407.

12. Garrett, "Visualizing Protest Culture in China's Hong Kong," 57.

13. To read more about the Party's numerous attempts to strip Hong Kong of its "special administrative region" title, see Frank Ching, "Misreading Hong Kong," *Foreign Affairs*, May 1, 1997; Warren I. Cohen and Li Zhao, *Hong Kong under Chinese Rule: The Economic and Political Implications of Reversion* (Cambridge: Cambridge University Press, 1997); Ralf Horlemann, *Hong Kong's Transition to Chinese Rule: The Limits of Autonomy* (New York: Routledge, 2003); "Who's the Boss? China's White Paper on Hong Kong," *Tibetan Political Review*, July 10, 2014.

14. See "Feeling Special," *The Economist*, June 4, 2009; Francois Gipouloux, *Gateways to Globalisation: Asia's International Trading and Finance Centres* (Cheltenham: Edward Elgar, 2011); Dan Steinbock, "Shanghai Free-Trade Zone Plan Offers New Challenges to Hong Kong," *South China Morning Post*, July 29, 2013.

15. Interview with the author, June 8, 2015, in Hong Kong. Horlemann, *Hong Kong's Transition*.

16. Gruber, "Beijing Wolf," 371.

17. Garrett, "Visualizing Protest Culture," 58.

18. Sharon LaFraniere, "Mainland Chinese Flock to Hong Kong to Have Babies," *New York Times*, February 22, 2012.

19. Tim Sullivan and Sylvia Hui, "Protests Reveal Unease over Hong Kong's Identity," *Washington Examiner*, October 12, 2014.

20. Zoher Abdoolcarim, "Hong Kong in Turmoil: 5 Takeaways from Weekend of Protests," *Time*, September 28, 2014.

21. The following authors all discuss Hong Kong's very public bathrooms: Daniel Garrett, *Counter-hegemonic Resistance in China's Hong Kong: Visualizing Protest in the City* (Singapore: Springer Singapore, 2015); Gruber, "Beijing Wolf"; Carol A. G. Jones, *Lost in China? Law, Culture and Identity in Post-1997 Hong Kong* (Cambridge: Cambridge University Press, 2015); Ishaan Tharoor, "Chinese Toddler Pees in Hong Kong Street, Stirs Online Firestorm," *Washington Post*, April 30, 2014.

22. Interview with the author, June 8, 2015, in Hong Kong.

23. Alex Liu and Chun Chiu, "Cause of Resentment between Hongkongers & Mainlanders," *China Daily*, September 26, 2012; Gruber, "Beijing Wolf"; Key, "Peking University Professor Says Some Hong Kong People Are Dogs," *ChinaHush*, January 25, 2012.

24. "Rift Developing between Hong Kong Residents, Mainland Chinese," *Public Radio International*, February 23, 2012.

25. Amy Li, "Rude Awakening: Chinese Tourists Have the Money, but Not the Manners," *South China Morning Post*, December 31, 2014.

26. Gwynn Guilford, "Chinese Government Publishes Guide on How to Avoid Being a

Terrible Tourist," *The Atlantic*, October 7, 2013.

27. "Chinese Tourists Spent 12% More in Travelling Abroad in 2016," *World Tourism Organization*, April 12, 2017. Li, "Rude Awakening."

28. Francis L. F. Lee and Joseph Man Chan, "The Political Consequences of Ambivalence: The Case of Democratic Reform in Hong Kong," *International Journal of Public Opinion Research* 21, no. 1 (March 1, 2009): 51. Alice Miller, "How's Hu Doing?," *Hoover Institution*, January 30, 2004, 84.

29. Xiao Shu, "Hong Kong's Civil Disobedience against 'Mainlandization,'" *Human Rights in China*, January 28, 2015.

30. See Suzanne Pepper, "The Kids Are Alright: Hong Kong's Latest Elections Are Proof the Umbrella Revolution Did Not Fail," *Hong Kong Free Press*, September 11, 2016; see also Stuart Lau and Shirley Zhao, "'It's a Miracle': Ex-Student Leader Nathan Law Celebrates New Status as Hong Kong's Youngest Ever Lawmaker," *South China Morning Post*, September 5, 2016.

31. Tom Phillips and Eric Cheung, "Hong Kong Elections: Anti-Beijing Activists Gain Foothold in Power," *The Guardian*, September 5, 2016.

32. Chris Lau and Kimmy Chung, "Court Ruling Disqualifying Hong Kong Lawmakers over Oath-Taking Controversy 'a Declaration of War,'" *South China Morning Post*, July 15, 2017.

33. Ibid.

34. Shirley Zhao, "Oath-Taking Antics: The Acts That Got Six Hong Kong Lawmakers Disqualified," *South China Morning Post*, July 14, 2017.

35. Lau and Chung, "Court Ruling Disqualifying."

36. For more information about the mainlandization of Hong Kong's education system, see Winnie Cheng and Janet Ho, "Brainwashing or Nurturing Positive Values: Competing Voices in Hong Kong's National Education Debate," *Journal of Pragmatics* 74 (December 1, 2014): 1–14; Thomas Kwan Choi Tse, "Remaking Chinese Identity: Hegemonic Struggles over National Education in Post-colonial Hong Kong," *International Studies in Sociology of Education* 17, no. 3 (September 1, 2007): 231–248; Joyce Lau, "Thousands Protest over China's Curriculum Plans for Hong Kong," *New York Times*, July 29, 2012; Tracy Lau, "State Formation and Education in Hong Kong: Pro-Beijing Schools and National Education," *Asian Survey* 53, no. 4 (2013): 728–753; Yew Chiew Ping and Kwong Kin-ming, "Hong Kong Identity on the Rise," *Asian Survey* 54, no. 6 (2014): 1088–1112; Thomas Kwan-choi Tse, "Constructing Chinese Identity in Post-colonial Hong Kong: A Discursive Analysis of the Official Nation-Building Project," *Studies in Ethnicity and Nationalism* 14, no. 1 (April 1, 2014): 188–206.

37. Andrew Higgins, "Hong Kongers Resist Pressure to Identify with 'Motherland,'" *The*

Washington Post, June 28, 2012.

38. Gerald Webster and Antoni Luna Garcia, "National Identity Case Study: How Is National Identity Symbolized?," *AAG Center for Global Geography Education*, accessed May 20, 2018.

39. Tse, "Constructing Chinese Identity," 188.

40. "Hong Kong Football Fans Boo China National Anthem," *BBC News*, October 6, 2017; Euan McKirdy and James Griffiths, "Hong Kong Football Fans Take a Stand as Chinese Anthem Law Looms," *CNN*, November 17, 2017.

41. McKirdy and Griffiths, "Hong Kong Football Fans."

42. Tse, "Constructing Chinese Identity," 188, 193, 198.

43. Ping and Kin-ming, "Hong Kong Identity," 1102; Thomas Kwan-choi Tse, "Constructing Chinese Identity in Post-Colonial Hong Kong: A Discursive Analysis of the Official Nation-Building Project," *Studies in Ethnicity and Nationalism* 14, no. 1 (April 1, 2014): 188.

44. Denise Ho, David Schlesinger, and Ho-Fung Hung, "Mao's Invisible Hand in Hong Kong," *Foreign Policy*, October 2, 2015.

45. Ibid.

46. Harriet Alexander, "Who Is CY Leung and Why Do the Hong Kong Protesters Want Him to Resign?," *The Telegraph*, October 1, 2014.

47. Yuen Chan, "Mother Tongue Squeezed out of the Chinese Classroom in Cantonese-Speaking Hong Kong," *Hong Kong Free Press*, July 22, 2015; Elaine Yau, "Cantonese or Putonghua in Schools? Hongkongers Fear Culture and Identity 'Waning,'" *South China Morning Post*, September 2, 2014.

48. Yau, "Cantonese or Putonghua in Schools?"

49. Edward Wong, "Move to Limit Cantonese on Chinese TV Is Assailed," *New York Times*, July 26, 2010; Yau, "Cantonese or Putonghua in Schools?"

50. Yau, "Cantonese or Putonghua in Schools?"

51. "The Joint Declaration," paragraph 3.5, government website, Constitutional and Mainland Affairs Bureau, July 1, 2007.

52. See Rick Carew, "Alibaba to Buy South China Morning Post," *Wall Street Journal*, December 11, 2015; Tom Phillips, "Mysterious Confession Fuels Fears of Beijing's Influence on Hong Kong's Top Newspaper," *The Guardian*, July 25, 2016.

53. Carew, "Alibaba to Buy."

54. Zheping Huang, "China Is Using Hong Kong's Media to Broadcast Its Smear Campaigns," *Quartz*, August 1, 2016; Phillips, "Mysterious Confession."

55. Phillips, "Mysterious Confession." Huang, "China Is Using Hong Kong's Media."

56. The assertion that Hong Kong's media outlets can no longer be fully trusted was made by

a subject during an interview with the author, June 8, 2015, in Hong Kong. This claim is furthered in Gruber, "Beijing Wolf."

57. Yonden Lhatoo, "Hong Kong's Appalling Wealth Gap Is a Burning Fuse for Revolution," *South China Morning Post*, October 13, 2016; "Local Wealth Inequality Worsens as Richest Earn 29 Times More than Poorest," *Oxfam Hong Kong*, October 11, 2016; Cannix Yau and Viola Zhou, "What Hope for the Poorest? Hong Kong Wealth Gap Hits Record High," *South China Morning Post*, June 10, 2017.

58. Interview with the author, June 8, 2015, in Hong Kong.

59. Ibid.

60. Celia Hatton, "Panama Papers: How China's Wealth Is Sneaked Abroad," *BBC News*, April 6, 2016.

61. "Planet Plutocrat—Our Crony-Capitalism Index," *Economist.com*, March 15, 2014. See also Stephen J. Hartnett and Laura A. Stengrim, *Globalization and Empire: The U.S. Invasion of Iraq, Free Markets, and the Twilight of Democracy* (Tuscaloosa: University of Alabama Press, 2006).

62. "Planet Plutocrat."

63. Laurel Moglen, "The Brilliant Billionaires of Hong Kong," *Forbes.com*, March 30, 2017.

64. See Yau and Zhou, "What Hope for the Poorest?"; "Hong Kong Poverty Situation," Government of the Hong Kong Special Administrative Region, 2016; Carrie Lam, "Government Measures to Cut Poverty in Hong Kong Are Delivering Results," *South China Morning Post*, December 1, 2014.

65. For information regarding Hong Kong's vast wealth disparity, see Yau and Zhou, "What Hope for the Poorest?" For more on CY Leung's thoughts on the city's poor, see Paul Krugman, "Plutocrats Against Democracy," *New York Times*, October 23, 2014.

66. Liz Dwyer, "The 10 Least Affordable Housing Markets in the World," *TakePart*, January 23, 2015.

67. Joyce Man, "Is It Time to Leave Beloved Hong Kong?," *South China Morning Post*, September 4, 2014.

68. Sullivan and Hui, "Protests Reveal Unease."

69. The following authors provide excellent work surrounding gentrification: Loretta Lees, Tom Slater, and Elvin Wyly, *Gentrification* (New York: Routledge, 2007); Loretta Lees, Hyun Bang Shin, and Ernesto López-Morales, eds., *Global Gentrifications: Uneven Development and Displacement* (Chicago: Policy Press, 2015); Kate Shaw, "Teaching and Learning Guide for Gentrification: What It Is, Why It Is, and What Can Be Done about It," *Geography Compass* 4, no. 4 (April 1, 2010): 383–387.

70. For more on China's gentrification, see David Ley and Sin Yih Teo, "Gentrification in Hong

Kong? Epistemology vs. Ontology," *International Journal of Urban and Regional Research* 38, no. 4 (July 1, 2014): 1286–1303; Michael J. Meyer, *The Last Days of Old Beijing: Life in the Backstreets of a City Transformed* (New York: Walker & Company, 2008); Minting Ye, Igor Vojnovic, and Guo Chen, "The Landscape of Gentrification: Exploring the Diversity of 'Upgrading' Processes in Hong Kong, 1986–2006," *Urban Geography* 36, no. 4 (2015): 471–503.

71. Ley and Teo, "Gentrification in Hong Kong?"

72. "Are the Rich Getting Richer?," *South China Morning Post*, November 19, 2015.

73. Grace Charles, "A 20% Rent Rise Has Forced Us out of Our Home," *The Guardian*, May 2, 2015; Zhou Mo, "Housing Costs Are Forcing Out Young Generation," *China Daily*, July 15, 2015.

74. Nick Enoch, "Hong Kong's Metal Cage Homes: How Tens of Thousands Live in 6ft by 2ft Rabbit Hutches," *Daily Mail*, February 7, 2013. For more information on Hong Kong's tiny residences, see Brian Cassey, "'From Mansions, to Cages, to Coffins—Hong Kong's Rotten Property Ladder' . . . ," *Brian Cassey Photographer*, June 29, 2013; Alan Taylor, "The 'Coffin Homes' of Hong Kong," *The Atlantic*, May 16, 2016.

75. Eric Cheung, "Family Firms Priced Out as Chain Stores Dominate up to 96% of Mall Space—Survey," *Hong Kong Free Press*, July 23, 2015; Jun Concepcion, "Soaring Rents in Prime Locations Push Out Local Shops and Restaurants," *South China Morning Post*, May 19, 2018; Lizzie Meager, "Hong Kong's Excessive Retail Rental Prices Are Damaging Local Trade," *European CEO*, September 25, 2014; Bettina Wassener and Mary Hui, "Hong Kong Rents Push Out Mom and Pop Stores," *New York Times*, July 3, 2013.

76. Ivan Broadhead, "Hong Kong Exodus: Middle Class Leave City for Freedoms Overseas," *VOA*, November 20, 2013; Te-Ping Chen and Chester Yung, "Politics, Cost of Living Push Hong Kong Residents Overseas," *Wall Street Journal*, August 21, 2013; Man, "Is It Time to Leave Beloved Hong Kong?"; Verna Yu, "Giving Up on Hong Kong," *New York Times*, February 18, 2015.

77. Man, "Is It Time to Leave Beloved Hong Kong?"

78. Sullivan and Hui, "Protests Reveal Unease."

79. Michelle Fei, "The Great Exodus," *China Daily*, April 20, 2011; He Huifeng, "Forgotten Stories of the Great Escape to Hong Kong," *South China Morning Post*, January 13, 2013; Gordon Mathews, Eric Ma, and Tai-Lok Lui, *Hong Kong, China: Learning to Belong to a Nation* (New York: Routledge, 2007).

80. Interview with the author, June 8, 2015, in Hong Kong; see also Verna Yu, "Veterans Who Fled Mainland for Hong Kong in 1970s Tell Their Stories," *South China Morning Post*, January 7, 2013.

81. Interview with the author, June 8, 2015, in Hong Kong.

82. Ibid.

83. See Marilynn Brewer, "Multiple Identities and Identity Transition: Implications for Hong Kong," *International Journal of Intercultural Relations* 23, no. 2 (March 1, 1999): 187–197; Tim Hamlett, "Hong Kong Identity . . . What Exactly Is It?," *Hong Kong Free Press*, June 18, 2017; Ping and Kin-ming, "Hong Kong Identity." For evidence of pro–Hong Hong chants, see Jennifer Creery, "Hong Kong Gov't Criticises 'Disrespectful, Sensational, Misleading' Chants at Annual Democracy Rally," *Hong Kong Free Press*, July 2 2018; "Occupy Central Protesters Chant in Hong Kong," *MSN.com*, March 2, 2015; "Watch: Local Soccer Fans Chant 'We Are Hong Kong!' during China National Anthem before EAFF Game against North Korea," *South China Morning Post*, November 12, 2016.

84. Edward Wong and Alan Wong, "Seeking Identity, 'Hong Kong People' Look to City, Not State," *New York Times*, October 7, 2014.

85. Mathews, Ma, and Lui, *Hong Kong, China*, 39.

86. Interview with the author, June 9, 2015, in Hong Kong.

87. Andrew Gilmore, "Romancing the Chinese Identity: Rhetorical Strategies Used to Facilitate Identification in the Handover of Hong Kong," in *Rhetorical Criticism: Exploration and Practice*, ed. Sonja K. Foss, 5th ed. (Long Grove, IL: Waveland Press, 2017), 476–486; Higgins, "Hong Kongers Resist Pressure"; Sebastian Veg, "Hong Kong's Enduring Identity Crisis," *The Atlantic*, October 16, 2013.

88. "Feeling Special." See also Higgins, "Hong Kongers Resist Pressure"; Wong and Wong, "Seeking Identity."

89. Wong and Wong, "Seeking Identity." "Feeling Special."

90. "數表 Table," *Hong Kong University Pop Site*, April 23, 2017, https://www.hkupop.hku.hk/english/header.html.

91. Higgins, "Hong Kongers Resist Pressure."

92. Ping and Kin-ming, "Hong Kong Identity," 1101.

93. J. F. Tsai, *Hèunggóngyàhn Jì Hèunggóngsí* [The Hong Kong People's History of Hong Kong, 1841–1945] (Hong Kong: Oxford University Press, 2001), 2.

94. Sergey Radchenko, "Why Hong Kong Showdown Could Never Have Morphed into Tiananmen 2.0," *Reuters Blogs*, October 10, 2014.

95. Ibid. Interview with the author, June 8, 2015, in Hong Kong.

96. Ibid.

97. Gruber, "Beijing Wolf," 378.

98. Katie Hunt, "C.Y. Leung: Hong Kong's Unloved Leader," *CNN*, October 3, 2014.

99. Te-Ping Chen, "New Hong Kong Leader Opts for Mandarin," *Wall Street Journal*, July 1,

2012; Gruber, "Beijing Wolf"; Hunt, "C.Y. Leung"; Mark McDonald, "A Telling Language Lesson in Hong Kong," *IHT Rendezvous*, Jauly 1, 2012.

100. Gruber, "Beijing Wolf," 371; Hunt, "C.Y. Leung"; Suzanne Sataline, "Heads, Beijing Wins. Tails, Hong Kong Loses," *Foreign Policy*, March 24, 2017.

101. See Jeffie Lam, "CY Leung Feels Heat over Donation to Karolinska Institute—Where His Son Studies," *South China Morning Post*, February 17, 2015; Lai Ying-kit, "C.Y. Leung Admits Liability for Illegal Structures," *South China Morning Post*, November 23, 2012; Raymond Cheng, "Hong Kong Chief Executive Denies Using Influence to Land Daughter Internship at Major Bank," *South China Morning Post*, November 24, 2016; "Everything You Need to Know about Hong Kong Leader CY Leung's HK$50 Million UGL Deal and More," *South China Morning Post*, May 23, 2017.

102. Hunt, "C.Y. Leung."

103. Alexander, "Who Is CY Leung?"; Te-Ping Chen, "Who Is Leung Chun-Ying?," *Wall Street Journal*, March 25, 2012; Hunt, "C.Y. Leung."

104. Hunt, "C.Y. Leung."

105. "Hong Kong's Irrational Election Process," *Asia Sentinel*, October 3, 2011.

106. See "HK to Limit China Birth Tourism," *BBC News*, April 25, 2012; Kris Cheng, "Ban on Mainland Women Giving Birth in HK to Remain as One-Child Policy Axed," *Hong Kong Free Press*, October 31, 2015; Ng Kang-chung, "Hong Kong Leader"; Emily Tsang, Thomas Chan, and Tony Cheung, "Government Set to Crackdown on Infant Formula Trading," *South China Morning Post*, February 1, 2015.

107. "China Seizes HK Novelty Toilet Rolls," *BBC News*, February 7, 2015. Chan Chi-kit, "Who Is Beijing Really Unhappy With? CY Leung or HK People?," *EJ Insight*, December 14, 2016.

108. Chi-kit, "Who Is Beijing Really Unhappy With?"

109. Alexander, "Who Is CY Leung?"

110. Interview with the author, June 8, 2015, in Hong Kong.

111. For Umbrella Revolution caricatures of CY Leung, see https://cdn.cnn.com/cnnnext/dam/assets/140310033121-hong-kong-parody-protest-3-horizontal-large-gallery.jpg (Mao); https://www.scmp.com/news/hong-kong/article/1103279/chief-executive-cy-leung-set-survive-no-confidence-vote (Pinocchio); https://media.gettyimages.com/photos/cardboard-figure-depicting-hong-kong-chief-executive-leung-chunying-picture-id459846735 (a wolf); https://coconuts.co/public/field/image/occupy_art_-_scary_cy.jpg (a zombie); https://www.scmp.com/news/hong-kong/article/1600540/students-march-cy-leungs-door-dissent-grows (a vampire).

112. Tom Phillips, "Hong Kong Protests: CY Leung Angers Activists and Says They Have 'Zero Chance' of Winning," *The Telegraph*, October 12, 2014.

113. *Hell money* is a Chinese ritual saved for the deceased and a serious insult when given to the living. Karen Cheung, "Man Who Attempted to 'Egg' CY Leung Sentenced to 80 Hours of Community Service," *Hong Kong Free Press*, April 13, 2016; Gruber, "Beijing Wolf"; Tom Grundy, "Why Are Hong Kongers Going Crazy for 'Lufsig' the Toy Wolf?," December 9, 2013; Jeffie Lam, "Police Called to Legco after Glass Thrown towards CY Leung amid Pan-Democrat Walkout," *South China Morning Post*, July 4, 2014. On Leung losing face: *face* is an important sign of respect in Chinese culture. To save face is to maintain reputation and to keep dignity and honor intact; to lose face is embarrassing and shameful.

114. See Amy Nip, "Cuddly Wolf Lufsig Becomes C.Y. Leung's Virtual Nemesis in Online Game," *South China Morning Post*, December 16, 2013; Andrew Gilmore, "Hong Kong's Vehicles of Democracy: The Vernacular Monumentality of Buses during the Umbrella Revolution," *Journal of International and Intercultural Communication* (2019), https://doi.org/10.1080/17513057.2019.1646789.

115. Nicole Kwok, "Hong Kong Handover: Memes Making Fun of Chinese President Xi Jinping and His Wife, CY Leung, and Others," *Quartz*, June 30, 2017; Peter Martinez, "Winnie the Pooh Censored in China after President Xi Jinping Comparisons," *CBS News*, July 17, 2017.

116. Nikhil Sonnad, "Here Is the Full Text of the Chinese Communist Party's Message to Hong Kong," *Quartz*, October 1, 2014.

117. Al Pessin, "Analysis: China Raises Hong Kong Rhetoric to Tiananmen Level," *VOA*, October 2, 2014.

118. Hanna Kozlowska, "Is Hong Kong's 'Umbrella Revolution' a New Tiananmen?," *New York Times*, October 2, 2014.

119. Rick Moran, "China's President Xi Threatens Crackdown on Hong Kong," *PJ Media*, July 1, 2017.

120. Danny Lee, "CY Leung Urges Hongkongers to 'Be Like Sheep' in Lunar New Year Message," *South China Morning Post*, February 18, 2015.

121. Gilmore, "Hong Kong's Vehicles."

122. "CY Leung Wins Nomination as Vice-Chairman of Top China Body," *South China Morning Post*, March 10, 2017.

Fragmentation and Convergence in the Construction of National Imaginaries in US and Chinese Documentaries

Zhi Li and Xi Wang

I n different contexts, the word "other" has different meanings. For example, in the modernist philosophy of Jean-Paul Sartre, the concept of the "other" was defined as indicating the opposite of the self, as something external and foreign.[1] Within the history of colonization and expansion, this philosophical understanding was loaded with Western notions of domination, often including a sense of Europe's assumed racial and cultural superiority.[2] In the specific context of the history of the British Empire, "other" has been positioned at the margins of political discourse, marking one extreme of what Stuart Hall has called "the West and the rest" discourse.[3] More recent scholarship has called such binaries into question, suggesting that the history of global imperialisms is in fact much more complicated than a monolithic "West" conquering various "others." Under the notion of "alternative modernities," this new thinking suggests that there have been multiple centers of power over the ages, and multiple sites of political struggle and resistance, hence rendering the notion of "others" and "otherness" less totalizing and more local.[4] Nonetheless, the notion of the other remains a powerful indicator of political oppression. According to Zhang, the notion of the other "implies the condition of marginalization, subordination, inferiority, being oppressed, and excluded." As a consequence, within a wide range of humanistic disciplines, working with and alongside those once deemed other has become a hallmark of scholars who, according to Zhang, are committed to "pursuing justice, equality, freedom and liberty."[5] Indeed, within this discursive context of scholars working for justice—and hence breaking down the notions of self and other, West and rest, powerful and powerless—emphasis is placed on examining cultural peculiarities, community progress, and lingering problems through a comparative lens that supports cross-cultural communication and understanding.

In the age of convergence, the notion of otherness is increasingly complicated, as global media flows enable consumers around the world to view images from almost limitless sources. Moreover, convergence means these global media streams are now multilayered, including local and national news, comedies, sports, weather, and more—hence rendering the notion of "others" more multiple, more complicated. The most obscure Balinese comedies, Hindu dance, Australian rugby, Nigerian folks songs, or American news are now just a click away—within this infinite data-stream, what is "other"? Nonetheless, documentary films have long served a key role in Western countries of conveying a normative sense of preferred—and sometimes oppositional—national imaginaries.[6] In China, on the other hand, documentaries have always been associated with the needs of the Communist Party of China (hereafter CPC or Party), rendering them, in the eyes of most viewers, as little more than propaganda. We are concerned, then, with the fascinating question of how a sense of the nation, a stable and coherent national self, is constructed in documentaries in America and China, in both cases by creating a sense of external others who threaten the nation. Our goal, then, is to address national image construction in both American and Chinese documentary films, offering a comparative analysis of how they construct senses of self and other, even while acknowledging the more complicated contexts of identification made possible by the age of convergence. In this way, our analysis contributes to the understanding of US–China relations, as we hope to show how each nation imagines itself in documentaries, and hence, at the same time, imagines the "other" as well.

Indeed, with the development of new media technologies, the paradox of convergence and fragmentation has become increasingly relevant in the new era. On the one hand, more voices from different social classes have been included in political debates via the online public sphere; on the other hand, the problems of low-quality information, fake news, and rumors bring great trouble for both citizens and governments. In terms of documentaries, the situation is ever more complicated because China's mainstream media is now governed by a central political power. This entails mainstream media sources producing monotonic national images with the hope that audiences will be inoculated against dissent by imbibing harmonious and prosperous imaginings of the country. But this outdated, direct-effects strategy generally backfires, as increasingly critical youth fight for a modernized and democratized China of the future. Within this context, China's young media consumers are fueling a golden age of documentary; the genre has become so popular that it can be regarded as providing a kind of media infrastructure, one that extends "the area of local intercourse, that engenders the need for combination and co-operation, communication and communion."[7] In the case of China's documentaries, it is necessary to notice that "infrastructures produce power relations," in the sense that power is something "that works not just negatively, by denying, restricting, prohibiting, or repressing, but also positively, by producing forms of pleasure, systems of knowledge, goods, and discourses."[8] This notion of power as productive and pleasurable is important to remember, as China's new youth generation emerges into itself as a force within global media and consumer cultures, and hence as hungry not for old-school, Party-style propaganda, but for something fresh and new. As Henry Jenkins has argued, "Convergence represents a cultural shift as consumers are encouraged to seek out new information and make connections among dispersed media content."[9] Documentaries are at the forefront of this new media moment in China and thus offer us rich opportunities for addressing how fragmentation and convergence are portrayed and visualized, in documentaries both about China and about China's relations with the United States and beyond.

To support our claims, we analyze documentaries that engage in national image construction strategies in the United States and China. Though it is impossible to reach any ultimate conclusions, our discussion attempts to shed light on how different documentary strategies point to corresponding national imaginaries and how these imaginaries in turn rotate around differing notions of fragmentation and convergence. Though we write as Chinese scholars, we find fault in traditional Chinese documentary styles, which have sought to build a sense of national harmony through propaganda. The American documentaries we consider demonstrate a much greater sense of faith in the nation and its people, and hence use fragmentation to strong effect. In our conclusion, we point to some recent Chinese documentaries that demonstrate a more modern, open-ended style, and which therefore give us hope that national imaginings in and of China, and about China's relations to the United States and beyond, may be maturing in exciting new ways.

National Image Construction in *America: The Story of Us*

In 2010, the History Channel produced a twelve-part documentary, *America: The Story of Us*, an epic that takes a sweeping approach to telling the story of American history.[10] *America* covers over four hundred years of American history, moving from 1607 to 2010. Some sixteen hundred actors were employed to represent the different figures populating these historical periods; due in part to its sheer size and scope, and to its heroic tribute to American democracy, the documentary was nominated in 2010 for four Emmy Awards, including Outstanding Cinematography, Outstanding Picture Editing, Outstanding Sound Editing, and Outstanding Writing for Nonfiction Programming.[11] Because *America* was so successful in depicting the history of the nation, gleaning collective memories and illustrating their significance from various microperspectives, we approach the documentary as a representative case study of how deploying fragmentation—a focus on small scenes, forgotten individuals, the mundane and humble parts of daily life—can add up to create a sweeping sense of convergence and national unity.

For example, the interviewees' viewpoints in *America* represent considerable walks of life, including businessmen Donald J. Trump (before he was elected president); the award-winning actor Meryl Streep; the founder of Wikipedia, Jimmy Wales; the American fashion designer Vera Wang; recording artist and musician John Legend; the host of NBC news programs Brian Williams; comedian, actress, and activist Margaret Cho; among many, many others. Additionally, political viewpoints are included from former US secretary of state Colin L. Powell and mayor of New York Michael R. Bloomberg. Finally, commentary from historians such as Annette Gordon-Reed and David Kennedy is also included. We have listed the names of some prominent Americans, but *America* includes lesser-known figures and a fair representation of ethnic and racial minorities as well. So the film's producers clearly tried to represent the panorama of American life, with historians standing as the providers of overarching historical narratives.

According to Elizabeth Jensen, writing for the *New York Times*, the documentary allotted celebrities too much time to address their opinions about America instead of giving historians the chance to display more accurate insights about specific historical events. However, on the inclusion of celebrity testimony, Nancy Dubuc, president and chief executive officer of A+E Networks, explained that "it sort of ups the entertainment value of the show."[12] Indeed, by fusing healthy doses of celebrity testimony and historian narration, by including figures from multifarious fields and ranges of social classes, professional areas, and vocational backgrounds, *America* found the right balance that captured mainstream America's attention, the first episode drawing 5.7 million total viewers during its original airing.[13] As Chinese scholars, we find it highly fascinating that the nation's story needed to be told by celebrities, as if the nation could not listen to ordinary people or scholars alone, but we understand the filmmakers' intentions to help sell the film to the public by including such figures. Moreover, the inclusion of celebrities in the narrative indicates another moment in communication convergence, as *America* incorporates staged dramatic reenactments, historical footage, historical commentary, and, yes, celebrities, hence embodying the interweaving of different forms of cultural production and knowledge in one piece.

Despite our comments about celebrities in *America*, among the people highlighted in the film we also find well-known historical figures positioned alongside humble and mundane people from everyday walks of life. For example, in the first episode, Benjamin Franklin's experiences are layered against the experiences of Edward Winslow, a twenty-four-year-old printing apprentice: the former stood out as one of the premier intellectuals, journalists, and activists of the Revolutionary era, whereas the latter toiled in obscurity. Such contrasts provide a range of vantage points for audiences to perceive the ups and downs of destiny against the resplendent backdrop of history. It appears that this layering is meant to show how individuals from different walks of life manage to converge at key points in time to create change, in essence showing viewers how disparate fragments accumulate into a national whole.

America also includes perspectives on slavery, postslavery apartheid, and the slaughter of Native Americans, hence tackling some of America's most violent and oppressive histories. Additionally, the film explores the deeper and complex reasons driving America's troubled past, hence asking serious questions about the practices and legacies of racism, structural inequality, religious oppression, sexism, and others. The courage of directly facing hidden and subjugated subject positions displays an honest, balanced, yet ultimately hopeful outlook on history, suggesting that part of the American story is the nation's tough-minded willingness to learn from past atrocities. Because of this perspective, *America* has become one of the most acclaimed educational works from the History Channel. DVDs were freely distributed to schools, colleges, and universities all over America; according to History executives, more than thirty thousand interested parties signed up to receive copies shortly after its first airing. According to Nancy Dubuc, president and general manager of the History Channel when the documentary was released, "The genesis of the idea for me came from this notion of showing people that you can get through difficult times and that this country has been in difficult times many, many times. And the perseverance and the strength and the determination and the sacrifice that so many millions of people have had to endure to form this country is far greater than anything that we can really imagine. I'm a big believer in: Show people that path and it becomes easier in some ways."[14] That is to say, in addition to showing where we are here and now, it is just as important to present what we have been through and how we finally triumphed, or at least persevered, in each particular situation, hence constructing the arc of national history.

What needs to be emphasized here is the constitutive nature of *America*. Since "the analysis of rhetorical documents should not turn inward, to an appreciation of persuasive, manipulative techniques, but outward to functions of rhetoric," so the documentary should not be merely regarded as an accumulation of visual and storytelling techniques but addressed as an attempt to create a coherent national narrative—as an attempt to create a sense of convergence around a network of fragments.[15] Thus, the main form of American national image construction in *America* is the presentation of everyday, ordinary people alongside the insertion of well-known landscapes, hence highlighting people constituting America in their daily lives. The people include the workers at the core of American culture, from farmers selling crops and fishermen distributing seafood, to baristas making the perfect cup of coffee and conductors driving the coaches to get people to the next station. Ordinary displays of people living mundane life with jubilant smiles represent the friendliness and spontaneity of daily life. These everyday images are used throughout the documentary, yet when events of great importance and significance are addressed by key figures in society, we find their voices providing the overarching narratives that are so important to national image construction.

From *America*, then, we can see that national image construction evolves through a complex layering of voices and images representing an epic sweep of American life.[16] In comparison to CPC-style propaganda, what makes this layering so interesting is the presence of disagreement, fundamental conflicts about what it means to be an American. The documentary therefore embodies the democratic process itself, showing us the give-and-take of ideas across time. *America* thus celebrates what Maurice Charland has called "the importance of discourse, culture, and history in giving rise to subjectivity," which is "always social, constituted in language, and exists in a delicate balance of contradictory drives and impulses."[17]

Demonstrating confidence in this uniquely and multilayered American subjectivity plays a key role in how *America* communicates a strong national identity. Indeed, *America* is interesting as a project in national image construction because it seems less interested in arguing for some grand and coherent narrative than in foregrounding how democracy is iterative, constitutive, self-generating, and (ideally) self-correcting. Within this framework, American subjectivities do not have to be generated by state media in accordance with state imperatives. The sense of national convergence emerges, then, from a love of its fragments.

Reflections on Contemporary Chinese Documentary Films

Having considered a US example of national image construction, we now transition to addressing Chinese documentary films. In China, most documentaries are made by television stations owned by the government, meaning they strive to establish a positive national image, as mandated by the Party (whose control over all facets of communication are detailed in Patrick Dodge's introduction to this book). But some other documentaries are produced by ordinary people, and many of these independent documentaries attempt to reveal the real conditions of Chinese society from diverse perspectives, even though sometimes they cannot obtain official approval of the government for circulating their work. And thus, as a result of the development of new social media, "The Chinese people are kind of split between evolving, but still old-fashioned and Party-controlled, offerings and emerging, innovative, new-media offerings."[18] As a result of this "split," Chinese audiences now have access to more choices of different kinds of domestic documentaries. However, when it comes to national image construction, propaganda continues to be the main approach of the Party, even in documentary production. Yet this approach has largely backfired, for the ideology packaged into Chinese documentary films has been rejected not only by domestic and Western audiences, but also by global audiences. Rare indeed is the Chinese documentary that finds traction in international markets.

In light of these findings, some Chinese documentary films are changing with the times by embracing multiple forms and content, arguably in an attempt to move past propaganda and toward more artful forms. However, this process is far from being accomplished. From our reading *America*, the essence of making documentaries for global communication has been articulated; no such global successes exist (yet) on the Chinese side. Bearing that fact in mind, it might be useful to discern some drawbacks in contemporary Chinese documentaries via comparison with *America*. Our purpose here is not to assail our Chinese colleagues, but—writing as teachers of, scholars of, and practitioners of documentary making—to prompt their adaptation, so that future national image construction in Chinese documentaries is more effective and more palatable to international audiences. To fulfill this task, our argument focuses on a few tendencies in contemporary Chinese documentaries. While critical of the overreliance on propaganda, we are also hopeful, for as Jing and Yun point out, "With the development of new technologies, especially the internet and digitalization, it is now also possible for documentary photography to bypass the threshold of infrastructure, institutional support, and capital to intervene directly in social processes within civil society."[19] We hope our arguments below aid our fellow documentary makers in improving the quality of such forthcoming "interventions."

Strong Emphasis on Party Ideology

It is obvious to audiences that some, probably most, Chinese documentaries, especially political films, lay great stress on reproducing Party ideology. Whereas this approach may have worked in the past to increase patriotism in domestic audiences, international audiences would be more likely to doubt the credibility of the narrative teeming with harmony and acclamation, and thus to lose their trust in Chinese voices, in turn broadening the gap in cross-cultural communication. For example, consider this paragraph of narration from the second episode of the political film *Tides of Centuries: Dreams of China*:

> The reason why China, the people and the history chose the Communist Party is that Chinese Communists faithfully represent the fundamental interests of the people, and open up a road towards prosperity, democracy, civilization and harmony for China. This road can be appreciated by the people of all ethnic groups, all political parties, all walks of life, all aspects—the widest majority of the Chinese people—and admired by people with rectitude and conscience all over the world. It is also the inevitable choice of realizing the *Two Centenary Goals* for China in the future.[20]

Produced in 2014 by China Central Television (CCTV) and the Publicity Department of the Communist Party of China Central Committee, this kind of propaganda celebrating the Chinese political system offers language familiar to most Chinese viewers yet hardly believable for international viewers. Indeed, the repetitive emphasis on political terms with Chinese characteristics can only bore Western viewers. Worse, the presumptuous and condescending tone is likely to sweep away any interest about China, working to broaden the gap between China and the West. As Cai stated, "The discourse of nationalism is a double-edged sword which must be dealt with carefully and intelligently when it is enlisted to resolve internal and external problems."[21] In this case, the "double-edged" nature of nationalism means that by trying so hard, and so didactically, to celebrate Chinese nationalism, the documentary ends up depicting the Party as overbearing.

For another example, let us turn to the Chinese documentary *A Year in Tibet*.[22] Before it aired on CCTV, it first premiered on BBC Four in 2008, afterward spreading to more than forty countries across Asia, Europe, America, and Africa. An essential factor of its circulation, acceptance, and recognition within China was the minimization of political ideology. For instance, in the very beginning of the documentary the vast earth, towering temples, and ordinary Tibetans are accompanied by placid and meaningful Tibetan folk songs. Although there was no overt trumpeting of a political tone, the story reproduces the Chinese state narrative of a "Leap Frog Style of Development," which is aimed at "harmoniously blending Chinese and Tibetan cultures through planned economic modernization in Tibet," and the achievements of "triumphant modernization," which "celebrates and performatively constitutes China's active development of Tibet."[23] Contrary to *America*, which directly reveals the dark sides of the United States' national history, *A Year in Tibet* avoids controversy by focusing on the nonpolitical, ordinary, and daily lives of local Tibetans, who appear to be thrilled to have been incorporated into China's forced modernization.[24] Thus, while less overt than *Tides of Centuries*, *A Year in Tibet* still fulfills heavily propagandistic purposes by offering visual evidence that, ultimately, only confirms Party ideology.

Lack of Objectivity

One of the recurrent problems in contemporary Chinese documentary films is what we will call a lack of objectivity. Unlike the direct confrontations with historical problems in *America*, for example, most mainstream documentary films in China celebrate the bright parts of national history without giving audiences a glance into the darker sides. Consider *The Road to Rejuvenation*,[25] the first contemporary Chinese political documentary to systematically discuss modern Chinese history. Several important topics are embraced, including the 1911 Revolution, the construction of the People's Republic of China, Deng Xiaoping's reform and opening policy, and the implementation of a socialist market economy, among others. However, the documentary mainly focuses on stages of China's great achievements and victories throughout history, thus showcasing the country's power and prosperity while also, at the same time, celebrating the visionary leadership of the CPC. Yet the film never traces back to the historical origins of the significant setbacks that once brought China's people tremendous trauma; for example, the catastrophic Cultural Revolution, the failed Great Leap Forward, and the still-forbidden 1989 Tiananmen Square student demonstrations—all of which are well known globally—receive no mention, as if they never happened. As Stephen J. Hartnett has pointed out elsewhere, the Chinese Communist Party fears the free flow of information in both domestic and international public spheres, prompting the Party to impose strict political regulations on all forms of media.[26] However, to truly be strong as a nation means reflecting on past misdeeds, both recovering from and learning from those pains, including domestic ones, and then replenishing the nation with courage and unremitting faith. Whereas *America* artfully leads viewers to this conclusion, *Road to Rejuvenation* forces it down their throats.

In contrast to this relentless Party propaganda, we believe the world would benefit from seeing the vivid and real details of Chinese people's lives, but they are oftentimes omitted or are altogether ignored in most Chinese mainstream documentary films. And yet, despite our critiques of the documentary, we argue that *A Year in Tibet* could serve as a gentle example of a needed turning point.[27] The documentary does not avoid problems and build mirages, but rather depicts ordinary people the way they are, reminding us that presenting taboo and sensitive topics in context, without garbling, shows confidence in viewers, allowing them to reach their own conclusions about past intercultural misunderstandings. For instance, though the documentary shows the relatively harmonious relationship between monks and the Communist Party, there are also clips presenting a taxi driver cheating customers, a young lama who found it boring to chant scriptures, Tibetan children who considered studying in the heartlands of China a heavy financial burden, and so on. Such scenes help build trust in foreign audiences by showing them real cultural and daily life in China, albeit in non-politically sensitive situations. During the process of cultural representation, these scenes of daily life might be considered negligible, but in fact, these details contribute to the moving power of attracting countless foreign audiences. In this instance, eschewing propagandistic grand narratives in favor of loving depictions of daily life makes for both a better film and a better piece of national image construction.

From the Obsession with Folklore to Delicious Tastes

Another common drawback in contemporary Chinese documentaries is that in some, directors overemphasize local cultural customs without situating them against larger humanistic concerns, thereby turning them into representations of superstition. For instance, the five-episode documentary *The Spring Festival*[28] showcases the customs of reunion, sacrificial rite, exorcism, blessing, and the celebration of the Lantern Festival during the Spring Festival. When it comes to sacrificial rites, the film places redundant attention on the details of the ceremony in a rural village, exhibiting the worship of Fuxi (a god in Chinese history) statues, people praying for peace, the process of parade, and so on, without pointing out the deeper cultural values engrained in these kinds of rites. In global communication contexts, while some foreign audiences may possess particular knowledge about Chinese history and culture, we assume most viewers will simply be lost within the folkloric details. By delving into the details of folklore without putting the rituals into detailed historical perspective, these kinds of representations could lead to biased understandings.

For a positive counterexample, consider *A Bite of China*,[29] which we believe provides a good example of how to situate local customs within the larger narratives that succeed in the global communication context. According to Fan Yang, the program "enacts the simultaneously homogenizing and heterogenizing mechanisms of globalization that intercept food and media at once."[30] For instance, season 1, episode 4, depicts food produced by secondary processing. It represented not only the production of food, but also the people and their stories behind the process, providing audiences with insights into the intimate relationships within Chinese food-producing communities and larger connections to the cultural heritages of food. In this way, the film depicts both local habits of food and their connections or similarities to more widespread cultural practices. For example, the end of this episode presents a lasting impression:

> It is the taste of salt, the taste of the mountains, the taste of the wind, the taste of clouds, the taste of time, and the taste of human emotions. They've been closely tied to the lands, to the people, hard work, and persistence for a very long time. They meet at the tip of the tongue and within the heart.[31]

"Taste" transcends the tongue and mouth; it is a set of beliefs and hopes and assumptions that have been transferred from people's palates through their experiences and emotions out into the world. Taste is a communicative process rooted in human beings' daily lives, and hence a treasured experience that spreads across international contexts in global communication. As represented here, even something as singular and personal as a taste on your tongue speaks to larger, even universal values. *A Bite of China* thus moves the viewer from fragmentation to convergence, from singularity to universality. By skipping the propaganda and savoring the delicious details, this documentary casts China in a truly positive light, one likely to contribute to positive feelings about the nation, its people, and our cultures.

Constructing Effective Narrative Frames

In order to construct national images efficiently, cultural barriers need to be addressed. In cross-cultural communication, it is a disservice if we fail to understand precisely the ways that specific audiences perceive audiovisual languages within their own cultural contexts. For instance, the original version of the twelve-episode historical documentary *The Imperial Palace* depicts more than six hundred years of history from its original construction up to present renovations.[32] The film lovingly showcases abundant historical records, exquisite images, architectural art, the functions of the palace, its collections of antiques, its transformation from palace to museum, and so forth. Although the documentary presents a high value on history and aesthetics, when put onto the global stage of communication, its shortcomings become obvious: due to a lack of knowledge about the Imperial Palace, voluminous historical details can be overwhelming for foreign audiences. Instead of bombarding viewers with huge amounts of information under verbose narration and countless detailed images, it would be more effective to present viewers logical and vivid stories that unveil the mysterious palace in a more accessible way. If *Road to Rejuvenation* is all propaganda and little detail, *Imperial Palace* is awash in so many details that no coherent narrative emerges.

In contrast, the global version of *Imperial Palace*, as adapted by the National Geographic Channel, has satisfied foreign audience's appetite. It condenses the twelve-episode documentary into two episodes of 120 minutes each, overturning the narrative order to tell a fascinating story. It asks the question, what happened in a majestic palace of former emperors? Unlike the considerable amount of historical information about architecture and multifarious aspects of the palace embraced in the Chinese version, this one selects the essence of Chinese characteristics and lays great stress on penetrating the Imperial Palace's mysteries. For foreign audiences, depicting the ups and downs during dynastic changes, hence explaining the history and politics of the site, is aesthetically effective. Although the Imperial Palace is one of the most gorgeous palaces throughout the world, it is not as well known to Western audiences as the Great Wall due to the prohibition against civilians entering the grounds during a long period of history. Therefore, leading audiences directly to the core of historical stories and linking them to the historical-political conditions of the time is an effective way to address cultural barriers, paving the way for establishing China's national image in global communication contexts. This specific example indicates a curious moment in the age of communication convergence, as we find the US-based National Geographic Channel editing a Chinese-made documentary about Chinese history, using Western editing and narrative techniques to help international audiences make sense of China's national history.

Song Leng has suggested that "people all over the world are looking forward to seeing the *Made in China* trend take root and expand in the documentary field just as it has been in the global production of commodities."[33] As *Imperial Palace* suggests, that outward reach of Chinese documentaries might best be achieved in collaboration with international colleagues, demonstrating how the age of convergence and globalization offers China excellent opportunities to reach both new collaborators and new audiences.

Conclusion: US–China Relations and the Future of Documentaries

We have argued herein that China's contemporary documentaries are playing catchup with American films, which tend to be much stronger at showcasing contrasting viewpoints. We have pointed to *America: The Story of Us* as a particularly good example. And we have argued that China's documentaries are most successful when they eschew Party-driven propaganda, which dominates *Road to Rejuvenation*, instead focusing on the humble details of daily life in China, as in certain scenes from *A Year in Tibet* and *Bite of China*. We have written both as scholars diagnosing the respective documentary trends in America and China and as advocates, calling upon our fellow Chinese filmmakers to show bravery in depicting the internal contradictions in contemporary Chinese life.

What we need now is a call upon American and Chinese documentary makers to begin the hard work of working together, entering a new phase of international collaboration and cooperation wherein we can begin to provide audiences with historically rich, aesthetically pleasing, and politically sophisticated portrayals of the US–China relationship. There are few good documentaries that proceed along these lines, yet the time is obviously ripe for such endeavors. In the age of communication convergence, the next step in global documentary filmmaking is clearly for US and Chinese artists to converge around the shared goal of making films that can build international peace.

NOTES

1. Jean-Paul Sartre, *Being and Nothingness*, Chinese trans. Xuanliang Chen (Beijing: SDX Joint Publishing Company, 2007).
2. See Edward W. Said, *Orientalism* (New York: Vintage Books, 1979).
3. Stuart Hall, "The West and the Rest: Discourse and Power," in *Formations of Modernity*, ed. Stuart Hall and Bram Gieben (Buckingham: Open University; Cambridge: Polity Press, 1992), 275–331.
4. Dilip Parameshwar Gaonkar, "On Alternative Modernities," *Public Culture* 11 (1999): 1–18; see also Stephen J. Hartnett, "Alternative Modernities, Postcolonial Colonialism, and Contested Imaginings in and of Tibet," in *Imagining China: Rhetorics of Nationalism in the Age of Globalization*, ed. Stephen J. Hartnett, Lisa B. Keränen, and Donovan Conley (East Lansing: Michigan State University Press, 2017), 91–137.
5. Jian Zhang, "Others," *Foreign Literature* 32 (2011): 118.

6. See Paula Rabinowitz, "Wreckage upon Wreckage: History, Documentary and the Ruins of Memory," in *They Must Be Represented: The Politics of Documentary* (New York: Verso, 1994), 16–32.

7. Lisa Parks and Nicole Starosielski, "Deep Time of Media Infrastructure," in *Signal Traffic: Critical Studies of Media Infrastructures* (Urbana: University of Illinois Press, 2015), 94–112.

8. Judy Wajcman, "'Anyone Can Edit,' Not Everyone Does: Wikipedia's Infrastructure and the Gender Gap," *Social Studies of Science* 47, no. 4 (2017): 511–527. Lila Abu-Lughod, "The Romance of Resistance: Tracing Transformations of Power through Bedouin Women," *American Ethnologist* 17, no. 1 (2015): 41–55.

9. Henry Jenkins, *Convergence Culture: Where Old and New Media Collide* (New York: New York University Press, 2006), 3.

10. *America: The Story of Us*, directed by Marion Milne, Clear Beavan, Jenny Ash, Andrew Chater, Nick Green, and Renny Bartlett (Nutopia, 2010), DVD.

11. National Academy of Television Arts and Sciences, "Awards Search," *Emmy Awards*, 2010, www.emmys.com.

12. Elizabeth Jensen, "History from Unexpected Characters," *New York Times*, April 16, 2010.

13. Alex Weprin, "Cable Ratings: 'America: The Story of Us' Delivers Big Ratings," *BroadcastingCable.com*, April 26, 2010.

14. Jensen, "History from Unexpected Characters."

15. Michael C. McGee, "In Search of 'the People': A Rhetorical Alternative," *Quarterly Journal of Speech* 61, no. 3 (1975): 235–249.

16. *America: The Story of Us.*

17. Maurice Charland, "Constitutive Rhetoric: The Case of the Peuple Québécois," *Quarterly Journal of Speech* 73, no. 2 (1987): 133–150.

18. Zhengrong Hu in discussion with Stephen J. Hartnett, May 2017.

19. Wu Jing and Guoqiang Yun, "Beyond Propaganda, Aestheticism and Commercialism: The Coming of Age of Documentary Photography in China," *Javnost: The Public* 14, no. 3 (2007): 31–48.

20. *Tides of Centuries; Dreams of China*, directed by the Publicity Department of the Communist Party of China Central Committee (China Central Television, 2014), DVD.

21. Shenshen Cai, "Analyzing the Nationalist Genre of Chinese Commercial Media: Case Study of Sohu Web Document—the Search for Modern China," *China Media Research* 11, no. 1 (2015): 36–45.

22. *A Year in Tibet*, directed by Suyun Sun (China Central Television, 2008), DVD.

23. Patrick Shaou-Whea Dodge and Lisa Keränen, "Sixty Years of 'Peaceful Liberation' at

the Tibet Museum in Lhasa: Triumphant Modernization at the Rooftop of the World," *Chinese Journal of Communication* 11, no. 3 (2018): 306–323. Lisa Keränen, Patrick Shaou-Whea Dodge, and Donovan Conley, "Modernizing Traditions on the Roof of the World: Displaying 'Liberation' and 'Occupation' in Three Tibet Museums," *Journal of Curatorial Studies* 4, no. 1 (2015): 78–106.

24. See Hartnett, "Alternative Modernities."

25. *The Road to Rejuvenation*, directed by Xuean Ren (China Central Television, 2007), DVD.

26. Stephen J. Hartnett, "Google and the 'Twisted Cyber Spy' Affair: US-Chinese Communication in an Age of Globalization," *Quarterly Journal of Speech* 97, no. 4 (2011): 411–434.

27. *A Year in Tibet.*

28. *The Spring Festival*, directed by China Central Television (China Central Television, 2014), DVD.

29. *A Bite of China*, directed by Xiaoqing Chen (China Central Television, 2012), DVD.

30. Fan Yang, "A Bite of China: Food, Media, and the Televisual Negotiation of National Difference," *Quarterly Review of Film and Video* 32, no. 5 (2015): 409–425.

31. *A Bite of China.*

32. *The Imperial Palace*, directed by Ming Luo and Hong Cheng (China Central Television, 2005), DVD.

33. Song Leng, "The Trending of Documentary Communication under Globalization," *China Media Report Overseas* 9, no. 2 (2013): 91–94.

PART 2

Communication and Crisis in the Age of Convergence

Dueling Narratives of Distrust, Hypocrisy, and Blame

The 2014 US–China Cyber Controversy

Michelle Murray Yang and Da Wang

R epresentations of US–China relations have historically vacillated between portrayals of the nations as stalwart enemies or as allies bonded by shared ideals, aims, and challenges.[1] New technology has further complicated fluctuations in the nations' relationship. More specifically, advances in cyber technology and cyberespionage have strained US–China relations as the nations grapple with delineating the tenuous divide between acceptable forms of national-security-enhancing cyberespionage and global-security-threatening acts of cyberwar.[2] A profound example of the nations' complex cyber relationship recently played out with the United States' indictment of five People's Liberation Army (PLA) officers for engaging in alleged cyberattacks against US companies. In May 2014, a grand jury in the Western District of Pennsylvania indicted the five officers on thirty-one counts. The counts included "conspiring to commit computer fraud; accessing a computer without authorization for the purpose of commercial advantage and private financial gain; damaging computers through the transmission of code and commands; aggravated identity theft; economic espionage; and theft of trade secrets."[3] The US Department of Justice accused the five PLA officers of belonging to Military Unit 61398 and of hacking into multiple US companies' computer networks, including Westinghouse Electric, United States Steel, SolarWorld, Alcoa, Allegheny

Technologies, and the United Steel, Paper and Forestry, Rubber, Manufacturing, Energy, Allied Industrial and Service Workers International Union (USW).[4] The cyber intrusions coincided with the companies' involvement in legal proceedings, partnerships, and negotiations with Chinese state-owned companies. The officers were accused of illegally accessing a variety of information including emails and trade secrets. Across the US intelligence community there was rare consensus: China was engaging in acts of cyber intrusion—whether called espionage, surveillance, theft, or hacking—that amounted to acts of war.

A milestone in US–China relations, the indictment of the Chinese officers was the first time that the United States charged a state actor with this kind of cyber hacking. The indictments enraged Chinese officials such as Qin Gang, spokesperson for China's Ministry of Foreign Affairs, who denounced the indictments as "purely ungrounded with ulterior motives," claiming "the Chinese government, the Chinese military and their relevant personnel have never engaged or participated in cyber theft of trade secrets."[5] The controversy marred China's twentieth anniversary of first participating in the World Wide Web and threatened to escalate tensions between the nations as US and Chinese officials accused one another of engaging in cyberespionage and cyberattacks.[6] These dueling representations of the indictment in Chinese and US media thus provide insight into the tensions underlying convergence, new technology, governance, and crisis in US–China relations. The incident also indicates how both US and Chinese institutional structures struggle to address the questions of ethics and security raised by advances in technology. The cyber controversy therefore raises important questions regarding how the United States and China reconcile disputes regarding new technologies and communication supply chains, indicating how the age of communication convergence is inherently fraught with confusions, complications, and controversies.

This chapter examines how the cyber controversy was portrayed in Chinese and US political discourse by undertaking a comparative framing analysis. The first portion of the chapter analyzes US media and political discourse regarding the indictments of the PLA officers, including statements by US political leaders and news coverage by the *New York Times*, the *Washington Post*, the *Huffington Post*, and the *Wall Street Journal*. The second half of the chapter examines coverage of the cyber controversy as portrayed in the Chinese version of the *People's Daily* and how Chinese state media used Western news reports to frame the controversy. In offering this comparative analysis, we attempt to chart how institutional structures in the United States and China responded to the unique challenges posed by new technology in matters of convergence, governance, and crisis. Moreover, because the question of "cyberwar" is so unstable—including competing definitions of cyberespionage, cyber surveillance, cyberattacks, cyber policing, cybertheft, and so on—our analysis touches upon the questions of ethics and truth in international communication, the relationship between communication and national security, and, ultimately, the very prospects of diplomacy and trade in the age of communication convergence.

Rhetoric and News-Framing Analysis

In this chapter we take a rhetorical approach in examining discourse concerning the 2014 cyber controversy. This method enables us to probe symbols at the level of their meaning, to explore how they function, and to examine the ways they are employed to discern relationships regarding language, power, and authority.[7] In doing so we combine a close textual analysis with news framing to analyze media articles and political statements. Close textual analysis requires the critic to examine discourse "microscopically—at the level of the sentence, phrase, word, and syllable."[8] Thus, this entails studying the syntax, imagery, language choice, figures, argument structure, and the development of ideas. This critical attention to the minute levels of language usage can yield new understanding of how texts function both rhetorically and politically.[9]

In combining close textual analysis with news-framing analysis, we find that language and communication play a significant role in the framing process. We approach frames as "discursive structures embedded in news discourses that function to convey meaning" that are integral to gaining and sustaining power.[10] How rhetors frame an issue can open avenues for deliberation or limit argumentative possibilities, as they can emphasize "specific values, facts, or other considerations and endow them with greater relevance to an issue than would an alternative frame."[11] Framing can also work to influence people's perceptions of social issues "by eliminating voices or weakening arguments of those attempting to generate news coverage for their candidate, cause, or policy."[12] This means that politicians can affect the framing process through their word choices. Thus, powerful political officials can promote or resist a specific frame through their language usage in public speeches and statements. Additionally, high-ranking political leaders whose remarks are pertinent to a specific news story may be more effective in influencing how a journalist frames the issue.[13] Examining how journalists and political officials use language to support, dispute, or counter the framing of issues is significant, as frames can influence the public's understanding of news and events by prioritizing "some facts, events, or developments over others, thereby promoting a particular interpretation."[14]

Combining rhetorical and news-framing analysis is a productive approach for examining discourse surrounding the cyber controversy, for the contested nature of representations distinguishing different types of cyber activity was a crucial part of the dispute. Indeed, the United States and China offered wildly divergent perspectives concerning what constitutes unacceptable cyberattacks and standard cyberespionage, further complicating deliberations between the two states. For most nation-states, including the United States, cyberespionage is a common part of intelligence-gathering operations—it is a form of spy-craft, but not war. However, trouble arises in defining what a cyberattack encompasses. Foreign policy analysts Kenneth Lieberthal and Peter W. Singer note that "a variety of like and unlike efforts have all been described as 'cyber attacks' simply because they involve the technology of the Internet at some point." In this study, we define cyberattack as a behavior in cyberspace that impedes, harms, and/or devastates a computer network or system; in contrast, cyberespionage compromises "cyber systems in order to monitor activities . . . and to extract information."[15]

To watch how these debates unfolded, we conducted a Google Images search for the FBI "Most Wanted" posters—which included images of the charged PLA officers—in order to locate US media in which the posters circulated. We also collected US political leaders' statements regarding the 2014 indictments. Additionally, we searched for, collected, and analyzed articles concerning the cyber controversy in the Chinese sphere that appeared in the *People's Daily*. As the newspaper of the Communist Party of China's Central Committee, the *People's Daily* is the Party's most authoritative and influential newspaper. We collected a sample of ninety-seven articles by searching network records and library back issues of the *People's Daily* between March 1, 2014, and October 1, 2015, with the keywords "America" (美国) and "internet" (网络).[16] We then analyzed the articles and statements in both data sets by using a rhetorical approach that combines elements of rhetorical and news-framing analysis.[17]

Our analysis of this data suggests that US political leaders relied on the frame of "criminality" to cast the PLA officers as well as the Chinese government as guilty of unlawful cyber behavior. American political officials also used the frame of "(un)acceptability" to differentiate between US cyberespionage for national security purposes and Chinese cyberespionage for economic advantages and financial gains. In so doing, US officials attempted to present a clear narrative that exonerated the United States while blaming China for criminal wrongdoings. US media outlets such as the *New York Times* and the *Wall Street Journal* provided a range of perspectives—some even challenging the US officials' narratives—by explaining similarities between US and Chinese cyberespionage and articulating the differences between how US and Chinese leaders define appropriate cyber activity. In contrast, Chinese state media used the frames of "US aggression" and "Chinese victimage" to counter the indictments of the PLA officers and refute allegations that China engages in cyberespionage.

By portraying the United States as an aggressive world power that routinely conducted surveillance on its own citizens as well as a number of other countries, the *People's Daily* characterized US leaders as hypocritical. In turn, the newspaper sought to exonerate China by denying that the nation engaged in cyberespionage and claiming that the nation was committed to peaceful development. The cyber controversy illustrates how both US and Chinese institutional structures struggled to navigate the challenges of convergence, governance, and crisis when faced with the potential and peril of new technology and global communication supply chains.

Cyber Controversy in US–China Relations

US–China relations include a complicated history of cyber controversies. Mandiant, a US computer security firm, first published a report in February 2013 linking Chinese Military Unit 61398 to the hacking of over one hundred US companies.[18] China's Foreign Ministry declared that China did not sanction cyberespionage and asserted that US hackers had also targeted China.[19] US–China relations were further strained when the Pentagon released its first report tracing cyberespionage to China's government.[20] According to the May 2013 report, Chinese government and military hackers gained access to information concerning US economic and defense systems, compromising the computer networks of 150 corporations and agencies.[21] In June 2013, Hua Chunying, a spokesperson for China's Foreign Ministry, responded to the allegations by explaining that "China is one of the most seriously cyber-attacked countries." She asserted that China opposed "all forms of hacker attacks."[22] Instead of "war and hegemony," she recommended that cyberspace needed "rules and cooperation."[23]

With the increasing threat of cyberattacks, US officials developed a five-point strategy that involved (1) creating legislation (2) highlighting trade secret thefts, (3) increasing public awareness of cyberthreats, (4) encouraging the private sector to bolster cybersecurity measures, and (5) privileging the investigation and prosecution of private sector and state-sponsored trade secret theft. With this strategy, the FBI's efforts yielded an increase of cyber trade theft investigations by 60 percent from 2009 to 2013.[24] In turn, Congress strengthened punitive measures for individuals engaging in cyberattacks under the Economic Espionage Act. As part of the act, those convicted of economic espionage face a $5 million penalty, substantially raising the penalty from the prior $500,000.

But US–China relations were already on edge. In 2013 former US National Security Agency (NSA) contractor Edward Snowden had leaked information to WikiLeaks revealing the NSA's extensive espionage activities, including the monitoring of networks in Germany, France, Hong Kong, and Beijing.[25] The timing came just two days prior to the US–China "Sunnylands Summit." Snowden's disclosure severely undercut US officials' portrayal of the United States as the victim of Chinese cyberespionage. Despite the damage, both Xi and Obama agreed that the nations must further cooperate on issues of cybersecurity. In a public statement at the Summit, President Obama acknowledged the complex terrain of international cybersecurity, characterizing it as "uncharted waters" since "you don't have the kinds of protocols that have governed military issues . . . where nations have a lot of experience in trying to negotiate what's acceptable and what's not." It was of "critical" importance, Obama maintained, "that China and the United States arrive at a firm understanding of how we work together on these issues."[26]

In similar fashion, President Xi agreed that the United States and China needed to work together to establish cybersecurity guidelines. China was also the "victim of cyber attacks," Xi explained, noting that both nations needed to "remove misgivings and make information security and cyber security a positive area of cooperation."[27] After the Summit, Yang Jiechi, Xi's foreign policy adviser, echoed the sentiment when he told reporters, "Cyber-security should not become the root cause of mutual suspicion and friction, rather it should be a new bright spot in our co-operation."[28] As a result of the Sunnylands Summit, Xi and Obama agreed upon the common ground that "international law applies to cyberspace," setting the groundwork for bilateral relations and US–China collaboration on issues of cybersecurity.[29]

Despite such positive strides, tensions increased the following year when US attorney general Eric Holder announced the indictment of five PLA officers for infiltrating US companies' computer networks to illegally acquire information that provided commercial advantages to Chinese businesses.[30] In response, China lodged a complaint with the United States criticizing the indictment, surmising that the move was based on fabricated facts, that it violated basic norms governing international relations, and that it jeopardized China-US cooperation. In protest, China announced that it would no longer take part in a bilateral working group with the United States on cyber behavior, urging the United States to immediately withdraw the indictment. Shortly thereafter, China's State Internet Information Office mandated new restrictions on foreign internet companies and the selling of foreign computer equipment in China.[31]

Accordingly, the Obama administration sent a stern warning to nations supporting cyberattacks. In response to North Korea's hacking of Sony Pictures that same year, President Obama pledged to take a "proportional response." Hours after the president's statement, North Korean computer networks were down for nearly ten hours.[32] Some speculated that the United States orchestrated the North Korea outage, although US leaders would not confirm the allegations.[33]

Further straining cyber relations in 2015, US officials linked Chinese hackers to "the largest cyber hack in U.S. history."[34] The intrusion compromised over four million US federal employees' records at the Office of Personnel Management (OPM) as well as another computer system encompassing records on federal employees' associates, friends, and family.[35] The OPM breach marked a sharp turn in Chinese cyberespionage efforts, from attacks on economic targets to ones focused on security and federal agents. According to Western news reports, the hacking of United Airlines, Sabre Corp., and OPM showed China's strategic and calculated efforts to create a vast database of US government employee information for intelligence-gathering purposes. US officials were increasingly alarmed by Chinese efforts to restructure state hacking groups into a central, militarized unit for what Gibson described as "traditional state espionage and politically-motivated cyber attacks."[36] These progression of events, actions, and comments thus point to a troubling pattern: US and Chinese leaders discuss cyber matters and even reach tentative agreements, then the US releases reports, warnings, and even indictments linking the Chinese government and PLA to illegal hacks and the cybertheft of industrial and military R&D. We highlight the notion that this pattern underwrites the now bipartisan anger in Washington, where China's cyber activities are perceived as nothing less than acts of war.

In response to the cyberattack, President Obama announced a national emergency, signing an executive order allowing the United States to impose financial sanctions against individuals and nations involved in cyber behavior that have caused or "materially contributed to, a significant threat to the national security, foreign policy, or economic health or financial stability of the United States."[37] The executive order allows the president to prohibit groups from purchasing US goods and technology, bar citizens from taking part in business dealings with individuals who engaged in cyberattacks, and freeze those individuals' or groups' financial assets. In taking these actions, the Obama administration applied efforts to hold parties accountable and to deter future attacks. Although international laws and treaties exist to govern traditional warfare, there are no similar agreements governing cyberwarfare.[38] The order was significant as it offered a framework to guide the greater international response to cyber hacking, cyberattacks, and cybertheft. In fact, President Trump's aggressive actions against Huawei were based in part on the legal and political groundwork established here by President Obama. Meanwhile the US response was framed as "escalatory," spun by Chinese state media in outlets like the *People's Daily* to draw attention to conflicting definitions of and approaches to cyberespionage. Accordingly, in the following sections we turn to an analysis of US and Chinese political and media discourse surrounding the 2014 cyber controversy.

US Political and Media Representations of the US–China Cyber Controversy

FBI Wanted posters of five PLA soldiers were released in 2014, when Attorney General Eric Holder announced their indictment in Shanghai during the Fourth Summit Conference on Interaction and Confidence-Building Measures in Asia.[39] The posters were reproduced in US media reports that covered the cyber controversy.[40] They provide a fruitful area of inquiry as they lend insight into how US political leaders and journalists (re)presented the cyber dispute and the responses elicited. We posit that the Wanted posters worked to reaffirm the "China threat" in US discourses and during the cyber controversy. While the CPC and Chinese state media outlets' responded to the indictments and Wanted posters by framing the United States as a hypocritical and aggressive foe that repeatedly victimized China, the indictments, Wanted posters, media representations, and government responses illuminate how converging communication systems, political rhetoric, and advances in technology reflect significantly complicated challenges to the US–China relationship.

Making Criminality Visible: The History of FBI "Most Wanted" Posters

"Most Wanted" FBI posters are perhaps the most widely recognized symbols denoting criminality, and they have a long history within the United States, where runaway slave posters were predecessors of the "Most Wanted" posters. Wanted posters were later used to locate outlaws like Jesse James and Butch Cassidy. In 1919, the FBI created Wanted posters for gangsters and deserters from the military. In 1930, the civic organization Chicago Crime Commission published public enemies lists featuring the notorious gangster Al Capone.[41] Over the years, Wanted posters have become an established convention in the United States, identifying individuals who have engaged in unlawful acts, denouncing them as dangers to society.

The contemporary "Top Ten Most Wanted" list almost did not come into being. Initially, FBI officials were wary of publicizing the nations' most formidable criminals, deeming it "undesirable to dignify Public Enemies by listing them."[42] However, the organization changed its approach in 1949 when an International News Service reporter asked FBI director J. Edgar Hoover to name the top ten men he wanted to apprehend. The FBI subsequently published its official "Ten Most Wanted Fugitives" list on March 14, 1950, in the *Washington Daily News*. Bank robber Thomas James Holden topped the list. Within a year, Holden was in custody.[43] Due to the high level of interest generated by the article, Hoover made the list a regular feature.[44] To date, the list has aided in the capture of over 150 criminals.

The FBI's "Most Wanted" list has evolved in relation to advances in technology. In 1996, the FBI began posting the list on its website. Contemporary iterations of the list can be found on the FBI's website and podcast as well as the agency's social media accounts. Additionally, on Facebook and Twitter platforms, users are able to access and share "Most Wanted Posters." Since first posting the list on its website, the agency has also broadened its efforts by creating different "Most Wanted" lists for specific types of crimes, including a list for cybercrimes. The development of multiple listings and formats has offered the FBI greater flexibility and visibility for targeting different types of criminals. When spots open on the "Most Wanted Terrorists" and "Most Wanted Fugitives" lists, "The FBI's 56 field offices submit nominations, which are subjected to several rounds of vetting at headquarters, and must finally get a stamp of approval from the FBI's top executives." In addition, "Any FBI agent can request that a fugitive be added to one of the crime-specific pages."[45] Advances in technology, combined with the creation of multiple lists, have increased the visibility and circulation of the FBI's "Most Wanted" lists. Adding an individual to the list is a serious affair that has profound consequences. By being named to a "Most Wanted" list, the individual is publicly conflated with criminality, classified as a dangerous criminal. The "Most Wanted" list's long history in US law enforcement and high visibility further heighten the gravity of being named to this list.

While not as extensive as some of the other lists, the "Cyber's Most Wanted" list has steadily grown. The FBI added the five PLA officers to the list in 2012. In March 2016, two Syrian men were charged with "attempting to hack U.S. companies and media organizations" and were added to the cybercriminals list. Later that month, Attorney General Loretta Lynch announced the indictment of seven Iranians for planning a cyberattack targeting New York financial institutions.[46] At the time of writing, the list includes over forty individuals and organizations.[47] The list's growth illustrates US officials' urgency in countering what they perceive as foreign cyberthreats. While the United States sought to send a strong message to China via the Wanted posters and the indictments, China denied allegations of engaging in wrongful cyber behavior. The *People's Daily* countered the US charges with claims that China is the victim of ongoing US cyber aggression and characterized itself as a world power committed to peaceful development.[48] In the following sections we examine the prominent news frames that dominated US media coverage of the cyber dispute, before turning to Chinese state media coverage.

"Criminality" and (Un)acceptability of Chinese Cyberattacks

In political discourse and media representations of the 2014 indictment of five PLA officers, the frames of criminality and (un)acceptability dominated US leaders' characterization of the cyber controversy. For instance, FBI director James Comey described the PLA officers' actions as "thievery" and pledged that the FBI would "investigate it and seek to prosecute it the way we do when anyone kicks in your door and steals something from your house or business."[49] Assistant Attorney General for National Security John Carlin added to the sentiment by comparing hardworking Americans who "spent their business days innovating, creating, and developing strategies to compete in the global marketplace" to Unit 61398 members who "spent their business days in Shanghai stealing the fruits of our labor." Furthermore, Carlin deemed China's actions as "criminal" and as representing "conduct that most responsible nations within the global economic community would not tolerate."[50]

Thus, the indictments, coupled with US leaders and media reports displaying the PLA officers as wanted criminals, worked to represent China's actions as unequivocally unacceptable and criminal. Furthermore, the combination of the indictment and posters displayed not only the Chinese military officers, but also the Chinese government and CPC as outlaws flagrantly violating US law. Furthermore, the indictment of the officers and the issuing of the "Most Wanted" posters are reflective of the Obama administration's shift to implementing policy, action, and the escalating consequences of cyberattacks from a matter of diplomatic governance to that of criminality (recall Obama's executive order in 2015 and the five-point strategy before that in 2013 to create legislation to fight cybertheft and cyberattacks and promote cybersecurity, among other actions).[51] As *Gizmodo* writer Adam Clark Estes sums up, "The very existence of these Wanted posters shows how the government wants everyone to view these suspects as serious criminals."[52]

Additionally, the indictments and Wanted posters worked to make cyber-crime and the US–China cyber controversy visible to a larger audience. As Carlin described, for "the first time, we are exposing the faces and names behind the keyboards in Shanghai used to steal from American businesses."[53] The publishing of the Wanted posters alongside news articles detailing the indictments visually affirmed the portrayal of the hackers and, by extension, the Chinese government as engaging in criminal behavior.

Additionally, and coupled with representations indicting the Chinese military and government through a criminality frame, US leaders and media representation used the frame of (un)acceptability to portray China's behavior as criminally dangerous and different from the United States' use of noncriminal cyberespionage. For example, Eric Holder described China's actions as appearing to have been done "for no reason other than to advantage state-owned companies and other interests in China, at the expense of businesses here in the United States."[54] Jay Carney, White House press secretary, reiterated this same differentiation, declaring, "We don't do what those Chinese nationals were indicted for." "We don't gather intelligence for the benefit of U.S. companies." Eric Holder's and Carney's testimonies strike the key distinction represented in the criminality and (un)acceptability frames and US–China cyber controversy—that the Chinese government, military, and Party benefit from cyber hacking, cyberattacks, and cyberespionage as the proprietors of state-owned enterprises.[55]

US officials attempted to differentiate the United States' cyber behavior from China's cyber actions by positing that there is a clear distinction between criminal and noncriminal cyberespionage. Speaking to the tensions underlying new technology, convergence, and governance, Carlin further justified the indictments by asserting that Chinese leaders had been unreceptive to the United States' previous efforts to raise concerns about Chinese cyber behavior. He explained how the Chinese government previously "responded by publicly challenging us to provide hard evidence of their hacking that could stand up in court."[56] Despite a decrease in Chinese hacking in the aftermath of the publishing of the Mandiant report and US leaders' expression of concern, Chinese hackers resumed cyber-hacking activity.[57]

A Range of Perspectives in US Media Discourse

US media outlets represented a range of perspectives, some challenging US leaders' dominant narratives, in opening dialogue about the similarities and differences between US and Chinese cyber behavior. For instance, *Wired* senior writer Andy Greenberg asserted that it was unclear whether the US effort to define acceptable hacking "helps to legally or diplomatically distinguish Chinese hacking activities from cyberespionage by America and its allies."[58] *Huffington Post* reporter Matt Sheehan argued that the United States' distinction between cyberespionage for national security purposes and for financial gain and commercial advantage became "increasingly difficult to maintain given recent revelations that NSA hackers broke into both Petrobras, Brazil's largest oil company, and Huawei, a Chinese telecom firm that has largely been stonewalled in American markets because of cyber-security fears." Referencing Snowden's earlier disclosure of intelligence information to WikiLeaks, cryptography specialist Bruce Schneier raised a similar issue, surmising the United States had lost "any moral high ground to complain about this stuff."[59] *New York Times* journalist Edward Wong pointed out that "China and other nations accuse the United States of being the biggest perpetrator of both kinds of espionage."[60] And from yet another perspective, Eric King, deputy director of Privacy International, affirmed that "there are real questions about whether these [Chinese] agencies' employees are independently criminally liable." King warned that China could very likely retaliate by targeting NSA employees, using "the exact same legal justifications as the Chinese who have been put on the FBI's most-wanted list."[61] As this diversity of perspectives suggests, US media outlets were critically and openly engaging in efforts to differentiate between cyberespionage for security purposes, financial gain, economic advantages, and the potential impacts all this might have on US–China cyber relations.

Moreover, Western news reports considered differences in political systems when interrogating the differences between the United States' and China's alleged cyberespionage. For instance, in the *Wall Street Journal* Barrett and Gorman pointed out that "in China, where many companies are state-controlled in some fashion," the strict divide between state and private sectors does not exist.[62] US media publications also reported on the pervasive nature of hacking in China such as when *New York Times* reporter Edward Wong reported how "hacking is as common in the corporate and criminal worlds as in the government. It is even promoted at trade shows, in classrooms and on Internet forums."[63] By providing more information regarding the political nuances informing the cyber controversy, journalists considered a range of perspectives to help complicate notions of (un) acceptability in cyberespionage.

Furthermore, US reporters also questioned the effectiveness of the indictments. They pointed out that it was highly unlikely that the Chinese officers would ever face a US judge, as the nations have no extradition treaty and the men were unlikely to visit the United States.[64] As *Washington Post* journalist Andrea Peterson reported, "The people who are charged in this case have never been inside the United States—and now that they're literally on wanted posters, they're probably not going to visit here anytime soon."[65] By questioning the effectiveness of the indictments, journalists further explored the criminality and (un)acceptability frames. In so doing, they created space and generated dialogue for alternative ways of interpreting the cyber controversy that critically expanded the range of deliberative possibilities—from criminality and condemnation—to understanding and reflection.

Retaliation and Chinese State Media Coverage of the US–China Cyber Conflict

While images of FBI Wanted posters featuring the indicted PLA officers circulated in US media discourse, a very different image appeared in the *People's Daily*. A silhouetted figure stands with his back to the viewer. A pair of headphones is perched on his head. The cords from the headphones stretch forward, encircling a globe positioned in front of him. As the cords wrap around the earth, they form the shape of an "X" on the continent of Asia. A circular crest of an eagle adorns the back of the silhouetted figure's jacket. The words "National Security Agency, United States of America" are clearly visible on the crest.[66]

Although the figure's face is not shown, the outline, the color of skin, and the NSA crest signify connotations of US president Barack Obama. Accompanying an article in the *People's Daily*, the image provides a powerful visual rebuttal to the Wanted posters of PLA soldiers circulating in US media.[67] In the picture, Obama serves as a symbol of the United States' NSA cyber surveillance. While the US Department of Justice indicted five PLA officers on accusations of engaging in military acts of cyberespionage for commercial gains, the *People's Daily*—directly representing the voice of the Party—responded with the image portraying the United States as cyber surveilling not just China, but having a wired chokehold on the entire world. Not only does the image depict global dominance of the US cyber surveillance program, it also is an attempt to portray the Obama administration as hypocritical for indicting the PLA officers. This evocative image encompasses many of the most prevalent frames that appeared in Chinese state media coverage of the 2014 US–China cyber controversy. In its attempts to create a dueling narrative to counter US allegations of PLA cyberespionage, the *People's Daily* implemented the media frames of US aggression and Chinese victimage to sway its readers. Representations characterized Obama and—by extension the US government and NSA—as hypocritical cyber aggressors. The dueling narratives engaged by US leaders and the *People's Daily* illustrate how advances in technology work to trigger new communication convergences as well as new challenges regarding cyber relations and sovereignty. Rather than dissipating tensions between the United States and China, both nations contributed to greater distrust in the relationship as each side rhetorically escalated the stakes of the controversy.

The Frame of US Aggression

People's Daily relied heavily on the frame of US aggression to rebut US allegations while portraying the United States as provocateur in the cyber conflict. Instead of acknowledging China and the PLA's use of cyber surveillance and espionage, the outlet instead focused on the United States' history of surveillance programs, citing evidence from both US and Chinese sources. Characterizing the United States as a dangerous aggressor that used technology for duplicitous means, *People's Daily* targeted domestic and international cases of US surveillance. Unlike US news outlets that provided a range of perspectives on issues of cyberespionage and security, the Party and Chinese state media directed the Chinese public to focus on US intelligence efforts at large. This included not only cyber surveillance but also intelligence gathering via other technological devices. For example, the *People's Daily* cited an August 2015 *New York Times* article detailing how American Telephone and Telegraph Company helped the US National Security Bureau monitor a large-scale collection of internet information.[68] Citing a piece from 2014, the *People's Daily* reported how Germany criticized the United States' NSA for implementing a broad program to monitor individuals' communications, using it to point the finger at the United States for violating individuals' human rights. The *People's Daily* attempted to draw parallels, echoing the 2014 report's concerns in criticizing the United States for engaging in a wide range of global monitoring.[69] Thus, these representations, among others, served to escalate the cybersecurity dispute from an issue between China and the United States to one about human rights and global monitoring between the United States and the international community.[70] These examples are indicative of the CPC's efforts in using state media outlets like the *People's Daily* to frame China as a victim in a larger global campaign, wherein the United States was portrayed as a dangerous and hypocritical aggressor against global world order.

The *People's Daily* further deflected attention from Chinese intelligence efforts by focusing attention on the United States and Germany, turning to a "Pew Global Attitude Survey" released in the spring of 2015. The data was used to frame US aggression, with the *People's Daily* report highlighting that at the time more than half of German citizens perceived the NSA's monitoring efforts to have had a significantly negative impact.[71] The newspaper implied that US intelligence's monitoring tactics were not only domestic, drawing associations to the Obama and NSA chokehold image in the *People's Daily*, but also affecting the global community.[72] By portraying the United States as an adversary engaged in extensive global surveillance programs, Chinese state media attempted to frame leaders in the US government as hypocritical when it came to the issue of cyber sovereignty. It was an attempt to articulate the United States as losing the trust of nations and the people around the world. By reconfiguring the scope of the conflict to other cases in other foreign nations, Chinese state media concocted the image of the United States as a dangerous aggressor that routinely violated the human rights of its own people as well as the citizens of other countries. Without any critical focus turned inward, the United States as hypocritical aggressor frame worked to dismiss the CPC's, PLA's, and Chinese government's roles in the cyber conflict and project any responsibility for the crisis onto the United States.

Additionally, the *People's Daily* published several commentaries by Chinese scholars and officials about the controversy to counter the FBI's indictment and, in an attempt to bolster the United States' "Global Monitoring Behavior Record," released a report by the China Internet Media Research Center (CIMR).[73] In great detail, the report provides an interrogation of the global monitoring behavior of the United States, again pulling from a plethora of Chinese and international sources, demanding that the United States "explain its surveillance activities, cease spying operations that seriously infringe upon human rights, and to stop creating tension and hostility in global cyber space."[74] The *People's Daily* covered the CIMR, using it to frame the United States as the real aggressor in mystical fashion and attempting to debunk US leaders' allegations of Chinese criminality and cyberespionage.

Chinese state media further supported its counter-US strategy by publishing framing statements from former CIA officer Ray McGowan and former secretary of state Madeleine Albright that called for the strengthening of mutual trust—front and center.[75] The story described Ray McGowan criticizing the United States' indictment of five Chinese army officers as childish, irresponsible, and contradicting its own aims. McGowan states, "From the documents released by Snowden, the U.S. government is collecting everything, including 'National Interests' and 'Commercial Interests.'"[76] Again, we see the deflection from China's role in the cyber controversy to the highlighting of the United States as the hypocritical aggressor. Similarly, Madeleine Albright's emphasis on the need for more US–China cooperation was used to reframe the issue. Albright asserted, "It is necessary for all of us to realize that the two countries have an unshirkable responsibility for reducing friction and strengthening cooperation."[77] By publishing critical comments by US officials— dressed up as Chinese victimage justifying China's position—the *People's Daily* attempted to cast doubt on the Obama administration's efforts to create a stark divide between acceptable and unacceptable cyberespionage. Quoting former US officials questioning the US standpoint—for Chinese readers—worked to strengthen China's efforts in framing the United States as a hypocritical aggressor rather than as the victim of cyberespionage.

Chinese journalists also cited frustrations regarding US cyber surveillance programs to counter US leaders' delineation of (un)acceptable cyberespionage and to reinforce the narrative of US aggression. For instance, the *People's Daily* published a report produced by China's State Council Information Office, *Human Rights Record of the United States in 2013*. Furthering the frame of the United States as a hypocritical aggressor, the report quotes a joint declaration from nine civil liberties groups criticizing the United States, declaring "such vast and pervasive state surveillance violates two of the most fundamental human rights: the right to privacy and to freedom of expression."[78] By highlighting civil liberties groups' concerns over US surveillance programs, the *People's Daily* and China State Council Information Office framed the United States as engaging in unacceptable cyberespionage.[79]

Framing Chinese Victimage

Unlike US media outlets that provided a range of perspectives, including ones that critically examined US leaders' accusations against China, the *People's Daily* served to bolster the claims of Chinese leaders through its reliance on the frame of Chinese victimage. This is, of course, unsurprising as the newspaper serves as the mouthpiece of the CPC. Thus, it is crucial to examine how the *People's Daily* depicted China in the cyber conflict in order to witness how the newspaper rhetorically deflected attention to and responsibility for China's role in the controversy.

When the US Justice Department announced the indictment against five Chinese military officers on allegations of cybertheft, the *People's Daily* hit back by publishing a report by China's National Information Office chronicling how the United States attacked China's cyber network. In citing the report, the *People's Daily* declared that "the U.S. must explain its own monitoring operations," accusing US leaders of engaging in violations of human rights at home and abroad and urging them to stop creating tensions and hostility in the global cyber arena. In so doing, the *People's Daily* attempted to cast the United States as hypocritical and unreasonable, victimizing its own citizens through its cyber programs, and thereby attempting to affirm the image that China was the victim in the cyber conflict.[80] A week after the indictment, the *People's Daily* followed up by publishing a report by the CIMR, reinforcing the frame that China was the victim of US cyberattacks. The report—published in Chinese and made available in the Chinese public arena—provided details on how the United States monitored various groups within China, including the Chinese government, enterprises, research institutions, ordinary internet users, and their mobile phones.[81] Tellingly, the report highlights a case from 1990—nearly thirty years ago—that frames the United States as planting optical fiber bugs in the office walls at the Chinese Embassy in Australia. According to the report and the corresponding newspaper story that points the finger at the United States as aggressor in the cyber conflict, China has historically been the victim. By casting the United States as a dangerous cyberthreat and China as a peaceful victim, the *People's Daily* worked as a mouthpiece for CPC attempts to justify the need for increased Chinese cyber defense programs. While criticizing US officials as making unjustified allegations, the newspaper argued for China's efforts to strengthen its own network security in the name of safeguarding Chinese networks.[82] Through its reliance on the frame of Chinese victimage, the *People's Daily* depicted China as the victim of US aggression, meanwhile framing the United States as a threat to China's cybersecurity.

Progress and Peril in US–China Cyber Relations

Chinese and US representations of the cyber controversy provide insight into the often- complicated intersections between convergence, new technology, and the global communication supply chain. While advances in technology create new possibilities and convergence points, they also often generate new challenges for institutional structures. Within the context of the 2014 controversy, developments in cyber technology required the nations to develop new guidelines delineating how such technological innovations should be used. Tensions arising from the countries' divergent perspectives magnified the challenges already embedded in US–China relations. The dispute brought to light the cultural differences, distrust, and competing and complimentary aims that inform US–China relations.

For Chinese leaders, and as represented in the *People's Daily*, the indictment of the PLA officers was yet another example of American hypocrisy and US aggression. Chinese officials viewed US leaders as hypocritically castigating China for cyber behavior from which the United States routinely benefits. US political leaders became increasingly frustrated as their previous efforts to address the cyber controversy appeared fruitless, as China refused to abide by the distinction between cybertheft for economic advantage and financial gains, and cyberespionage for national security purposes. Due to mounting frustrations, US officials believed it was increasingly unlikely that Chinese leaders would engage in substantive action regarding the 2014 cyber disagreement. As both US and Chinese leaders jockeyed to safeguard each nation's respective power, neither side was willing to yield advantage to the other.

US and Chinese representations of the cyber controversy offer important insight into the complexities of US–China relations. The cyber conflict illuminates the limitations of simplistic binary narratives often employed to make sense of the nations' complicated relationship. As this chapter has demonstrated, the frames of criminality and (un)acceptability positioned China as an outlaw deserving of punishment. The US media's inclusion of a range of perspectives helped to open up space for dialogue and debate in defining the parameters of cyber relations. In turn, coverage in the *People's Daily* obscured vantage points by framing China as the victim and criticizing the United States as a hypocritical aggressor. The cyber controversy illustrates the misguided assumptions that such one-dimensional representations yield.

Since the 2014 indictments, the United States and China have experienced progress and setbacks in their cyber relations. In the wake of the OPM breach, the Obama administration contemplated levying sanctions against China. US and Chinese leaders were concerned such action would jeopardize relations and impede President Xi Jinping's first state visit to the United States. In the weeks preceding Xi's September 2015 visit, Chinese and US officials met in Beijing and Washington to craft an agreement governing cyber behavior.[83] The delegation, including high-ranking Chinese Politburo official Meng Jianzhu, created an accord to guide US–China relations in cyberspace.[84] As part of this agreement, the nations pledged their respective governments would not "conduct or knowingly support cyber-related theft of intellectual property, including trade secrets or other confidential business information, with the intent of providing competitive advantages to companies or commercial sectors."[85] The accord was an important breakthrough, as it represented the nations' first step in negotiating the configuration of cyber behavior. It also signified a significant change in China's perception of cyberespionage. Neither President Xi nor President Obama commented on the indictment of the PLA officers or the Wanted posters during their joint press conference announcing the accord.

As part of the agreement, Chinese leaders agreed to the US view distinguishing between cyberespionage for national security and commercial purposes. Critics pointed to several possible reasons to explain China's shift, including advances in the NSA's capabilities to identify those responsible for cyberattacks and the threat of sanctions.[86] Under the agreement, US and Chinese leaders approved developing a cyber hotline to improve communication between the nations on cyber issues, participating in regular meetings regarding aggressive cyber behavior, combating cyberthreats from both countries, and readily responding to menacing actions in cyberspace.[87] The agreement did not entirely resolve the cyber controversy, as it skirted complicated issues such as delineating acceptable cyberespionage for economic and national security means. However, the accord did represent significant progress in the nations' handling of the dispute. But, as we move to the next saga in US–China cyber relations, controversies over technology and security continue—for example, clashes over ZTE, 5G networks, Huawei, and China's "Made in China 2025" program—show us a future rife with ongoing clashes and fragmentation.

Today, the United States and China continue to struggle with challenges regarding convergence and cyber sovereignty. In December 2018 the Trump administration accused China of violating the 2015 cyber agreement to end cyberespionage for economic purposes.[88] The US Department of Justice indicted two Chinese nationals for allegedly breaking into the computer systems of US government agencies and major internet providers. The *New York Times* reported that the suspected individuals were connected with China's Ministry of State Security. In 2019, the debates have shifted to global 5G networks and Huawei, recharging similar debates on cyber relations and (inter)national security concerns in the global arena. Despite these setbacks, we argue that engagement between the United States and China must continue. The United States and China must continue to deliberate, negotiate, and compromise in order to effectively face the demands of convergence in the twenty-first century.

NOTES

1. Jeffrey N. Wasserstrom, "Dreams and Nightmares: History and U.S. Visions of the Beijing Games," in *Owning the Olympics: Narratives of the New China*, ed. Monroe E. Price and Daniel Dayan (Ann Arbor: University of Michigan Press, 2008), 163–184. For rhetorical scholarship examining the tension within and the evolution of US–Sino relations, see Robert P. Newman, "Lethal Rhetoric: The Selling of the China Myths," *Quarterly Journal of Speech* 61, no. 2 (1975): 113–128; Denise M. Bostdorff, "The Evolution of a Diplomatic Surprise: Richard M. Nixon's Rhetoric on China, 1952–July 15, 1971," *Rhetoric & Public Affairs* 5, no. 1 (2002): 31–56; Xing Lu and Herbert Simons, "Transitional Rhetoric of

Chinese Communist Party Leaders in the Post-Mao Reform Period: Dilemmas and Strategies," *Quarterly Journal of Speech* 92, no. 3 (2006): 262–286; Kent A. Ono and Joy Yang Jiao, "China in the U.S. Imaginary: Tibet, the Olympics, and the 2008 Earthquake," *Communication and Critical/Cultural Studies* 5, no. 4 (2008): 406–410; Xing Lu, "From 'Ideological Enemies' to 'Strategic Partners': A Rhetorical Analysis of U.S.-China Relations in Intercultural Contexts," *Howard Journal of Communications* 22, no. 4 (2011): 336–357; Michelle Murray Yang, "President Nixon's Speeches and Toasts during His 1972 Trip to China: A Study in Diplomatic Rhetoric," *Rhetoric & Public Affairs* 14, no. 1 (2011): 1–44; Stephen John Hartnett, "Democracy in Decline, as Chaos, and as Hope; or, US-China Relations and Political Style in an Age of Unraveling," *Rhetoric & Public Affairs* 19, no. 4 (2016): 629–678; Stephen J. Hartnett and Bryan R. Reckard, "Sovereign Tropes: A Rhetorical Critique of Contested Claims in the South China Sea," *Rhetoric & Public Affairs* 20, no. 2 (2017): 291–338; Michelle Murray Yang, "At War with the Chinese Economic Yellow Peril: Mitt Romney's 2012 Presidential Campaign Rhetoric," *Journal of Intercultural Communication Research* 45, no. 1 (2016): 45–69; and Michelle Murray Yang, *American Political Discourse on China* (New York: Routledge, 2017).

2. See Nancy Marion, "The Council of Europe's Cyber Crime Treaty: An Exercise in Symbolic Legislation," *International Journal of Cyber Criminology* 4, nos. 1–2 (2010): 699–712; Benjamin Mueller, "Why We Need a Cyberwar Treaty," *The Guardian,* June 2, 2014; and Greg Austin, "What the U.S. Gets Wrong about Chinese Cyberespionage," *The Diplomat,* May 22, 2015.

3. "Most Wanted: Sun Kailiang," FBI, 2014. You can find the FBI charts here: https://www.fbi.gov/wanted/cyber/sun-kailiang.

4. "U.S. Charges Five Chinese Military Hackers for Cyber Espionage against U.S. Corporations and a Labor Organization for Commercial Advantage," US Department of Justice, May 19, 2014, https://www.justice.gov/opa/pr/us-charges-five-chinese-military-hackers-cyber-espionage-against-us-corporations-and-labor.

5. "China Reacts Strongly to US Announcement of Indictment against Chinese Personnel," Ministry of Foreign Affairs of the People's Republic of China, May 20, 2014, http://www.fmprc.gov.cn/mfa_eng/xwfw_665399/s2510_665401/t1157520.shtml.

6. In 1994, China established its first World Wide Web server. The next decade yielded rapid advances in China's internet. The twentieth anniversary of China's web server in 2014 signaled a series of achievements and setbacks. In 2014, China set up a security leadership group at the national level, issued internet reports, and made network security policies to strengthen control over the internet. However, Chinese internet officials also faced a series of complex issues. These concerns included internet privacy,

internet management, Xue Manzi's arrest for his messages on social media, network rumors, and the transformation of pornography online. There was a surge in news coverage of network security, especially articles examining how network governance could be strengthened.

7. Kenneth Burke, *A Grammar of Motives* (Berkeley: University of California Press, 1969).

8. Stephen Lucas, "The Stylistic Artistry of the Declaration of Independence," in *Readings in Rhetorical Criticism,* 2nd ed., ed. Carl Burgchardt (State College, PA: Strata, 2000), 564.

9. Michael C. Leff and Gerald P. Mohrmann, "Lincoln at Cooper Union: A Rhetorical Analysis of the Text," *Quarterly Journal of Speech* 60, no. 3 (1974): 346–358; Martin Medhurst, "Reconceptualizing Rhetorical History: Eisenhower's Farewell Address," in Burgchardt, *Readings in Rhetorical Criticism*, 579–602; and Amy Slagell, "Anatomy of a Masterpiece: A Close Textual Analysis of Abraham Lincoln's Second Inaugural Address," *Communication Studies* 42, no. 2 (1991): 155–171.

10. Min Wu, "Framing AIDS in China: A Comparative Analysis of U.S. and Chinese Wire News Coverage of HIV/AIDS in China," *Asian Journal of Communication* 16, no. 3 (2006): 253. Richard Entman explains how "frames define problems—determine what a causal agent is doing with what costs and benefits, usually measured in terms of common cultural values." He asserts that frames also "identify the forces creating the problem," make moral judgments that "evaluate causal agents and their effects," and offer solutions. Journalists endow news stories with meaning through their choice of frames. See Richard M. Entman, "Framing: Toward Clarification of a Fractured Paradigm," *Journal of Communication* 43, no. 4 (1993): 52.

11. Elizabeth Powers, Vincent Price, and David Tewksbury, "Switching Trains of Thought: The Impact of News Frames on Readers' Cognitive Responses," *Communication Research* 24, no. 5 (1997): 481.

12. James W. Tankard, "The Empirical Approach to the Study of Media Framing," in *Framing Public Life: Perspectives on Media and Understanding of the Social World*, ed. S. D. Reese, O. H. Gandy Jr., and E. Grant (Mahwah, NJ: Lawrence Erlbaum Associates, 2001), 97.

13. Kathleen Hall Jamieson and Paul Waldman, *The Press Effect: Politicians, Journalists, and the Stories That Shape the Political World* (Oxford: Oxford University Press, 2002), xiii.

14. Pippa Norris, "The Restless Search: Network News Framing of the Post–Cold War World," *Political Communication* 12, no. 4 (1995): 358.

15. Kenneth Lieberthal and Peter W. Singer, "Cybersecurity and U.S.-Sino Relations," Brookings Institution, February 2012, https://www.brookings.edu/wp-content/uploads/2016/06/0223_cybersecurity_china_us_lieberthal_singer_pdf_english.pdf, 8, 9.

16. Our data set includes news reports, opinions and comments, and interviews. Several

prominent categories were derived from the sample. The analysis includes statistics and description of the categories, including time when reported, which page the story was reported on, the type of report, and the author of the report.

17. Frames bundle "key concepts, stock phrases, and stereotyped images to reinforce certain common ways of interpreting developments." Norris, "The Restless Search," 358.

18. Frank Langfitt, "U.S. Security Company Tracks Hacking to Chinese Army Unit," *NPR*, February 19, 2013, http://www.npr.org/2013/02/19/172373133/report-links-cyber-attacks-on-u-s-to-chinas-military.

19. "China Reacts Strongly."

20. Jonathan Marcus, "U.S. Accuses China Government and Military of Cyber-Spying," *BBC News*, March 7, 2013, http://www.bbc.co.uk/news/world-asia-china-22430224.

21. See Marcus, "U.S. Accuses China"; and Cheng Li and Ryan McElveen, "A New Type of Cyber Relations," Brookings Institution, October 2015, http://www.brookings.edu/research/articles/2015/10/new-type-cyber-relations-li-mcelveen.

22. Ministry of Foreign Affairs of the PRC, "China Opposes All Forms of Hacker Attacks, and Will Have In-Depth Communication with the U.S.," *People.com*, June 14, 2013, http://js.people.com.cn/html/2013/06/14/234715.html.

23. Ministry of Foreign Affairs of the PRC, "China Opposes All Forms." See also Stephen J. Hartnett's "Google and the 'Twisted Cyber Spy Affair': U.S.-China Communication in an Age of Globalization," *Quarterly Journal of Speech* 97, no. 4 (2011): 413–434.

24. Nicole Perlroth, "An Obama Plan to Stop Foreign Hackers Has Mixed Results," *New York Times*, May 11 2015, B9.

25. "U.S. 'Spied on French Presidents'—Wikileaks," *BBC News*, June 24, 2015, http://www.bbc.com/news/33248484.

26. Barack Obama, "Remarks by President Obama and President Xi Jinping of the People's Republic of China After Bilateral Meeting," White House, June 8, 2013, https://obamawhitehouse.archives.gov/the-press-office/2013/06/08/remarks-president-obama-and-president-xi-jinping-peoples-republic-china-.

27. Xi Jingping, "Remarks by President Obama and President Xi Jinping of the People's Republic of China after Bilateral Meeting," White House, June 8, 2013, https://obamawhitehouse.archives.gov/the-press-office/2013/06/08/remarks-president-obama-and-president-xi-jinping-peoples-republic-china-.

28. "Obama and Xi End 'Constructive' Summit," BBC News, June 9, 2013, https://www.bbc.com/news/world-us-canada-22828678.

29. Li and McElveen, "New Type of Cyber Relations."

30. "U.S. Charges Five Chinese Military Hackers."

31. See Austin Ramzy, "China Pulls Cisco into Dispute on Cyberspying," *New York Times*, May 28, 2014, http://www.nytimes.com/2014/05/28/business/international/china-pulls-cisco-into-dispute-on-cyberspying.html?_r=0; and Chris Buckley, "China Plans Security Checks for Tech Firms after U.S. Indictments," *New York Times*, May 23, 2014, http://www.nytimes.com/2014/05/23/world/asia/china-threatens-security-checks-for-tech-firms-after-us-indictments.html?_r=0.

32. Nicole Perlroth and David Sanger, "North Korea Loses Its Link to the Internet," *New York Times*, December 22, 2014, http://www.nytimes.com/2014/12/23/world/asia/attack-is-suspected-as-north-korean-internet-collapses.html.

33. Leslie Wroughton and Megha Rajagopalan, "Internet Outage Seen in North Korea Amid U.S. Hacking Dispute," *Reuters*, December 22, 2014, https://www.reuters.com/article/us-sony-cybersecurity-northkorea/internet-outage-seen-in-north-korea-amid-u-s-hacking-dispute-idUSKBN0K01WA20141222.

34. Julie Hirschfeld, Michael Shear, and Michael Schmidt, "Hacking Exposed 21 Million in U.S., Government Says," *New York Times*, July 10, 2015, A1.

35. Julie Hirschfeld Davis, "Hacking of Government Computers Exposed 21.5 Million People," *New York Times*, July 9, 2015, http://www.nytimes.com/2015/07/10/us/office-of-personnel-management-hackers-got-data-of-millions.html?_r=0;%20; and Michael Shear and Scott Shane, "White House Weighs Sanctions after Second Breach of a Computer System," *New York Times*, June 13, 2015, A7.

36. Tremayne Gibson, "2015 a Pivotal Year for China's Cyber Armies," *The Diplomat*, December 17, 2015, http://thediplomat.com/2015/12/2015-a-pivotal-year-for-chinas-cyber-armies/.

37. Barack Obama, "Statement by the President on Executive Order 'Blocking the Property of Certain Persons Engaging in Significant Malicious Cyber-Enabled Activities,'" White House, April 1, 2015, https://www.whitehouse.gov/the-press-office/2015/04/02/statement-president-executive-order-blocking-property-certain-persons-en.

38. See Mueller, "Cyberwar Treaty"; and Marion, "Cyber Crime Treaty."

39. Ellen Nakashima and William Wan, "U.S. Announces First Charges against Foreign Country in Connection with Cyberspying," *Washington Post*, May 19, 2014, https://www.washingtonpost.com/world/national-security/us-to-announce-first-criminal-charges-against-foreign-country-for-cyberspying/2014/05/19/586c9992-df45-11e3-810f-764fe508b82d_story.html.

40. "Most Wanted: Sun Kailiang."

41. Erin Blakemore, "'Most Wanted': The Long History of the FBI's Top Ten List," *Time*, March 13, 2015, http://time.com/3742696/history-fbi-top-ten-list/.

42. "National Affairs: Leopard Hunt," *Time*, August 21, 1939, http://content.time.com/time/magazine/article/0,9171,762448,00.html.

43. Blakemore, "Most Wanted."

44. Kaveh Waddell, "The FBI's Most-Wanted Cybercriminals," *The Atlantic*, April 27, 2016, http://www.theatlantic.com/technology/archive/2016/04/the-fbis-most-wanted-cybercriminals/480036/.

45. Waddell, "FBI's Most-Wanted Cybercriminals." See "Ten Most Wanted," FBI, 2016 https://www.fbi.gov/wanted/topten; "FBI—Federal Bureau of Investigation," Facebook, 2016, https://www.facebook.com/FBI; and @FBI, Twitter, 2016, https://mobile.twitter.com/FBI.

46. Ibid.

47. "Cyber's Most Wanted," FBI, 2018, https://www.fbi.gov/wanted/cyber.

48. Internet Media Research Center, "The United States' Global Surveillance Record," qtd. in *People's Daily*, May 27, 2014, 22.

49. Devlin Barrett and Siobhan Gorman, "U.S. Charges Five in Chinese Army with Hacking," *Wall Street Journal*, May 19, 2014, http://www.wsj.com/articles/SB10001424052702304422704579571604060696532.

50. John Carlin, "Assistant Attorney General for National Security John Carlin Speaks at the Press Conference Announcing U.S. Charges against Five Chinese Military Hackers for Cyber Espionage," US Department of Justice, May 19, 2014, https://www.justice.gov/nsd/pr/assistant-attorney-general-national-security-john-carlin-speaks-press-conference.

51. Perlroth, "Obama Plan."

52. Adam Clark Estes, "The FBI Just Issued Wanted Posters for 5 Chinese Army Officers," *Gizmodo*, May 19, 2014, http://gizmodo.com/the-fbi-just-issued-wanted-posters-for-5-chinese-army-o-1578448066.

53. Carlin, "Assistant Attorney General."

54. Eric Holder, "Attorney General Eric Holder Speaks at the Press Conference Announcing U.S. Charges Against Five Chinese Military Hackers for Cyber Espionage," U.S. Department of Justice, May 19, 2014, https://www.justice.gov/opa/speech/attorney-general-eric-holder-speaks-press-conference-announcing-us-charges-against-five.

55. Barrett and Gorman, "U.S. Charges Five."

56. Carlin, "Assistant Attorney General."

57. Edward Wong, "U.S. Case Offers Glimpse into China's Hacker Army," *New York Times*, May 22, 2014, http://www.nytimes.com/2014/05/23/world/asia/us-case-offers-glimpse-into-chinas-hacker-army.html?_r=0.

58. Andy Greenberg, "U.S. Indictment of Chinese Hackers Could Be Awkward for the NSA," *Wired*, May 19, 2014, https://www.wired.com/2014/05/

us-indictments-of-chinese-military-hackers-could-be-awkward-for-nsa/.

59. Matt Sheehan, "China Mocks U.S. 'Hypocrisy' on Hacking Charges, *Huffington Post*, May 20, 2014, http://www.huffingtonpost.com/2014/05/20/china-cyber-spying_n_5356072.html.

60. Wong, "U.S. Case Offers Glimpse."

61. Greenberg, "U.S. Indictment."

62. Barrett and Gorman, "U.S. Charges Five."

63. Wong, "U.S. Case Offers Glimpse."

64. Jason Bellini, "#TheShortAnswer," *Wall Street Journal*, May 20, 2014, http://www.wsj.com/articles/SB10001424052702304422704579573650764970552; and Barrett and Gorman, "U.S. Charges Five."

65. Andrea Peterson, "Everything You Need to Know about the Alleged Chinese Military Hacker Squad the U.S. Just Indicted," *Washington Post*, May 19, 2014, https://www.washingtonpost.com/news/the-switch/wp/2014/05/19/everything-you-need-to-know-about-the-alleged-chinese-military-hacker-squad-the-u-s-just-indicted/.

66. "The World's Most Famous Network Thief 'Calls Thieves,'" *People's Daily*, May 22, 2014, 21, http://www.peopledaily.eu/yw/rd/20140522_16316.html. You can find the image accompanying the same *People's Daily* story.

67. Ibid.

68. Ma Dan, "U.S. Telecommunications Giant Helps Intelligence Agencies to Monitor," *People's Daily*, August 17, 2015, 21.

69. Huang Fahong, "Germany Issued the '2014 Basic Rights Report,'" *People's Daily*, June 6, 2014, 21.

70. Hong Yanqing, "How Long Can the U.S. Internet 'Decentralization' Go," *People's Daily*, March 25, 2014, 22.

71. Zhang Penghui and Zheng Hong, "The Image of the United States Is 'Discounted' Again in Europe," *People's Daily*, July 4, 2015, 11.

72. Liao Zaijun, "Obama Proposed to Terminate the Large-Scale Monitoring Program," *People's Daily*, March 27, 2014, 22.

73. "Network Sovereignty: An Unavoidable Topic," *People's Daily*, June 23, 2014, 23.

74. Internet Media Research Center, "The United States' Global Surveillance Record," qtd. in *People's Daily*, May 27, 2014, 22.

75. "Developing Sino-U.S. Relations Needs to Strengthen Strategic Mutual Trust," *People's Daily*, September 19, 2014, 23; and Ray McGowan, "The United States Is Not Responsible for the 'Indictment' of Chinese Soldiers," *People's Daily*, June 6, 2014, 21.

76. McGowan, "United States Is Not Responsible," 21.

77. "To Develop Sino-U.S. Relations, The Two Countries Need to Consolidate Strategic Mutual Trust," *People's Daily*, September 19, 2014, 23.

78. State Council Information Office of the People's Republic of China, "Human Rights Record of the United States in 2013," *People's Daily*, March 1, 2014, 11.

79. To further bolster the narrative of the United States as a hypocritical aggressor, the *People's Daily* published an article explaining how US citizens were protesting against the United States' surveillance efforts at home in Washington. See Liao Zhengjun and Li Yingqi, "U.S. Security Is Exposed to Be Able to Listen to All of a Country's Phones," *People's Daily*, March 20, 2014, 21. A close-up photograph accompanying the article showed a woman at a protest rally wearing a huge pair of fake glasses with two words, "STOP SPYING," on the lenses. The *People's Daily* published this story and image to illustrate the hypocrisy of the United States' position and American citizens' resistance to the US government's invasion of privacy.

80. National Information Office, "The Latest Data of the United States to Attack on China's Network," *People's Daily*, May 20, 2014, 4.For another example of how the *People's Daily* used US citizen protests out of context to frame the United States as hypocritical aggressor and human rights violator, see Liao Zhengjun and Li Yingqi, "U.S. Security Is Exposed."

81. Zhang Yang, "Internet Media Research Center Issued a Report on the U.S. Intelligence Agencies' 'Unscrupulous' Surveillance Over the Rest of the World," *People's Daily*, May 27, 2014, 1.

82. "The Future of the Internet Will Face Their Own Development, Network Security and Privacy Ethics and Many Other Challenges," *People's Daily*, June 23, 2014.

83. See David Sanger, "Path Set by U.S. and China to Limit Security Breaches May Be Impossible to Follow," *New York Times*, September 26, 2015, A9; and Greg Austin, "China's Cyber Turn: Recognizing Change for the Better," *The Diplomat*, December 21, 2015, http://thediplomat.com/2015/12/chinas-cyber-turn-recognizing-change-for-the-better/.

84. Austin, "China's Cyber Turn."

85. Barack Obama, "Remarks by President Obama and President Xi of the People's Republic of China in Joint Press Conference," White House, September 25, 2015, https://www.whitehouse.gov/the-press-office/2015/09/25/remarks-president-obama-and-president-xi-peoples-republic-china-joint.

86. See Sanger, "Path Set"; and Graham Webster, "Has U.S. Cyber Pressure Worked on China?," *The Diplomat*, December 10, 2015, http://thediplomat.com/2015/12/has-u-s-cyber-pressure-worked-on-china/.

87. See Office of the Press Secretary, "Fact Sheet: President Xi Jinping's State Visit to the

United States," White House, September 25, 2015, https://www.whitehouse.gov/the-press-office/2015/09/25/fact-sheet-president-xi-jinpings-state-visit-united-states; Li and McElveen, "New Type of Cyber Relations."

88. David Sanger and Katie Benner, "U.S. Accuses Chinese Nationals of Infiltrating Corporate and Government Technology," *New York Times*, December 20, 2018, https://www.nytimes.com/2018/12/20/us/politics/us-and-other-nations-to-announce-china-crackdown.html?smid=nytcore-ios-share.

Huawei and the 2019 Cybersecurity Crisis

Sino–US Conflict in the Age of Convergence

Jufei Wan and Bryan R. Reckard

A diplomatic crisis between the United States and China erupted on December 1, 2018, when Meng Wanzhou, chief financial officer of the Chinese tech giant Huawei, and daughter of Huawei founder, Ren Zhengfei, was arrested in Canada. Accused of violating US sanctions on Iran, Meng's arrest was part of a larger investigation conducted by the US government that initially focused on the Chinese telecommunications giant ZTE Corporation.[1] In 2017, ZTE paid a $1.2 billion fine for violating US sanctions on North Korea and Iran. Later, among the documents seized from a ZTE laptop, US officials identified Huawei as having used a shell company in Hong Kong to do business with Iran.[2] Meng's connection to evading American sanctions on Iran further discredited Huawei's international reputation, increased US suspicions about its relationship with the Chinese government, and deepened America's concerns about Huawei and the Chinese government's alleged cyberespionage activities. Signaling deteriorating US–China relations, Meng's arrest and the controversy surrounding Huawei indicate how the age of convergence rotates around murky cybersecurity crises.

Although the US Justice Department argues that the case of Meng Wanzhou is "free of any political interference and follows evidence and the law,"[3] China frames the case as a serious political issue, both denouncing American hegemony and

Meng's detention, in which the CPC portrays Meng as a scapegoat for Huawei's challenge to US tech dominance. For example, a spokesperson for the Chinese embassy argued that the arrest of Huawei's CFO illustrated a politically motivated effort to intervene in Chinese high-tech enterprise, claiming that it did not adhere to "the principle of rule of law and judiciary independence" and constituted a violation of Meng's human rights.[4] Public outcry regarding Meng's arrest was prevalent in China as well as in the international Chinese community. Parker Li, a student who studies China's political economy at the University of British Columbia, stated that "many Chinese people from mainland China feel she is being unfairly bullied by the United States."[5] The discourse revolving around the detention of Meng indicates how the United States and China are interdependent yet also absorbed in the global competition for technological and economic supremacy, hence illustrating communicative patterns that are deeply rooted in contradiction and conflict in the age of convergence.

Indeed, as Stephen Hartnett and Bryan Reckard have noted, "the U.S.–China relationship has been marked for more than sixty years by entrenched misunderstanding, unproductive communication patterns, and simmering rivalries."[6] Furthermore, long-standing and seemingly irreconcilable conflicts—economic, political, diplomatic, cultural, and military—continue to impact the relationship between the two global powers. In fact, for more than two centuries the two nations' histories have intertwined. As American journalist and China expert John Pomfret posits, "Americans and Chinese have been enchanting each other and disappointing each other since they first met in 1784." "If there's a pattern to the relationship," he explains, "it has been rapturous enchantment followed by despair."[7]

When President Richard Nixon visited China in 1972, many agreed that an open, transparent, and prosperous China was in the United States' interests.[8] In the nearly five decades that have passed since the Nixon-Mao meeting, the United States and China have repeatedly drifted apart and at times moved closer together. For instance, tensions between the two nations increased after the Tiananmen Square massacre in 1989, in the aftermath of the accidental US bombing of the Chinese embassy in Belgrade in 1999, and after a midair collision between US and Chinese military aircraft near Hainan island in 2001.[9] However, the tethers of economic benefit and our mutual "enchantment" have reinvigorated the partnership time and again. Despite these periodic upswings, the past five years have seen increased concerns about global economic competition, contested military hegemony, and rapid changes to the balance of the world order.

While some US commentators hold out hope "that China will become 'more like us' as it is more integrated into the U.S.–led liberal international system," other Americans have begun "to feel disappointed, uneasy, and threatened."[10] Nonetheless, Cheng Li, director of the John L. Thornton China Center and a senior fellow with Brookings, has argued that "positive U.S.–China relations" are "vital to the two countries and to the world at large." In 2016, Li explained, "Forty-four years after establishing diplomatic relations, the world's two greatest economic powers [had] forged unprecedentedly close ties."[11] Yet even during President Obama's tenure, tensions caused by disagreements concerning climate change, disputes between rival claimants in the South China Sea, the Obama administration's "Pivot to Asia," and attempts to establish the Trans Pacific Partnership trade agreement did little to assuage fears regarding China's growth and the potential for conflict.

With the arrival of Trump in the White House, concerns quickly departed from previous US policy, which had sought "a constructive relationship" that "mitigated risk" and "maximized opportunities for cooperation" with China.[12] Instead, the Trump administration "adopted an increasingly zero-sum, unilateralist, protectionist, and nativist 'America first' approach to the relationship."[13] Take for example, when on October 4, 2018, Vice President Mike Pence delivered a damning address denouncing Beijing's political dictatorship, its unfair trade practices, currency manipulation, military expansion, diplomatic strategies, surveillance mechanisms, religious oppression, forced technology transfers, and intellectual property theft, among others. Amid his machine gun barrage of criticism, Pence argued that it was "America [that] rebuilt China over the last 25 years" in the hope that "freedom in China would expand in all of its forms"; however, America's hopes for a prodemocratic China, Pence suggested, had been dashed.[14] In the US–China relationship, plagued by enduring distrust and culminating in Pence's latest challenge, we hear overlapping yet also conflicting interests in the rhetorical tropes and communication patterns that attempt to justify each sides' respective actions, meanwhile accusing the other of wrongdoing.

In our examination of US–China discourse, our shared communication patterns, and the rhetorical maneuverings surrounding the Huawei controversy, we hope to contribute to a burgeoning area of research that has emerged in the communication discipline. For instance, Denise Bostdorff's work has analyzed the evolution of Richard Nixon's rhetoric on China from the early 1950s, when Nixon emerged as a rising political figure in US politics to his visit to China in the early 1970s as president.[15] More recently Michelle Murray Yang's work has explored

Nixon's speeches and toasts over the course of that China visit.[16] Yang's work is particularly relevant to our analysis in this chapter, as she shows how President Nixon was able to overcome the ideological differences between the United States and China "by using the definitional power of epideictic rhetoric to craft a positive view of Sino-American relations," hence creating "a new definition of the nations' relationship that focused on the countries' shared values and common goals."[17] Yet, whereas Yang illustrates Nixon's rhetorical successes in bridging cultural chasms to build international ties, our analysis emphasizes a breakdown in US–China relations, an instance where rather than coming together, the two countries are moving apart at an increasingly rapid rate.

In fact, the highs and lows of the US–China relationship are front and center in Lu Xing's research examining the "dynamics of U.S.–China relations" over a period of more than sixty years from 1940 to the end of the twentieth century.[18] Examining converging and diverging rhetorical patterns, Lu notes that in the US–China relationship "the two countries have evolved from 'military allies' to 'ideological enemies' from 'moral adversaries' to 'strategic partners' in response to international and domestic rhetorical exigencies."[19] Similarly, Stephen Hartnett has focused on US–China communication patterns comparing and contrasting discourses of democracy as exemplified in coverage of the Hong Kong protests, the discourse of US secretary of defense Chuck Hagel, and the CPC's responses to Hagel and the protests.[20] More recently, Hartnett and Reckard's research exploring US and Chinese discourse and the rhetorical battle as it pertains to growing rivalries in the South China Sea illustrates the clash between an increasingly powerful and progressively more assertive China, and a US military hell-bent on maintaining the regional status quo.[21] And so, in an effort to shed light on the future of US–China communication in the age of convergence, we build upon Lu Xing, Murray Yang, Hartnett, and Hartnett and Reckard's work to make sense of the multinational dispute concerning Huawei and the ongoing rhetorical conflict between the United States and China.

In the following sections of this chapter we analyze the rhetorical strategies deployed by the Trump administration, China, Huawei, and other international communities. We argue that the detention of Huawei's CFO Meng Wanzhou and the Trump administration's anti-Huawei campaign are synecdochical symbols for souring Sino–US relations. On the one hand, we show that US discourse revolving around this international trade and cybersecurity crisis is based on threat construction.[22] Embodying what Hartnett refers to as "the rhetoric of warhawk hysteria," this "imperial rhetorical style" is brimming with features and characteristics in which US policymakers seek to build support for uncompromising trade policies through anxiety-producing rhetoric that establishes China as a threat to US interests (as well as global democratic interests).[23] On the other hand, we turn to Huawei and attempts by its founder, Ren Zhengfei, to distance the Chinese tech company from the Chinese Communist Party–led government with the hopes of repairing Huawei's international corporate image amid US allegations that Huawei collaborates with the CPC, Chinese military, and Chinese spy agencies to skirt US sanctions. We highlight Ren's and Huawei's attempts, in a series of interviews in 2019 intended to rebuild its image in the international sphere as an ethical, high-tech company, at removing doubt about linkages to the Chinese government—a systematic PR and marketing strategy—through denial, dissociation, avoidance, and redirection.

Furthermore, we contend that the Party has adopted a "tit for tat" rhetorical strategy to downplay the seriousness of America's accusations and to highlight American hypocrisy. In this rhetorical bout, the "tit for tat" trope appropriates common rhetorical themes used by America in Sino–US discourse, transforming what were at one time criticisms of China into rhetorical tools used to denounce the United States. While the discourse surrounding Huawei shows us fragmented US and China interests despite the two countries being intertwined both economically and technologically, ultimately we argue that the ongoing rhetorical battle exemplifies the degradation of the US–China relationship, wherein both nations inch further away from a cooperative partnership and move closer to geopolitical rivalry marked by competition and conflict.

To support our thesis, we first explore the rhetorical tactics Huawei employed as the company addressed US allegations and attempted to maintain and repair its international reputation. Next, we examine the controversies surrounding China's alleged cybercrimes, Huawei's dubious relationship with the Chinese state, and Vice President Pence's rhetoric of "warhawk hysteria," hence illustrating the Trump administration's emphasis on directly confronting China as a threat to US interests. Third, in an attempt to illuminate a wide range of perspectives, we examine the opinions and arguments stressed by different media factions and the international community with respect to Huawei and the Meng Wanzhou crisis. We analyze American mainstream media viewpoints, Chinese official state/Party media representations, and perspectives from state actors outside of and separate from the United States and China. We believe this study, by incorporating multiple perspectives making different arguments, can shed light on the rhetorical tensions between the United States and China while also highlighting some potential openings for improving Sino–US discourse in the age of convergence.

"Made in China 2025" and Efforts to Reform Huawei's International Image

Two central tropes within Confucian rhetoric and traditional Chinese culture—peace and harmony—pervade customary Chinese adages and ancient idioms. In this ancient discourse, harmony is prized as a precious social good, while peace is touted as a cherished goal in both domestic and international political arenas. However, public memory of China's "century of humiliation"—a period marked by foreign imperialism and colonialism as European and Japanese powers repeatedly invaded the Chinese mainland beginning in the early nineteenth century until the rise of Mao and the CPC—significantly influences the CPC's outlook today. Thus, what Harnett has termed the rhetorical trope of "traumatized nationalism"—"wherein contemporary CPC leaders strive to justify geo-political aggressions by framing them as dignity-restoring and sovereignty-protecting attempts to erase the stain of prior humiliations"[24]—is deeply rooted in contemporary Chinese politics and the Party's rhetorical choices. Domestically, this means that the concepts of peace and harmony have been transformed, coded into rhetorical justifications for continued CPC control. Internationally, these concepts have become part of the rhetorical strategy designed to support China's global expansion and regional dominance.[25] In short, ancient Confucian values have been repurposed for contemporary needs, albeit turning them into tools for the Communist Party's global ambitions.

Given this historical-tactical-rhetorical context, our chapter is driven by these questions: How does the trope of traumatized nationalism impact China and the CPC in their pursuit of peace and harmony? Moreover, will China's global ambitions entail a future of peace and harmony or something more resembling hegemony and dominance?[26] The seemingly inevitable rise of China as a global power suggests that the answer to these questions will very likely have significant impacts on the world community. In exploring the answer to these questions, we first consider China's technological ambitions and its "Made in China 2025" plan before turning to the drama surrounding tech-giant Huawei, which, in the fall of 2018, became the focal point of international debates concerning China's global intentions and ambitions.

In line with Huawei's rise, "Made in China 2025" is a state-led industrial policy (released in 2015) that aims to reduce China's dependence on foreign technology, to catch up with and then surpass Western high-tech industries, and to seek a dominant position in the global high-tech marketplace. As McBride and Chatzky suggest, this program will "use government subsidies, mobilize state-owned enterprises, and pursue intellectual property acquisition" to "update China's manufacturing base by rapidly developing ten high-tech industries."[27] Of course, new fifth-generation cellular networks (5G) and telecommunications—Huawei's bread and butter—are included in this list of high-tech industries. Envisaged as the "network of networks,"[28] 5G impacts data traffic in many different high-tech devices, including industrial robots, security cameras, drones, and cars. With this in mind, China's blurring of the lines separating civilian and military technologies potentially poses a threat to developed countries' national security. For example, in April 2018, US intelligence agencies warned that Chinese recruitment of foreign scientists, their theft of US intellectual property, and their targeted acquisition of US firms constituted an "unprecedented threat" to the US industrial base.[29] Vice President Pence detailed the threat, noting that the "Made in China 2025" plan encroaches on America's global technical and economic leadership position and does so in dubious and suspicious ways, because "Beijing has directed its bureaucrats and businesses to obtain American intellectual property by any means necessary."[30] While China has described the "Made in China 2025" program as inspiring growth, strengthening the nation's technological power, and pursuing unaided innovation—think Huawei as one of the leading tech giants[31]—the United States has deemed it a serious threat to national security and global technological stability.

Huawei, one of world's largest telecommunications companies, operates in more than 170 countries and regions. It is regarded as the face of China's technological prowess and a source of national pride. As a leader of technological innovation in China, Huawei is at the center of the fight over the future of 5G. As illustrated by De Cremer and Wu, Huawei's objectives converge with the Party's communication infrastructure and technology goals. Indeed, Ren Zhengfei created the company "with the aim of becoming the backbone of the People's communications industry."[32] Yet because of the strong connections between Huawei's objectives and the CPC's ambitions, Huawei's advanced 5G technology has prompted national security concerns among Western countries. Furthermore, Huawei's alleged ties to China's People's Liberation Army, its politically oriented business models in foreign markets, and its infringement on intellectual property rights discredit the company's overseas reputation, sap the tech giant's economic strength, and impede Huawei in its global expansion efforts. Moreover, China's intelligence law, passed in 2017, has amplified concerns about Huawei's cyberespionage activities. For instance, Article 7 of China's National Intelligence Law declares, "Any organization and citizen shall, in accordance with the law, support, provide assistance and cooperate in national intelligence work, and guard the secrecy of any national intelligence work that they are aware of."[33] In this chain of events, a corporation like Huawei has a legal responsibility to aid the Chinese state and Party in intelligence work. Thus, as a key player competing for global technological supremacy, Huawei has become increasingly scrutinized by foreign nations the world over. This key point merits repeating: according to the Chinese law, Huawei is required to do the CPC's bidding—as we will see below, Huawei has tried to distance itself from the Party, yet the National Intelligence Law makes such distancing difficult, if not impossible.

Confronted by the Trump administration's global anti-Huawei campaign,[34] and shackled by the Party's intelligence law, the Chinese tech giant has favored two defensive strategies. On the one hand, Huawei has a propensity for taking legal action, suing some governments for allegedly damaging its corporate image.[35] On the other hand, it has pursued a systematic strategy to reform its image into that of an ethical high-tech company that strives for openness, transparency, and the highest cybersecurity standards. Indeed, even the construction of Huawei's headquarters illustrates the major rebranding efforts sought by the company. Linking traditional European architecture and Chinese technology, visitors are able to visit Huawei's newest campus in China's tech megacity, Shenzhen. The campus features picturesque Parisian building facades and manicured grounds dotted with Budapest-inspired bridges. Upon entering the campus, visitors can board Huawei's own vintage-style red train—complete with old-fashioned train whistle—to take a Disneyland-like ride through the campus.[36] The scope of the project reflects the size of Huawei's massive economic footprint too, as demonstrated by a new European-style "castle" that stretches across land equivalent to a whopping 345 football fields.[37] Huawei's Shenzhen campus thus points—like Google's, Apple's, and Facebook's headquarters in America—to a massive international company trying to use architecture to brand itself as a cheerful, innovative, and classy member of the international community.

But architecture is not enough, and so Huawei has been practicing US-style public relations spectacles as well. For example, with the hope of drawing domestic and, particularly, positive international attention to the company and its new campus, in July of 2018, Huawei held the "To the Explorers: 5G Polar Code and

Fundamental Research Awards" ceremony at its headquarters in Shenzhen.[38] More than one hundred experts received awards in basic research and communication standards at the ceremony, including Turkish professor Dr. Erdal Arikan, the father of polar codes and the official coding scheme for 5G standardization. As much an award ceremony as a concentrated public relations stunt, the event highlighted international collaboration and the benefits of technological progress not only for China but also the world. Upon arrival at Huawei's campus, two commissionaires in white suits opened Dr. Erdal's door as he stepped out of a shiny, streamlined car; then, accompanied by Huawei's concurrent rotating chairman, Guo Ping, Dr. Erdal walked the red carpet to a grandiose auditorium where he was met with thunderous applause.[39] Crystal chandeliers, live symphonies, stunning European-style decorations, and the efforts of well-trained PR personnel came together to illustrate Huawei as an exemplar of ethical technological progress, a company that stays abreast of Western standards, that values innovation, and both works with and is beloved by international intellectuals.

In his award acceptance speech, Dr. Erdal praised Huawei for its future-facing outlook and service to civilization: "Without vision and technical contributions of Huawei's directors and engineers, polar codes would not have made it from the lab to 5G in less than 10 years."[40] Huawei, Erdal continued, makes it "possible for so many researchers from around the globe to collaborate for a common cause in service to humanity."[41] We highlight this example to stress the significance of Huawei's image maintenance efforts in light of its tarnished reputation. From the pomp and circumstance surrounding Erdal's arrival at the ceremony to his own comments emphasizing Huawei's focus on the global good, the display was a calculated and sustained PR effort to present itself as an ethical corporation contributing to the global good of humanity, dedicated to the international community.

Denial, Dissociation, Avoidance, Redirection and The Ren Zhengfei Interviews

In contrast to the publicity Huawei hoped the award ceremony would encourage, Huawei's founder has typically preferred to stay out of the limelight. From the founding of Huawei in 1987, Ren Zhengfei has accepted few interviews, avoiding speaking to the news media until 2013.[42] Yet because of intensifying pressure from the international community to address concerns related to technology and security issues, Ren has recently been interviewed by dozens of domestic and foreign broadcasters, including the United Kingdom's BBC, the United States' CBS and CNBC, and China's CGTN. From the perspective of many media groups, Ren presented himself as an ambitious leader. For instance, CBS reporters reacted positively to Ren, noting how engaging and humorous he seemed.[43] During his interviews, Ren reflected on the demanding situation Huawei faced as a start-up company in 1987. Regarding himself as a hardworking person and branding Huawei as an advanced innovative technology company, he denied any connections between Huawei and Chinese state intelligence efforts, international espionage, or intellectual property theft. Responding to interviewers, Ren also repudiated his ties to the Chinese government and the People's Liberation Army. In playing down the connections, Ren recounted, "At that time, I was a very low-ranking officer in the People's Liberation Army. After leaving there, I have [had] no interaction with them."[44] Ren attributed Huawei's successes to hard work rather than special ties to the Party, state, or military and, as he pointed out, "Even 100% state-owned companies have failed."[45] Notably, he even turned down an award as one of China's one hundred reform pioneers recognized by the CPC Central Committee and the State Council in 2018. And so, as exampled in the interviews, Ren utilized the strategy of dissociation to distance Huawei from the Chinese government, military, state, and Party, all the while emphasizing Huawei's independence as a company free from political intervention.[46]

When asked about Huawei's cyberespionage allegations, Ren firmly rebuffed accusations of wrongdoing and utilized Chinese law to support his claims. Ren maintained that, according to statements made by a "member of the Political Bureau of the CPC Central Committee," the "Chinese government always required Chinese firms to abide by international rules, laws, and the regulations of the country where they operate."[47] Noting that China had no law requiring companies to install backdoors in their technology products to collect foreign intelligence, Ren claimed that he would refuse to do so if the state or Party ordered Huawei to include such technology in its products, echoing Apple's and Tim Cook's stance in a 2016 interview with ABC.[48] In fact, Ren's response highlights the ambiguity and imprecision embedded in the characteristics of some Chinese laws. As Tanner suggests, the Chinese intelligence law, passed in 2017, places vaguely worded, ill-defined, and open-ended new security obligations on domestic as well as foreign firms.[49] For example, this law does not explicitly reference the consequences for failing to support the nation's intelligence work, nor does it distinguish "obstruction" from failure to assist.[50] Thus, across multiple interviews, Ren claimed the Chinese telecommunications tech giant would not cooperate with the Chinese state and CPC for intelligence work and would rather violate state regulations than emerging international norms.[51] In this way, Ren sought to dissociate Huawei from the Chinese state and Party.

With regard to accusations of intellectual property theft, Ren utilized the strategy of avoidance to suggest that he believed in US law and the legal process, redirecting the conversation to express his appreciation of "U.S. help" for a "huge advertisement at a very cheap price" in making Huawei visible in some countries, even where Huawei has not yet launched advertising campaigns.[52] BBC's Karishma Vaswani posed a more pointed question concerning Cisco, Nortel, and Motorola's accusations that Huawei had stolen intellectual property and technology from them. This time, Ren reframed the issue by denying the allegations, asking, "How can we steal what they don't have?" Ren called the US allegations "marginal," surmising that "they are not enough to say that Huawei has become what it is today by stealing from the U.S." Ren's redirection pointed out that "lots of Huawei's technologies are far ahead of those in Western companies . . . therefore, it is impossible for Huawei to steal technologies that Western companies do not have."[53] By using the strategies of denial, dissociation, avoidance, and redirection, Ren's interviews illustrate the rhetorical work put forth to rebrand Huawei on the international stage as an ethical tech company disconnected from the Chinese state, military, and Party.

Rebuilding Huawei's Image and Legal Action

Huawei has also conducted substantial advertising campaigns and created the hashtag #HuaweiFacts, which trended on social media.[54] In an effort to rebuild Huawei's image, Catherine Chen, who was then on the Board of Directors at Huawei, wrote an open letter to the US media inviting them to visit Huawei's campus. Focusing on Huawei's attempts to show its transparency and openness, Chen beseeched US media groups not to "believe everything you hear and Huawei's doors are always open."[55] Addressing US cybersecurity concerns, Chen argued that since 1987 "there has not been a single major cyber security incident" concerning Huawei, explaining that Huawei would annually spend 5 percent of its research and development budget on a global cybersecurity assurance system.[56] Ultimately,

Chen indicated that Huawei would "abide by all applicable laws and regulations in the countries and regions where it operates, including all export control and sanction laws and regulations of the UN, US, and EU."[57]

In addition to Chen's open letter and the Ren Zhengfei interviews, Huawei has concentrated its campaign on appealing to the media, responding to accusations of wrongdoing, and attempts to refashion itself into a tech company that plays by international rules. Furthermore, its actions in the courts exemplify an offensive to thwart the United States' global anti-Huawei campaign. On March 6, 2019, Huawei sued the United States for allegedly ruining its image due to claims it was a security threat, and for allegedly violating constitutional principles on the "separation of powers and the bill of attainder clause, which prohibits legislation that singles out a person or entity for punishment without trial."[58] Huawei's offensive was not confined to the United States alone, threatening legal action against the Czech Republic after the country issued a formal warning regarding Huawei's cybersecurity threat.[59] Additionally, Guo Ping, Huawei's rotating chairman, accused American intelligence agencies of hacking Huawei's services and insisted that the United States also needed to be scrutinized for its previous espionage activities.[60] In tandem with actions to deny, disassociate, avoid, and redirect, the lawsuit is part of Huawei's overall strategy to push back against America's global anti-Huawei campaign.

With its advanced 5G technology, Huawei is representative of one of the Party's greatest ambitions for the PRC, to be a powerful nation on the world stage built on a foundation of scientific and technological advancement. Although Ren Zhengfei has tried to embody Confucian values in his interview testimonies, suggesting that "a technological competition is a peaceful competition,"[61] Huawei's suspected ties to the People's Liberation Army, its politically oriented business models in foreign markets, its infringement on intellectual property rights, and its complicity in violating international trade sanctions against Iran have continued to arouse Western countries' national security concerns. Indeed, with the arrest of Meng Wanzhou in Canada, with a Huawei employee in Poland accused of spying for China, with the Czech Republic issuing a formal warning about Huawei as a cybersecurity risk, and with the United States, Japan, Australia, and New Zealand in some form blocking Huawei from building 5G networks in their countries, it seems clear that many nations continue to view Huawei as a CPC-linked security threat.[62]

China's Cyber Offensives and Mike Pence's Speech on Policy toward China

From as early as 1995, President Bill Clinton had recognized that "cyber-wars would likely be among the deciding factors of twenty-first century global power."[63] Indeed, cyber offensives disrupt the free flow and exchange of information and could lead to the dysfunction of a state.[64] As a growing economic, military, and technological power, China's rise has triggered increasing concerns in the West about the potential for foreign meddling in the democratic process and even the possibility of massive cyberwar. For instance, on October 4, 2018, Vice President Mike Pence delivered a scathing speech at the Hudson Institute laying out the Trump administration's policy toward China.[65] Replete with assertions of Chinese threats to American and international welfare, Pence's address embodies the rhetoric of "warhawk hysteria."[66] Stuffed with counterthreats of direct action, Pence's speech escalated tensions between Washington and Beijing, in large part by announcing that the Trump administration would not turn a blind eye to China's alleged infractions.

Highlighting China's attempts to influence American public opinion, and especially its interference in America's 2018 midterm elections, Pence shared that a senior member of the US intelligence community had told him that "what the Russians are doing pales in comparison to what China is doing across this country."[67] Framing Chinese efforts as aggressive interference in US domestic policy, politics, and domestic affairs, Pence explained the meddling as "China's comprehensive and coordinated campaign to undermine support for the President, the administration's agenda, and the nation's most cherished ideas."[68] Ryan Hass, a senior fellow at the Brookings Institution and a former member of the National Security Council in the Obama administration, notes that "the vice president attempted to shift public scrutiny from Russia to China."[69] Yet when asked to explain what the Chinese did in the 2018 elections, Dan Coats, US director of national intelligence, avoided any potential contradictions by sending a classified answer,[70] leaving the public wondering about the authenticity and potential dangers of such a Chinese threat to American democracy.

Bill Priestap, the FBI's assistant director in the Counterintelligence Division, argues the Chinese government learned from the Cold War that "economic strength is the foundation of national power," and thus China's cyberwarfare program has prioritized the advancement of economic supremacy through the targeting of foreign military technology, business secrets, and personal information.[71] And so

China's cyber operations have emphasized strengthening the economy and bridging the gap between China and the United States, in large part by stealing American R&D in the hope of jump-starting Chinese advancements in business and military technology.[72] Thus, Pence's address, presenting China as the gate-crasher that interfered in American domestic politics, illustrates America's increasing anxieties regarding China's systematic threats to national security. Given this context, the Trump administration's calculated move of escalating the animosity in the Sino–US relationship marks a shift into a long, drawn-out struggle over trade, technology, geopolitics, and security, thus pointing to what many observers are now calling a "New Cold War."[73]

Further highlighting Beijing's theft of American intellectual property, Pence's address targeted how Chinese hacking was detrimental to "the foundation of America's economic leadership."[74] As Coats has suggested, Beijing's hacking agenda was focused on pilfering information and stealing technical advancements: "Fortune 500 companies [that] were being hit at shockingly high rates."[75] Moreover, since 2012, Chinese hackers have transitioned from only targeting "companies and government agencies in the defense, energy, and aerospace sectors" to pursuing organizations charged with securing Americans' personal data.[76] Indeed, the September 2018 Marriott data breach demonstrates how Chinese intelligence agencies amass American personal data for tracking travel habits and movement across borders, for future use and the targeting of American spies.[77] As Townsend indicates, "China's access to large volumes of personal data—especially business and government employees—opens the opportunity for future stealthy operations against specific companies or government agencies."[78] Unlike Russia's cyber activities, which focused on meddling in the 2016 presidential elections, China's cyber priorities are to surpass America economically and to target its intelligence communities by collecting America's business information, military technology, and citizens' personal data. Across all of America's various intelligence agencies, then, the new consensus is that China is a bad actor, especially in the realm of cyber activity. The question is to what extent Huawei is complicit in this New Cold War.

The Multiple Perspectives of American Media

In stories about the Huawei cyberespionage crisis, American mainstream media have represented the spread of Huawei's 5G networking from multiple perspectives, including framing Huawei as (1) a CPC-linked national security threat, (2) a largely independent technological and economic challenge, and (3) a private business with a Communist-based culture and loose ties to the Party.[79] Across these three portrayals, some American media framings of Huawei's 5G global ambitions align with the views held by the Trump administration. As one article in the *New York Times* suggested, according to Mike Pompeo, the US secretary of state, Huawei is a puppet controlled by China's central government to promote its authoritarian regime, to seek economic dominance, and to threaten other nations' cybersecurity infrastructure.[80] Allowing Huawei to participate in 5G construction is tantamount to permitting China "to control the internet of the future," posing a wide range of economic and security threats to the world.[81] Furthermore, in the *Washington Post*, King and Moritz have argued that Huawei's ties to the Chinese government and China's 2017 intelligence law make it extremely risky for the United States to allow Huawei to enter its critical cyber infrastructure systems.[82] Presenting a range of alternative perspectives, some of the opinions advanced in the *New York Times* are consistent with Chinese media tropes that frame Huawei's 5G expansion as a technological challenge devoid of political motivation. Some of these stories also highlight cases of American hypocrisy and denounce America's past espionage activities.[83] Satariano showcases claims that the White House's accusations against Huawei are based on weak evidence. Suggesting that "nobody appeared to be won over" by the White House's "case against Huawei" when the Trump administration attempted to persuade other countries to ban the Chinese company at a Barcelona tech conference in February 2019, Satariano also emphasized Huawei's critiques of US cyberespionage and claims that "the United States had a more checkered history of espionage than Huawei" ever had.[84] In these instances, the United States' history of cyber activities serves as evidence of a nation willing to call others to task for the same offenses it routinely commits.

Yet another perspective attempts to illuminate Huawei's suspicious ties to the Party and central government. For example, some articles in the *New York Times* have focused on investigating Huawei's ideology, internal structure, and corporate culture.[85] As Zhong suggests, although Huawei has posited that it is entirely owned by its employees and has no affiliation with the Chinese government, its ownership remains murky because the company has never sold shares to the public.[86] Furthermore, the *New York Times* has represented Huawei's organizational structure as based on "traditional political and communist party culture for guidance."[87] In this line, Huawei refers to its management training program as the Central

Party School, the name of the Communist Party institution that trains promising CPC recruits. The casual reader of mainstream newspapers in America would therefore be understandably confused, as Huawei was portrayed in the *Times* and *Post* as either a CPC-linked intelligence agency threatening US national security, or a super-advanced tech giant challenging US international market leadership, or a shadowy entity with opaque financing and an authoritarian management culture—or all of these. Across the US media we examined, then, there was a shared sense of concern, a palpable sense of crisis, but no consensus as to Huawei's roles in the drama.

Chinese State Media, "Tit for Tat" Rhetorical Strategies, and the International Reframing of Huawei's Image

Whereas US media sources present multiple perspectives on Huawei, in response to Pence's inflammatory address, Chinese state media utilize the rhetorics of dissent and strategic silence to mitigate tensions between the United States and China. For instance, in an article published by *China Daily*, Pence's speech is framed as preposterous: "Mike Pence's speech arouses laughter on China's social media."[88] In the article, "laughable" or "laugh" appeared six times, "joke" appeared twice, and "ridicule" appeared three times.[89] Pointedly, the article only collected Chinese netizens' online responses to less sensitive portions of Pence's address, using them to illustrate the Party's attempts to portray Pence's comments as bordering on the absurd. As we will see in this section, the Party's rhetorical strategy is largely based on misdirection: on trying to discredit US claims by muddying the waters, confusing the categories of analysis, shifting attention to other claims, and otherwise shrouding the cyber controversy in confusion.

Within this campaign of misdirection, much Chinese state media avoided analysis of Huawei's actions altogether, instead focusing on the political and cultural tensions inherent in US discourse. With regard to cybersecurity concerns, Chinese state media have framed them as US political and ideological conspiracies channeling "American evidence" to support its claims. For example, Xinhua News Agency cites a CNN online poll as evidence that the US global anti-Huawei campaign is politically motivated.[90] *China Daily* reporters then heavily referenced Eric Xu, deputy chairman of the board and rotating CEO of Huawei. Mirroring Ren's attempts at dissociation, Xu attempted to separate Huawei from politics, suggesting that cybersecurity is a technical problem rather than a political or ideological problem.[91] Likewise, Hu Xijin, editor in chief at the *Global Times*, commented on Twitter that "Huawei has been trying to distance itself from politics, but it has grown too big [so] that politics is coming to its door. Huawei is innocent."[92] Furthermore, the editors of *China Daily* have argued that when America discriminates against Chinese tech giants like Huawei, the United States violates its own free market principles."[93] Borrowing rhetorical tropes from American discourse, Chinese state media's "tit for tat" approach adopts often-used US rhetorical strategies to attack America. And so, as these examples highlight, Chinese state media have utilized a "tit for tat" rhetorical strategy to denounce the United States' anti-Huawei global campaign and to point the finger at the United States' campaign as politically motivated, all the while framing Huawei as wholly concerned with technology alone, thus isolating the business from any notions of Party politics. It is of course ironic that these pronouncements regarding Huawei's alleged independence from Party control have all been issued in Party-controlled outlets.

Repentance and atonement also appear as major foci in Chinese state media framings of Huawei. State media pronounce Huawei as an advocate embracing openness and transparency, as adhering to foreign policies and international principles, and as incorporating ethical practices in its improvement of cybersecurity standards worldwide. But such claims to adhere to international standards contrast sharply with the Party's mandate that state media "align their ideology, political thinking, and deeds to those of the CPC Central Committee," and with President Xi Jinping's pronouncement that state media's responsibilities include "focusing on the Party's major task and serving the interests of the country," among others.[94] And here, in this tension, we stumble into one of the driving contradictions of the age of convergence: as markets interweave, creating new international networks and norms (convergence), so nation-states seek to marshal these markets for local advantage (hence fragmenting these new networks), meaning the national and the international exist in tension, and convergence and fragmentation exist in tension. As we have shown here, Huawei claims to be acting in the interests of international convergence, yet many observers fear it is a Party-controlled agent, making it a force of fragmentation.

Some Chinese media have sought to massage this contradiction by representing Huawei as both an agent of international convergence and an agent of national advancement. For instance, consider the *Global Times* representation of Huawei's launching of new cybersecurity centers—in Brussels in March 2019 and in Germany in November 2019—as illustrating the company's following both Party mandates and international principles.[95] According to the story, Huawei hopes to collaborate internationally across the industry to improve cybersecurity standards, underscoring Huawei's investment of at least $2 billion toward improving cybersecurity.[96] At the same time, the presence of such Huawei leadership in Europe signifies a major political gain for the PRC, a new foothold in new territory. In this way, the story portrays Huawei as advancing both Chinese and international interests.

As Huawei's 5G global expansion and the Trump administration's global anti-Huawei campaign have grown to represent the US–China technological and geopolitical competition for global leadership, international communities are cautiously considering Huawei's participation in their nation's 5G network construction, meticulously balancing their relationships with the United States and China. Although the Trump administration has made countless efforts to persuade, pressure, and even threaten its allies to ban Huawei's equipment, international attitudes toward Huawei's 5G global plan vary from country to country. For instance, Britain has considered the potential of allowing Huawei to have some access to nonessential elements of its new 5G system, positing that "the security risks could be managed by closely scrutinizing the company and its software."[97] Germany, in considering possibilities, claims that it might allow Huawei to enter its 5G networks, but only after implementing a formal "no spy" deal with Huawei.[98]

In *China Daily*, the editor cites Huawei's potential partnerships with the UK government as an exemplar highlighting Huawei's ethical practices in the cybersecurity sector."[99] Meanwhile, an article in *The Economist* considers Britain's cautious approach with Huawei as a potential model for other countries. In terms of cybersecurity, the article suggests, fully banning Huawei would not guarantee risk relief since hackers usually attack networks "through flaws in software coding."[100] The argument, rather, is that any ban on Huawei could possibly heighten security risks by discouraging intellectual cooperation, thereby preventing technological advancement. As Nicholas surmises, an embargo on Huawei would be detrimental to all nations' technological innovation and development, because "a ban would exclude a major source of innovation—ideas, people, and products—from the technology market."[101] From this perspective, supporting free markets trumps national security, and even underwrites it. And so, as the United States and the international community considers banning Huawei, the issue has become laced with concerns about fragmentation and the potential impact on the global communication system. Because telecommunication supply chains and markets are so heavily intertwined with each other across markets and countries, this argument goes, banning Huawei would hurt everyone.[102] For example, if a full ban on Huawei is imposed, *The Economist* warns, then at least 180,000 jobs would be cut, mainly in China.[103] Also, considering the cost-effectiveness of Huawei's products and services, companies that serve sparsely populated areas would suffer the most, as many alternatives to Huawei's telecommunication equipment are costly and less affordable. Speculation suggests that American farmers—assumedly Trump voters—might suffer great financial losses if they were forced to replace Huawei kits with more expensive products and services in order to collect data and monitor crop yields and productivity.[104] As these examples indicate, some die-hard free marketers are more worried about what a ban on Huawei would do to international commerce than what allowing Huawei's 5G technology into their systems might do to their national security.

Instead of a full ban on Huawei, Britain and Germany have suggested a softer approach, one that could be more effective by first calling for government co-operation to improve international cybersecurity standards. The United States has pushed its allies to adopt shared security and policy measures.[105] Similarly, the German regulations read, "Systems may only be sourced from trustworthy suppliers whose compliance with national security regulations and provisions for the secrecy of telecommunications and for data protection is assured."[106] As Britain's and Germany's stances suggests, in the age of convergence it is more important for governments to make efforts to work together to incorporate international cybersecurity standards and to standardize global telecommunications regulations than to let things spiral out of control into a New Cold War that could fragment the global communication system. This approach suggests doing the hard work of collaborating across differences rather than pushing for all-out confrontation.

Conclusion: The Spinning Wheel of Convergence and Fragmentation

The detention of Huawei's CFO Meng Wanzhou and the Trump administration's anti-Huawei campaign are symbolic of the ever-evolving Sino–US relationship and the paradox of convergence and fragmentation, wherein technology and the global economy simultaneously pull the two powers together while clashing national security concerns continue pushing the two countries apart. In this case, the US Justice Department has argued that the arrest of Meng is based on evidence and the law, and is merited by the right of national self-defense, while Chinese state media and Huawei have claimed that the case is politically motivated, yet another example of the United States trying to bully China. While we have tried here to represent the many sides of this controversy, it is hard not to recall Vice President Pence's lament that "China has taken a sharp U-turn toward control and oppression of its own people" and "has built an unparalleled surveillance state" by means "of U.S. technology."[107] By stressing Beijing's "theft of American intellectual property" and its "predatory practice of forced technology transfer," Pence argues that China's technological strength is based not on Chinese innovation, but the illegal seizure of US technologies.[108] Pence's concerns have legitimate grounding in regards to China's state surveillance mechanism, Huawei's past theft of intellectual property, the forced transfer of technology, and lingering concerns about Huawei's role in evading international sanctions by providing Iran with prohibited technologies.[109] Hearing such claims, it is hard not to conclude that Huawei is complicit with a wide range of China's rogue behaviors. At the same time, Pence's overblown argument that without American assistance there would not be a modern China closely aligns with what Hartnett calls an "imperial rhetorical style."[110] Indeed, even while leveling serious charges against China, Pence's arrogant claims highlight the Trump administration's sense of superiority, which rests directly in the heart of America's current foreign policy rhetoric.[111] Indeed, China's modernization and economic miracle rely on globalization and Western-led resources, yet Pence's framing of China, we argue, is excessively negative in plotting China as a geopolitical rival. The rhetorical posture of Pence and Trump thus risks destroying any possibility of cooperating as strategic partners.

Faced with cybersecurity accusations and a potential ban from participating in international 5G networks, Huawei, on the one hand, has not shied away from taking legal action against governments for allegedly damaging its corporate image. On the other hand, Ren and Huawei have attempted to rebrand Huawei as a tech company devoid of political motivations and as adhering to international regulations. Evident in their systematic campaign and PR plan to reform its global image and reputation we find the use of the rhetorical tactics of denial, disassociation, avoidance, and redirection. The fact that all of these claims are made in Party-controlled media, of course, compromises such claims to independence. Indeed, just as we find that the Trump administration is needlessly pursuing conflict, so we conclude that the Party's commitment to propaganda overwhelms any hope for genuine dialogue.

In this regard, it is important to note that China has taken its own aggressive measures to strike back, including most pointedly by practicing "hostage diplomacy" against Canada.[112] Following Meng's arrest, China detained two Canadians, accusing them of espionage, while resentencing another to the death penalty, thus signaling a "new age of hostility."[113] Canadian prime minister Justin Trudeau, commented, "We will consistently and always stand up for Canadians, particularly those Canadians who have been arbitrarily detained."[114] The US–China cyber controversy over Huawei has accordingly expanded to include Canada, and, as noted above, has become a central part of technology conversations in Great Britain, Germany, Australia, and other countries. The laws of convergence dictate that the damage will continue to spread, enveloping more and more players.

Recognizing this dynamic, in May 2019, the Trump administration exerted the full force of the US government in a bid to choke off Huawei's access to American suppliers, including chipmakers like Intel and Qualcomm and Google's Android software system, which Huawei has relied on. Today, as global supply chains are more interconnected than ever before, America's export control list also inhibits UK, German, and Japanese companies from selling equipment to Huawei. For example, UK chip designer Arm announced it would stop licensing key technology to Huawei because part of its designs were derived from "US origin technology" and were therefore subject to US export controls.[115] Arm's break with Huawei comes as a major blow to the Chinese tech giant, as few other tech companies produce complex processors such as those produced by Arm.[116] Nevertheless, as the anti-Huawei campaign continues, American tech companies have argued that such a ban could lead to massive financial losses for the United States, so they are now searching for legitimate ways to do business with Huawei without violating US regulations.[117] Notably, the Trump administration has suggested that it would relax restrictions on Huawei "where there is no threat to national security."[118]

But it may be too late. In the southern cities of Dongguan and Shenzhen, Huawei employees are already in full "war mode," with working hours extended to midnight.[119] Confronted by an increasing series of crackdowns, Huawei has responded by ramping up efforts to develop its own chips, operating systems, and other key technologies, pushing it closer to the goals of the Made in China 2025 plan. And so the wheel of convergence and fragmentation turns round, with Huawei as a potent symbol indicating the confusions and contradictions in US–China relations.

NOTES

1. Nigel Inkster, "The Huawei Affair and China's Technology Ambitions," *Survival* 61, no. 1 (2019): 105–111.

2. Ibid.

3. Rob Gilles, "Canada Allows Extradition Case against Huawei CFO to Proceed," *AP News*, March 1, 2019, https://www.apnews.com/c8d05e8406ed4e318a94634b36b6c50a.

4. "China Opposes Canada's Authority on Huawei CFO Case: Embassy," *Xinhua News Agency*, March 2, 2019, http://www.xinhuanet.com/english/2019-03/02/c_137862820.htm.

5. Dan Bilefsky, "Meng Wanzhou's Cushy Bail Is Raising Hackles in Canada," *New York Times*, March 4, 2019, https://www.nytimes.com/2019/03/04/world/canada/huawei-canada-meng-wanzhou.html.

6. Stephen J. Hartnett and Bryan R. Reckard, "Sovereign Tropes: A Rhetorical Critique of Contested Claims in the South China Sea," *Rhetoric & Public Affairs* 20, no. 2 (2017): 291–338.

7. John Pomfret is quoted in Edward Wong's "In the History of U.S.-China Relations, a Pattern of Enchantment and Despair," *New York Times*, November 24, 2016, https://www.nytimes.com/2016/11/24/world/asia/china-us-history-john-pomfret.html.

8. Zhiqun Zhu, "The Growing U.S.-China Conflict: Why, and Now What?," *National Interest*, June 5, 2019, https://nationalinterest.org/feature/growing-us-china-conflict-why-and-now-what-61227.

9. Ibid.

10. Ibid.

11. Cheng Li, "Assessing U.S.-China Relations under the Obama Administration," *Brookings*, August 30, 2016, https://www.brookings.edu/opinions/assessing-u-s-china-relations-under-the-obama-administration/.

12. David Dollar, Ryan Hass, and Jeffrey A. Bader, "Assessing U.S.-China Relations 2 Years into the Trump Presidency," *Brookings*, January 15, 2019, https://www.brookings.edu/blog/order-from-chaos/2019/01/15/assessing-u-s-china-relations-2-years-into-the-trump-presidency/.

13. Ibid.

14. Mike Pence, "Remarks by Vice President Pence on the Administration's Policy toward China," speech delivered at the Hudson Institute, Washington, DC, October 4, 2018, White House, https://www.whitehouse.gov/briefings-statements/remarks-vice-president-pence-administrations-policy-toward-china/.

15. Denise M. Bostdorff, "The Evolution of a Diplomatic Surprise: Richard M. Nixon's

Rhetoric on China, 1952–July 15, 1971," *Rhetoric & Public Affairs* 5, no. 1 (2002): 31–56.

16. Michelle Murray Yang, "President Nixon's Speeches and Toasts during His 1972 Trip to China: A Study in Diplomatic Rhetoric," *Rhetoric & Public Affairs* 14, no. 1 (2011): 1–44.

17. Ibid., 3.

18. Lu Xing, "From 'Ideological Enemies' to 'Strategic Partners': A Rhetorical Analysis of U.S.-China Relations in Intercultural Contexts," *Howard Journal of Communication* 22 (2011): 336.

19. Ibid., 337.

20. Stephen J. Hartnett, "Democracy in Decline, as Chaos, and as Hope; or, U.S.-China Relations in an Age of Unraveling," *Rhetoric & Public Affairs* 19, no. 4 (2016): 626–678.

21. Hartnett and Reckard, "Sovereign Tropes."

22. See also Bill Gertz, *The China Threat: How the People's Republic Targets America* (Washington, DC: Regnery Publishing, 2000).

23. Stephen J. Hartnett, Lisa B. Keränen, and Donovan Conley, eds., *Imagining China: Rhetorics of Nationalism in an Age of Globalization* (East Lansing: Michigan State University Press, 2017), 14. Hartnett, "Democracy in Decline."

24. Stephen J. Hartnett, "Google and the 'Twisted Cyber Spy' Affair: US-Chinese Communication in an Age of Globalization," *Quarterly Journal of Speech* 97, no. 4 (2011): 411.

25. For instance, see Zhao Tianyang's *The Tianxia System: An Introduction to the Philosophy of World Institution* (Beijing: China Renmin University Press, 2011); and Zhao Tianyang, "A Political World Philosophy in Terms of All-under-Heaven (Tianxia)," *Diogenes* 221 (2009): 5–18.

26. On this question see William A. Callahan's "Chinese Visions of World Order: Post-hegemonic or a New Hegemony?," *International Studies Review* 10, no. 4 (2008): 749–761.

27. James McBride and Andrew Chatzky, "Is 'Made in China 2025' a Threat to Global Trade?," *Council on Foreign Relations*, March 7, 2019, https://www.cfr.org/backgrounder/made-china-2025-threat-global-trade.

28. As cited in Raúl Chávez-Santiago, Michał Szydełko, Adrian Kliks, Fotis Foukalas, Yoram Haddad, Keith E. Nolan, Mark Y. Kelly, Moshe T. Masonta, and Ilangko Balasingham, "5G: The Convergence of Wireless Communications," *Wireless Personal Communications* 83, no. 3 (2015): 1617.

29. McBride and Chatzky, "Made in China 2025."

30. Pence, "Remarks by Vice President Pence."

31. In many ways we see Made in China 2025 (MIC 2025) as a central component of President Xi Jinping's China Dream of national rejuvenation. Xi has said that to achieve

the China Dream "we must spread the Chinese spirit, which combines the spirit of the nation with patriotism as the core and the spirit of the time with reform and innovation as the core." So MIC 2025's focus on pursuing unaided innovation and achieving regional and global supremacy in all sectors, including the technology sector, appears to directly support Xi's goals of national rejuvenation. See "What Does Xi Jinping's China Dream Mean?," *BBC*, June 6, 2013, https://www.bbc.com/news/world-asia-china-22726375.

32. Tian Tao, David De Cremer, and Chunbo Wu, *Huawei: Leadership, Culture, and Connectivity* (Los Angeles: Sage, 2017), 5.

33. Samantha Hoffman and Elsa Kania, "Huawei and the Ambiguity of China's Intelligence and Counter-espionage Laws," *Australian Strategic Policy Institute*, September 13, 2018, https://www.aspistrategist.org.au/huawei-and-the-ambiguity-of-chinas-intelligence-and-counter-espionage-laws/.

34. For more on Trump's anti-Huawei campaign see David E. Sanger, Julian E. Barnes, Raymond Zhong, and Marc Santora, "In 5G Race with China, U.S. Pushes Allies to Fight Huawei," *New York Times*, January 26, 2019, https://www.nytimes.com/2019/01/26/us/politics/huawei-china-us-5g-technology.html; Elias Groll, "Washington Tries a Softer Approach in Anti-Huawei Campaign," *Foreign Policy*, April 11, 2019, https://foreignpolicy.com/2019/04/11/washington-tries-a-softer-approach-in-anti-huawei-campaign/; and Graham Webster, "It's Not Just Huawei: Trump's New Tech Sector Order Could Ripple through Global Supply Chains," *Washington Post*, May 18, 2019, https://www.washingtonpost.com/politics/2019/05/18/its-not-just-huawei-trumps-new-tech-sector-order-could-ripple-through-global-supply-chains/.

35. For instance, see Paul Mozure and Austin Ramzy, "Huawei Sues U.S. Government over What It Calls an Unfair Ban," *New York Times*, March 6, 2019, https://www.nytimes.com/2019/03/06/business/huawei-united-states-trade-lawsuit.html; and Marc Santora, "Huawei Threatens Lawsuit against Czech Republic after Security Warning," *New York Times*, February 8, 2019, https://www.nytimes.com/2019/02/08/business/huawei-lawsuit-czech-republic.html.

36. Jeanne Whalen, "Huawei Digs In for a Long Battle with the U.S.," *Washington Post*, June 23, 2019, https://www.washingtonpost.com/business/2019/06/23/huawei-digs-long-battle-with-us/.

37. Ren Zhengfei, "Asia's Tech Titans: The Man Who Built Huawei," interview by Karishma Vaswani, *BBC*, February 23, 2019, video, https://www.youtube.com/watch?v=15rmE_Qijk8.

38. As a testament to the event's function as a public relations affair, much of the US coverage of the To the Explorers: 5G Polar Code and Fundamental Research Awards

ceremony and Dr. Erdal's award actually appeared as paid advertising in US periodicals. For instance, see "Huawei Rolls Out the Red Carpet for Science," *Financial Times*, n.d., https://www.ft.com/brandsuite/huawei/huawei-rolls-out-the-red-carpet-for-science/index.html (accessed August 20, 2019); "Huawei Rolls Out the Red Carpet for Science," *Bloomberg*, October 11, 2018, https://www.bloomberg.com/news/sponsors/huawei/huawei-rolls-out-the-red-carpet-for-science/?adv=6699&prx_t=0iMEAtywsAYikPA; and "The Father of Polar Codes for 5G Outlines the Approach to New Discoveries in Basic Research," *Wall Street Journal*, December 6, 2018, https://partners.wsj.com/huawei/news/the-father-of-polar-codes-for-5g-outlines-the-approach-to-new-discoveries-in-basic-research/.

39. See "Huawei Founder Ren Zhengfei Honors Father of Polar Codes and Scientists," *Huawei*, August 9, 2019, video, https://www.youtube.com/watch?v=8I2lg7Biyts.
40. Ibid.
41. Ibid.
42. Raymond Zhong, "Huawei's Reclusive Founder Rejects Spying and Praises Trump," *New York Times*, January 15, 2019, https://www.nytimes.com/2019/01/15/technology/huawei-ren-zhengfei.html.
43. Ren Zhengfei, "Huawei CEO: 'We Will Never' Provide Chinese Government with Any Information," interview by Bianna Golodryga, *CBS This Morning*, February 19, 2019, video, https://www.youtube.com/watch?v=UONBm56Wh5A.
44. Ibid.
45. Ren Zhengfei, "Asia's Tech Titans."
46. Yet the fact is that while Ren emphasized Huawei's distance from politics and government intervention, playing to Western audiences and Western values, as a Chinese tech giant, Huawei remains tethered to the state, Party, and government.
47. Ren Zhengfei, "Asia's Tech Titans."
48. For Tim Cook's ABC interview with David Muir see https://www.youtube.com/watch?v=tGqLTFv7v7c. Cook's testimony was in response to the FBI pressuring Apple to unlock Syed Tarook's iPhone after the December 2015 terrorist attack in San Bernardino, California.
49. Murray Scot Tanner, "Beijing's New National Intelligence Law: From Defense to Offense," *Lawfare*, July 20, 2017, https://www.lawfareblog.com/beijings-new-national-intelligence-law-defense-offense.
50. Ibid.
51. However, the line is that Huawei would be required to comply if the state requested any intelligence in the name of state security, as anything less could be considered

obstruction.

52. Ren Zhengfei, "Asia's Tech Titans."

53. Ibid.

54. "Huawei Facts," Twitter, https://twitter.com/HuaweiFacts?ref_src=twsrc%5Egoogle%7Ctwcamp%5Eserp%7Ctwgr%5Eauthor. For more on Huawei's advertising campaigns see "Huawei Launches Charm Campaign in US," *Nikkei Asian Review*, March 1, 2019, https://asia.nikkei.com/Economy/Trade-war/Huawei-launches-charm-campaign-in-US.

55. "'Come and See Us,' Huawei Says in Open Letter to U.S. Media," *Xinhua News Agency*, February 29, 2019, http://www.xinhuanet.com/english/2019-02/28/c_137858107.htm.

56. Ibid.

57. Ibid.

58. Mozur and Ramzy, "Huawei Sues U.S. Government."

59. Santora, "Huawei Threatens Lawsuit."

60. Mozur and Ramzy, "Huawei Sues U.S. Government."

61. Ren Zhengfei, "Asia's Tech Titans."

62. For instance, see Adam Satariano and Joanna Berendt, "Poland Arrests 2, Including Huawei Employee, Accused of Spying for China," *New York Times*, January 11, 2019, https://www.nytimes.com/2019/01/11/world/europe/poland-china-huawei-spy.html; Santora, "Huawei Threatens Lawsuit"; Sanger et al., "5G Race with China"; and Vicky Xiuzhong Xu, "New Zealand Blocks Huawei, in Blow to Chinese Telecom Giant," *New York Times*, November 28, 2018, https://www.nytimes.com/2018/11/28/business/huawei-new-zealand-papua-new-guinea.html.

63. Hartnett, "Google," 417.

64. Ellada Gamreklidze, "Cyber Security in Developing Countries, a Digital Divide Issue: The Case of Georgia," *Journal of International Communication* 20, no. 2 (2014): 200–217.

65. Pence, "Remarks by Vice President Pence."

66. Hartnett, "Google."

67. Pence, "Remarks by Vice President Pence."

68. Ibid.

69. Ryan Hass is quoted in Jane Perlez, "Pence's China Speech Seen as Portent of 'New Cold War,'" *New York Times*, October 5, 2018, https://www.nytimes.com/2018/10/05/world/asia/pence-china-speech-cold-war.html.

70. David E. Sanger, "Mystery of the Midterm Elections: Where Are the Russians?," *New York Times*, November 1, 2018, https://www.nytimes.com/2018/11/01/business/midterm-election-russia-cyber.html.

71. Bill Priestap, "China's Non-traditional Espionage against the United States: The Threat and Potential Policy Responses," Statement before the Senate Judiciary Committee, December 12, 2018.

72. Kevin Townsend, "The United States and China—a Different Kind of Cyberwar," *Security Week,* January 7, 2019, https://www.securityweek.com/united-states-and-china-different-kind-cyberwar.

73. For more on the New Cold War, see Perlez, "Pence's China Speech"; Jane Perlez, "Xi Jinping Extends Power, and China Braces for a New Cold War," *New York Times*, February 27, 2018; and Mark Landler, "Trump Has Put the U.S. and China on the Cusp of a New Cold War," *New York Times*, September 19, 2018.

74. Pence, "Remarks by Vice President Pence."

75. Dan Coats is paraphrased in Julian E. Barnes, "'Warning Lights Are Blinking Red,' Top Intelligence Officer Says of Russian Attacks," *New York Times*, July 13, 2018, https://www.nytimes.com/2018/07/13/us/politics/dan-coats-intelligence-russia-cyber-warning.html. Miriam Wugmeister, a cybersecurity specialist, is quoted in Nicole Perlroth, "This Week in Tech: Chinese and Iranian Hackers Have Returned," *New York Times*, February 22, 2019, https://www.nytimes.com/2019/02/22/technology/china-iran-hackers.html.

76. David E. Singer, Nicole Perlroth, Glenn Thrush, and Alan Rappeport, "Marriott Data Breach Is Traced to Chinese Hackers as U.S. Readies Crackdown on Beijing," *New York Times*, December 11, 2018, https://newsupdates365days.blogspot.com/2018/12/marriott-data-breach-is-traced-to.html.

77. Ibid.

78. Townsend, "United States and China."

79. Primarily, we chose to focus our analysis on articles published in the *New York Times* and the *Washington Post*, as they both enjoy a reputation for reliability and trustworthiness. Furthermore, the *Times* and the *Post* are repeatedly ranked as two of the top digital news outlets according to the number of unique viewers that read each newspaper's content, attesting to each newspaper's ability to shape public opinion. See Ken Doctor, "Is The Washington Post Closing in on the Times?," *Politico*, August 6, 2015, https://www.politico.com/media/story/2015/08/is-the-washington-post-closing-in-on-the-times-004045.

80. Mike Pompeo's comments are featured in Stephen Castle, "Pompeo Attacks China and Warns Britain over Huawei Security Risks," *New York Times*, May 8, 2019. See also Mike Pompeo, "Secretary Pompeo Remarks in London," *C-SPAN*, May 8, 2019, https://www.c-span.org/video/?460532-101/secretary-state-pompeo-delivers-margaret-thatcher-lecture-london.

81. Pompeo, "Secretary Pompeo Remarks."

82. Lan King and Scott Moritz, "Why 5G Phones Are New Focus of Freakouts about Huawei," *Bloomberg*, February 13, 2019, https://www.bloomberg.com/news/articles/2019-02-14/why-5g-phones-are-new-focus-of-freakouts-about-huawei-quicktake.

83. Adam Satariano, "The Week in Tech: How Can America Make the World Shun Huawei?," *New York Times*, March 1, 2019, https://www.nytimes.com/2019/03/01/technology/huawei-mwc-barcelona.html.

84. Ibid. Guo Ping, Huawei's rotating chairman, is paraphrased in Satariano, "The Week in Tech."

85. See Raymond Zhong, "As Trump and Xi Talk Trade, Huawei Will Loom Large," *New York Times*, June 28, 2019; and Li Yuan, "Huawei's Communist Culture Limits Its Global Ambitions," *New York Times*, May 1, 2019, https://www.nytimes.com/2019/05/01/technology/huawei-china-communist-party.html.

86. Zhong, "As Trump and Xi Talk."

87. Li Yuan, "Huawei's Communist Culture."

88. "Mike Pence's Speech Arouses Laughter on China's Social Media," *CGTN*, October 14, 2018, www.news.cgtn.com. See also stories of the same name reprinted in other Chinese outlets: Zhang Jianfeng, "Mike Pence's Speech Arouses Laughter on China's Social Media," *CCTV*, November 1, 2018, www.english.cctv.com; and "Mike Pence's Speech Arouses Laughter on China's Social Media," *China Daily*, November 2, 2018, www.chinadaily.com.cn.

89. Ibid.

90. "6 in 10 Say Politics behind U.S. Campaign against Huawei: CNN Poll," February 22, 2019, *Xinhua News Agency*, http://www.xinhuanet.com/english/2019-02/22/c_137842537.htm. Xinhua cites a Twitter poll carried out by #CNNJoin and tweeted by *The Quest Means Business*, a CNN business show. See Quest Means Business @questCNN, Twitter post, February 19, 2019, 12:47 p.m., https://twitter.com/questCNN/status/1097960963725316096.

91. Edith Mutethya, "Huawei to Invest $2 Billion in Cybersecurity," *China Daily*, February 21, 2019, http://www.chinadaily.com.cn/a/201902/21/WS5c6e6bb0a3106c65c34eaa2d.html.

92. Hu Xijin is quoted in Satariano and Berendt, "Poland Arrests 2."

93. "6 in 10 Say Politics."

94. See Dodge's introduction to this book for a discussion on Xi Jinping and the Party's mission and responsibilities for state media, the Party's mandate that all news produced must support the rejuvenation of China, and the requirement that state media avoid criticizing the Party.

95. See Chen Qingqing, "Huawei Launches Cybersecurity Center in Brussels to Quash US

Allegations," *Global Times*, March 5, 2019, http://www.globaltimes.cn/content/1141038.shtml.

96. Ibid.
97. Julian E. Barnes and Adam Satariano, "U.S. Campaign to Ban Huawei Overseas Stumbles as Allies Resist," *New York Times*, March 17, 2019, https://www.nytimes.com/2019/03/17/us/politics/huawei-ban.html.
98. Guy Chazan, "German Cyber Security Chief Backs 5G 'No Spy' Deal over Huawei," *Financial Times*, February 28, 2019, https://www.ft.com/content/5a0fe826-3b34-11e9-b856-5404d3811663.
99. Mutethya, "Huawei to Invest."
100. "Britain Strikes an Artful Compromise on Huawei and 5G," *The Economist*, April 27, 2019, https://www.economist.com/leaders/2019/04/27/britain-strikes-an-artful-compromise-on-huawei-and-5g.
101. Nicholas Negroponte, "Don't Ban Huawei. Do This Instead," *Fastcompany*, May 8, 2019, https://www.fastcompany.com/90344450/dont-ban-huawei-do-this-instead.
102. Cecilia Kang, "Delay in Huawei Ban Is Sought by White House Budget Office," *New York Times*, June 09, 2019, https://www.nytimes.com/2019/06/09/business/huawei-ban-delay.html.
103. "How to Handle Huawei," *The Economist*, January 31, 2019, https://www.economist.com/leaders/2019/01/31/how-to-handle-huawei.
104. Cecilia Kang, "Huawei Ban Threatens Wireless Service in Rural Areas," *New York Times*, May 25, 2019, https://www.nytimes.com/2019/05/25/technology/huawei-rural-wireless-service.html.
105. See Kanishka Singh, "U.S. Intelligence Says Huawei Funded by Chinese State Security: Report," *Reuters*, April 19, 2019, https://www.reuters.com/article/us-usa-trade-china-huawei/u-s-intelligence-says-huawei-funded-by-chinese-state-security-report-idUSKCN1RW03D; and Michael Kahn and Jan Lopatka, "Western Allies Agree 5G Security Guidelines, Warn of Outside Influence," *Reuters*, May 3, 2019, https://www.reuters.com/article/us-telecoms-5g-security/western-allies-agree-5g-security-guidelines-warn-of-outside-influence-idUSKCN1S91D2.
106. Groll, "Washington Tries a Softer Approach."
107. Pence, "Remarks by Vice President Pence."
108. Ibid.
109. For more on Huawei and the US government's controversial history, see Kate Fazzini, "Why the U.S. Government Is So Suspicious of Huawei," *CNBC*, December 6, 2018, https://www.cnbc.com/2018/12/06/huaweis-difficult-history-with-us-government.html. For

more on Huawei's Iran sanctions violations specifically, see Patricia Hurtado, "Huawei Iran-Sanctions Evidence Deemed Too Risky for China to See," *Bloomberg*, June 19, 2019, https://www.bloomberg.com/news/articles/2019-06-19/huawei-iran-sanctions-evidence-deemed-too-risky-for-china-to-see.

110. Hartnett, "Democracy in Decline."
111. Ibid.
112. Steve LeVine, "A New Age of Hostage Diplomacy," *Axios*, January 11, 2019, https://www.axios.com/international-arrests-poland-china-hostage-diplomacy-e1f249f0-6a45-430d-88e2-aed7ce4ecfc3.html.
113. Ibid.; Chris Buckley and Catherine Porter, "China Accuses Two Canadians of Spying, Widening a Political Rift," *New York Times*, March 4, 2019, https://www.nytimes.com/2019/03/04/world/asia/china-canada-michael-kovrig-huawei.html?module=inline.
114. Trudeau's quote comes from "Justin Trudeau Vows to Stand Up to Beijing over 'Unacceptable' Arrest of Two Canadians Accused of Spying in China," *South China Morning Post*, May 17, 2019, https://www.scmp.com/news/china/article/3010580/justin-trudeau-vows-stand-beijing-over-unacceptable-arrest-two-canadians.
115. Madhumita Murgia and Nic Fildes, "Huawei Chip Unit Hit as Arm Withdraws Licences," *Financial Times*, May 22, 2019, https://www.ft.com/content/a566bb84-7c88-11e9-81d2-f785092ab560.
116. Ibid.
117. Paul Mozur and Cecilia Kang, "U.S. Tech Companies Sidestep a Trump Ban, to Keep Selling to Huawei," *New York Times*, June 25, 2019, https://www.nytimes.com/2019/06/25/technology/huawei-trump-ban-technology.html.
118. Jim Tankersley and Ana Swanson, "Trump Administration Will Allow Some Companies to Sell to Huawei," *New York Times*, July 9, 2019, https://www.nytimes.com/2019/07/09/business/huawei-donald-trump.html?searchResultPosition=1.
119. Zhong, "As Trump and Xi Talk."

Evolving Forms of Citizen Engagement in the Age of Convergence

The 2016 Baidu and Ctrip Crises as Case Studies in Critique, Trust, and Hope in Contemporary China

Jack Kangjie Liu and Dan Wang

The age of convergence in contemporary China has been hailed by some observers as a golden opportunity for the flowering of civic engagement.[1] Within this notion of convergence, communication entails an unending stream of reports, responses, and rebuttals about critical, and perhaps criminal, failings within China—amounting to a genre we call herein "crisis communication." For example, consider these three incidents from 2016. First, toxic running tracks in the sport field at Changzhou Foreign School in Jiangsu province were found to be the cause of over a dozen students' sudden sickness, some even suffering from leukemia.[2] It turns out that to reduce production costs, the factory made the running track by using substandard plastics rich in health-threatening toxins. In this case, the story touched a raw nerve about the dangerous rush to make profits by producing deadly materials.[3] Second, a troubled patient in Guangzhou slaughtered the innocent Dr. Chen, an experienced dentist. Reports indicated that the murderer was a former patient of Dr. Chen and had been plotting revenge for more than twenty years. In this case, the story touched upon questions of mental health and issues of vengeance, anger, and retribution.[4] Third, Lei Yang, a twenty-nine-year old man, was beaten to death by police in Beijing on May 21, 2016. The police apparently mistook Lei for a criminal engaged in running a prostitution ring; when he resisted arrest, the police beat him to death. In this case, the story touches upon rising fears about state authority and wrongful arrest.[5] While incidents like these do not always make the headlines, they occur at an alarming rate, and increasingly—from legacy and social media news in China—we learn that each day brings new reports of a crisis of some kind. From this perspective, we argue in this chapter that it is important to analyze crisis communication, for these scandals and controversies tell us a great deal about the age of convergence in contemporary China. Indeed, this emerging genre of crisis communication opens up a rich window of opportunity for watching how Chinese netizens debate issues of ethical behavior, health care, and even guilt and innocence, amounting to nothing less than an ongoing debate about the health of the nation-state.

This fascinating new age of convergence and crisis communication in China is driven in large part by the fact that China has become a "mobile Internet country."[6] Data from the Ministry of Industry and Information Technology in 2016 show that there were 780 million mobile internet users in the country.[7] In addition, Chinese social media platform use has skyrocketed. Two social media platforms have dominated Chinese cyberspace this past decade: Weibo and WeChat. These social media platforms in particular, and the mobile internet more broadly, have empowered netizens across the country to communicate about the latest crisis events in real time, offering running commentaries and debates about daily life in China. The government has gone to great lengths to try to control communication in China, with leaders telling the media they have six basic responsibilities, working together to promote the "Chinese Dream" and a culture of "harmony."[8] Contrary to this Party mandate of upbeat and always positive news, media coverage of and netizen debate about the latest crises potentially spread depression, unease, and antagonism throughout society, amounting to a powerful counternarrative to the political leaders' preferred messages. In short, crisis communication is a rich terrain for political criticism in contemporary China.

We argue that crisis communication is particularly interesting as it offers pointed, albeit sometimes veiled, political commentary on daily life in China, thus amounting to a kind of subtle and highly mediated civic participation. To pursue this thesis, we turn to two crises that occurred in 2016. The first regards Baidu, one of the ten largest IT companies worldwide, and the most popular search engine in China. On January 9, 2016, in the online medical forum "Baidu Illness," an administrator revealed that he was dismissed from Baidu, which followed his firing by appointing questionable people into its administration. This new administrative group had the capability to promote fake medical advertisements and cancel any posts they deemed appropriate. Netizens questioned the group's authenticity and credibility, worrying especially about misleading information that could taint the quality of information and, ultimately, corrupt the medical information they accessed.[9] So, on January 9, netizens disclosed this information in the online forum Zhihu (知乎社区). The story was quickly reposted, and went viral on Weibo and WeChat. The mainstream media in China, including the *Beijing News* and the Xinhua News Agency Network, then reported that Baidu had sold the "Illness" forums to advertising companies. Then, in these for-sale forums, these companies were able to post fake advertisements for their products and services while also deleting complaints.[10] These online forums thus quickly changed from providing visitors with legitimate medical resources into corporate tools for earning money. In fact, administrators were promoting commercial products and services, some of which were uncertified, while others were highly suspect.[11] In this first Baidu crisis, a platform for distributing quality health communication was sold to the highest bidders, leaving Chinese netizens with bad advice and, hence, diminished health care.

In a similar move, media coverage confirmed that Baidu had also sold its "Baidu City" forum.[12] Originally an online platform where people shared ideas through multiple forums, "Baidu City" offered a textbook example of communication convergence, wherein a virtually limitless stream of user commentary touched upon issues of health, entertainment, interpersonal, cultural, and other forms of communication. It was a raucous free-for-all. But then city governments paid a great deal of money to acquire "Baidu City" forums, where they could cancel negative posts and maintain control over a positive image of their cities. As with the health forums noted above, Baidu's handling of these city forums provoked netizens to speak out through other social media channels, where they condemned Baidu in scathing testimony. Thus, by the end of 2016, Baidu had become a target of netizen anger, for the company was perceived as selling out its users' goodwill.[13] In this case, as we will demonstrate below in more detail, the crisis communication about Baidu spoke directly to questions of trust and accountability in contemporary China.

Around the same time, Ctrip, China's largest online travel agency, was encountering trouble of its own. Miao Li, an everyday citizen, revealed online that he had inadvertently purchased two fake airline tickets for his friends through Ctrip. As his friends were checking in to their flight, they found out that they had been swindled.[14] With Miao Li publicizing his wayward experience on Weibo, other customers throughout China shared similar stories about Ctrip issuing fake tickets and booking fake hotel reservations, derailing their travel and accommodation plans.[15] Throughout the country netizens converged on social media platforms and channels to condemn Ctrip. If the Baidu cases touched upon both health communication and urban living, then the Ctrip case illustrated—like the toxic track crises mentioned earlier—how many companies in China are perceived as engaging in unethical business practices, even going so far as to steal air miles to sell fake products. Like the Baidu cases, the Ctrip case spoke directly to a crisis in trust, with netizens going online to express their anger.

And so we offer the Baidu and Ctrip cases as examples for the comparative study of crisis communication and convergence in China. Both instances deal with high-profile companies in China, both are registered NASDAQ companies, and both occupy the leading positions in their respective online markets. The crises occurred around roughly the same time, harmed both company's image, provoked netizens to question the companies involved, and, more significantly, served as platforms for netizens to criticize the government's mismanagement of these crises. Indeed, whereas we assume that some Western readers perceive China's communication environment as one-dimensional and government-controlled, these cases of crisis communication indicate a lively public sphere—Patrick Dodge has called it an ever-changing terrain of dissent, a veritable "cat-and-mouse game" of political positioning—full of citizen feedback and, occasionally, political anger.[16] From this perspective, the landscape of netizen participation in contemporary China is happening in large part via responses to crisis communication.

Theoretical Terrain

Crises are events that seriously threaten fundamental societal values, living standards, and daily behaviors.[17] The typical example is the terrorist attacks of September 11, 2001. The crisis significantly changed the lives and worldviews of everyday US citizens, as well as citizens around the globe, profoundly shaping the world we live in. Post-9/11, Americans had a deeper awareness and stronger sense of terrorism, domestic security, and international politics. Moreover, in the United States the event triggered profound transformations in the budgets, projects, and outlets of federal, state, and local governments. Thus, national security and the "war on terror" became everyday topics, debated both in domestic contexts and in the international arena.[18] Along these lines, crises usually involve some unexpected negative event—a devastating tornado or earthquake, a terrorist attack, a political scandal, and so on—that triggers widespread public debate, often leading to the fragmenting of public values, conventions, and sometime rules. When the post-crisis discourse goes badly, it can lead to significant harm to society and personal well-being. On the other hand, some crises bring communities together, as they rally around shared norms and values.[19] Regardless of their long-term outcomes, during most crises, individuals seek out information through various channels and methods, meaning crises usually lead to spikes in communication.[20] In this sense, crises are significant moments of communication convergence, as they tend to lead to citizens seeking information, counseling, and advice across a wide range of platforms, while simultaneously using other platforms to express fear, anger, and political criticism.

Steve Fink has categorized four phases in crisis communication with his "four stages theory."[21] In the first period, the "prodromal" phase, a crisis emerges as the nature of the event generates negativity. In the second period, the severity of an event causes harm, "acute" harm, often at the societal level. Third, the acute severity of the crisis affects people, causing "chronic" harm, oftentimes both mental and physical suffering. Finally, there is some "resolution," when the crisis approaches its gradual finish. Whereas Fink's four stages theory of crisis communication is descriptive of the phases and effects of crisis communication, other scholars have built upon Fink's theory. For example Mitroff created the fives stages of crisis management system that incorporates five mechanisms, including detection, prevention/preparedness, damage containment, recovery, and learning.[22] For Fink, Mitroff, and other scholars of crisis communication, even while each crisis is unique and distinct, they also share certain generic similarities in terms of their stages and patterns.

Starting in the 1980s, crisis communication research gradually made its way to Chinese contexts. Because the Chinese political system, history, and culture vary greatly from those in Western countries, Chinese studies in crisis communication need to be highly contextualized. Recent research in China can be divided into macro, meso, and micro levels of analysis. While the former scrutinizes crisis communication in and by social structures, political system, and history, the meso level investigates strategies and relations at the intersections of crisis communication and public relations.[23] The micro level of analysis focuses on specific characteristics of "hot" issues. By "hot" issues we are referring to the specific crises that are happening in the age of convergence and social media. These noticeable events significantly threaten people's livelihood, assets, and safety, and can damage societal values, providing real and latent harm to both citizens and governments. For example, when looking at online reports of crisis events in China, Lan and Zeng characterize three insights: (1) a crisis usually peaks within ninety-six hours; (2) then it regresses after an average period of eight days; and (3) this pattern happens along a communication trend of three periods—prodromal, spreading, and regression.[24] Lan and Zeng's model of three periods in the Chinese context has been used to describe the general trend of the 2012 Nong Fu poisonous spring water crisis. For instance, Wang and Shen used the model to conclude that there were five spikes (peaks) in the online coverage pointing to patterns in the prolonged duration of the crisis.[25] This is just one case, however, and Chinese research on crisis communication and convergence trends is lacking.

Scholars have paid attention to social media crisis communication research in other countries and contexts. For instance, Graham, Avery, and Sejin conclude their study with strategies and skills that can help local governments in crisis.[26] Similarly, Liu, Fisher, Austin, and Jin have conceptualized a framework for understanding social media crisis communication.[27] Their model incorporates essential details encompassing connections between traditional and social media, media users, and crisis organization. Most useful to our study is their interpretation of two fundamental relationships, namely the connections between traditional and social media, and the relationship between social media topic creators and followers. From these two relationships, we are able to explore influential factors in our Baidu and Ctrip crises. Thus, for the purposes of our analysis we employ a loose framing that encompasses Liu, Fisher, Lucinda and Jin's research; Fink's four stages theory; Fisher, Liu, Austin, and Jin's social media crisis communication model;[28] and Lan and Zeng's model in the Chinese context.

Data Collection

Our research team collected online reports surrounding the Baidu and Ctrip crises in Guangzhou and Beijing between January 10 and March 16, 2016. We gathered news stories and comments on Weibo and WeChat platforms and from the general internet.[29] Furthermore, we collected data on the Chinese internet from traditional state media sources, namely the *People's Daily*, Xinhua News Agency, China News

Services, and various other metropolitan TV stations and newspapers. Gathering a range of reports and information from traditional state media news sources and comments on social media platforms has enabled us to compare and contrast data sets at the macro, meso, and micro levels. Considering that our data collection period was from January 10 to March 16, 2016, and that the Baidu and Ctrip crises significantly damaged customer-company relations, we were curious to examine netizens' reactions in the following months, especially with March 15 being World Consumer Rights Day.

To focus on relevant data, we used the keyword combinations "Baidu and web forum" and "Ctrip and fake air ticket" to search the Weibo postings, which consisted of more than one million user-generated posts, and searched over seventeen thousand official WeChat accounts.[30] For comparison, we collected news and comments from internet forums and state media news sources. Our collective search resulted in 19,002 hits for the Baidu crisis on Weibo; 4,590 hits on state media news sources; and 4,980 hits on WeChat. For Ctrip, the search yielded 15,050 hits from Weibo; 3,170 from state media; and 7,940 on WeChat. Subsequently, our team conducted data filtering and omitted items that did not contain content relevant to the two events. Thus, we confirmed qualified data for the Baidu crisis at 15,573 hits on Weibo, 4,290 on the internet state media news sites, and 4,598 hits on WeChat. Regarding the Ctrip crisis we confirmed 15,050 hits on Weibo, 3,170 hits on the internet state media news sources, and 7,940 hits on WeChat. While our data set cannot capture the entirety of public discourse in the nation, these numbers do indicate a massive sampling of opinions in contemporary China.

The Pulse of Convergence in the Baidu Crisis: Explosion, Spreading, and Regression

Our team used both quantitative (correlation analysis) and qualitative methods to analyze our data sets. In figure 1 the x-axis represents the independent variable, "time," and Y1, Y2, and Y3 represent the dependent variable, "report quantity." Also, we have listed the days with numerical significance on reports and comments of the three platforms from January to March in table 1. We combined our data analysis in figure 1 and table 1 with a textual analysis of the online reports and comments. We categorized the patterns across three general periods, and thus categorized the pulse of convergence as explosion, spreading, and regression. Taken together,

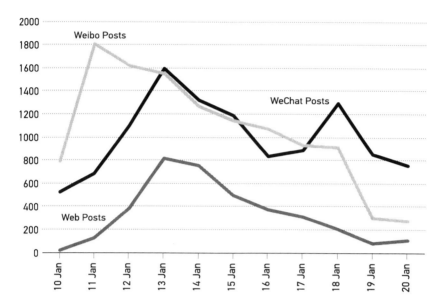

FIGURE 1. The Baidu Crisis: Convergence Period on Weibo, WeChat, and Internet Reports/Comments, January 10–20, 2016

these three phases evolved over roughly two weeks, with the most intense period of action falling between January 10 and January 20 (see figure 1).

Between January 10 and January 20 the phases of "explosion" and "spreading" were most prominent between January 10 and 14. The Baidu event was first revealed in internet forums and then was immediately reposted on Weibo. From Weibo posts it spread through WeChat. We posit that netizen awareness of the event increased dramatically once it was reposted from internet forums to social media platforms. With continual reposts and consistent commenting on day 2, the peak point materialized with 1,803 items on Weibo. We see the magnitude of this posting force on the carryover from Weibo, with significant impact, to WeChat and further internet reports on state media news sites. The convergence trend on WeChat and the internet dramatically increased, then peaking with 1,595 and 811 reports and comments, respectively. After January 14, relevant posts and articles reduced sharply. The overall "convergence period"—the range when "explosion" and then "spreading" came together across media—occurred between January 10 and 14. In this frenzied five-day period, the quantity of reports accounted for nearly 50 percent of the entire data set (see table 1).

TABLE 1. Report and Comments by Quantity on Important Days during the Baidu Crisis (January, February, and March 2016)

DAY/ MEDIA	1/10	1/11	1/12	1/13	1/14	1/15	1/16	1/17	1/18	1/19	1/20	2/20	3/15	3/16
WeChat	526	680	1094	1595	1318	1187	835	883	509	303	98	36	13	13
Internet	20	129	379	811	752	495	376	311	203	81	16	5	9	8
Weibo	790	1803	1622	1549	1262	1142	1069	927	913	309	91	38	30	28

Comparing the internet reports on state media sites and the two social media platforms proved revealing in a few ways. First, the Baidu crisis raised much attention on traditional state media platforms. Various investigative reports, analytical articles, and viewer comments were posted in the online versions of *People's Daily*, Xinhua News Agency, and CCTV. Professional news media contributed to exclusive reports, for instance The Paper (澎湃) and The Huxiu (虎嗅), the former being an online media outlet specifically covering the news, and the latter focusing on IT news. Personal, professional, and organizational Weibo and WeChat accounts across various sectors and industries then reposted these critical reports about Baidu. We call these reports "critical" because of the insightful, exclusive, or significant stories that critiqued Baidu as a corrupt, money-focused company, and the "explosive" and "spreading" periods that followed. For instance, during the explosive and spreading periods, the *Guangming Daily*, a paper affiliated with China's Ministry of Science, revealed that Baidu manager Guo Cheng Ma was sentenced to seven years in jail. Authorities charged Ma with accepting illegal commissions for helping an internet company, a subsidiary advertising agent of Baidu, obtain revenue from advertising advantages during the crisis.[31] They found that Ma had accepted a bribe of roughly 3.95 million RMB, which authorities found hiding in his niece's bank account. As this example indicates, while the state-run media are loath to allow articles questioning the legitimacy of the Communist Party, they are quick to notice instances of individual wrongdoing—for this enhances President Xi's much-publicized campaign to root out corruption.[32]

After the convergence period of January 10–15, the trend sharply dropped into the "regression" period. After January 20, the topic frequency returned to normal rates, as reports and comments fell below one hundred per twenty-four-hour period. This pattern of explosion, spreading, and regression illuminates just one beat in the pulse of communication convergence across platforms. It is telling that two months later, on March 15, 2016, on World Consumer Rights Day, there were relatively few hits or new postings about the Baidu crisis: thirty, nine, and thirteen, on Weibo, the internet state media news sites, and WeChat, respectively.

Influential Factors in the Baidu Crisis

We now turn our attention to some of the factors impacting the convergence periods and communication trends. Based on the social media crisis communication model (SMCC), we posit that the relationship between topic creators and followers in the Baidu crisis offers clues to what triggered the pulse of convergence. Recall that in the Baidu crisis, topic creators were fired from their forum administrator positions. These administrators insisted on revealing the stories behind their dismissal. To the followers—netizens seeking medical information—the forum not only served as a communication arena in which you could find helpful medical information, it quickly became a platform that sparked political participation where forum administrators denounced their replacements. And so both the original administrators and followers engaged in the forum to air Baidu's dirty laundry and learn about Baidu's problems of trust and accountability, then moved onto other platforms to spread the warning.

Dishonest business practices, a lack of trust and accountability, and advertising forums spreading misinformation were some of the factors that triggered the Baidu crisis. Additionally, we argue that because of the internet state monopoly, the government is also partially responsible for constraining the choice of everyday internet users. Since Google was forced to leave China in 2009, Baidu has become the biggest search engine in the country. The way Baidu controls, shields, and filters information, the way it reproduces fake advertisements and false information, and the way it disseminates misleading messages has exasperated internet users. Because of the Party's control of information, netizens have had to bear a distorted internet search process marked by misleading promotions. So when the Baidu crisis occurred in 2016, netizens across the country converged on social media platforms and the internet to collectively express their anger at both companies for ethical violations, and at the government for setting the parameters of a system where information is easily manipulated.

Concurrently, we turn to the connections between traditional state media outlets and social media platforms to highlight another influential factor in social media crisis communication. In our analysis, we found that the stories posted on Weibo provided the beginnings to many reposts converging with and on traditional media platforms. The internet sites of Sina, Sohu, and 163.com, for example, all published detailed news reports based on those first Baidu crisis stories on Weibo. One popular newspaper in China, the *New Beijing Daily*, published an exclusive report disclosing that some municipal governments bought the City Forum, outing government staff who became administrators and "fans" on the forum.[33] Thus, when netizens found out that government staff were deleting negative posts from the forum and intentionally publishing posts that supported either the government or the companies involved, there was an explosion of (re)posts revealing the scandal, with the story spreading like wildfire across social media platforms. And so while the Party's mandates have led to more control of communication platforms in contemporary China, netizens have taken to Weibo online forums and WeChat to voice their anger and to advocate for more ethical communication practices.

The Pulse of Convergence in the Ctrip Crisis

As with the Baidu crisis, the data in figure 2 and table 2 represent three periods in the pulse of convergence during the 2016 Ctrip crisis. In addition, the figure and table show dual peaks in Weibo and internet traffic. Like the Baidu convergence periods, Weibo posts peaked one day after Miao Li, the wronged, exposed the event. We posit that it was Miao Li's article coupled with Ctrip's insufficient and untimely reply that triggered the initial explosion and spreading periods, and then the subsequent second spike in hits.

Facing public anger (first spike on January 11) for selling fake tickets, Ctrip responded on January 12 that the case was just a random mistake in which "one of its suppliers had illegally exchanged air miles for tickets."[34] The company representative stated that the mistake was not intentional and framed it as a "two in ten thousand" mistake. However, to their surprise, this response provoked strong reactions of public anger. On WeChat accounts and online forums, people from various industries posted articles condemning the company. They viewed Ctrip's response as dishonest and dishonorable, and as evidence that Ctrip was trying to placate its customers by offering false explanations.

On top of the perception of Ctrip's disingenuous apology, Miao Li posted another article, again criticizing Ctrip's business practices, on January 13. The

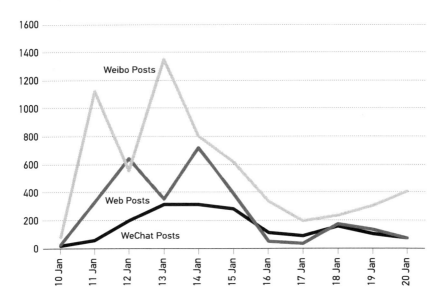

FIGURE 2. Ctrip Crisis: Convergence Period on Weibo, WeChat, and Internet Reports/Comments (January 10–20, 2016)

TABLE 2. Report and Comments by Quantity on Important Days during the Ctrip Crisis (January, February, and March 2016)

DAY/MEDIA	1/10	1/11	1/12	1/13	1/14	1/15	1/16	1/17	1/18	1/19	1/20	2/20	3/15	3/16
WeChat	17	58	199	314	315	279	111	89	59	39	13	10	9	11
Internet	21	327	639	356	722	388	51	31	20	11	7	5	8	5
Weibo	83	1122	552	1354	801	619	338	194	103	49	23	15	12	12

five-thousand-word article analyzed the process he went through in purchasing the air tickets, cross-referencing it with data from Ctrip's annual report to show that it had 4.3 billion RMB annual income in 2015.[35] In the article, Miao Li argued that Ctrip's staff intentionally deceived its customers by selling fake tickets, casting Ctrip as a company that condones criminal behavior. If there was a 0.02 percent (two in ten thousand) chance for the mistake of a fake ticket, he argued, it would mean substantial impacts in the millions of RMB in illegal income. Moreover, if Ctrip were inputting this illegal income into their total earned revenue, it would constitute a serious crime by both Chinese and US standards. Thus, with these explosive allegations drawing attention, Miao Li's article went viral, triggering a second spike in traffic, this one peaking on January 13.

Chen Caiyin, Ctrip's PR director, responded with a statement "express[ing] my deep sorrow for the inconvenience it has brought to all the passengers involved," saying, Ctrip would "offer triple compensation and full refund to customers . . . whose trips have been affected in the incidents."[36] But by then the damage was done. Whereas the Baidu crisis resulted in one explosion of information converging across communication platforms, the Ctrip crisis resulted in two distinguishable peaks spreading across Weibo posts, WeChat, and the internet. With no new topics or follow-up, the flow of communication dropped to under twenty reports or comments per day and gradually flattened out. As in the Baidu crisis as well, then, the Ctrip crisis evolved across initial "explosion" and "spreading" stages, which covered five intense days of public communication, followed by a longer and slower "regression" phase.

Influential Factors in the Ctrip Crisis

We posit that the relationships between topic creators and followers, and traditional media and social media, significantly impacted the period of communication convergence across platforms during the 2016 Ctrip crisis. In the first relationship, Miao Li played the role of a public figure influencing his followers. Each time Miao Li released scathing reports, traffic spiked, thereby triggering the pulse of convergence across platforms—explosion, spreading, and regression. Customers who had been cheated by Ctrip were enthusiastic participants, reposting Miao Li's articles and sharing stories of their own. Although there were many who reported that Ctrip did not cheat them, there were many posts in which customers questioned Ctrip's ethics and management practices. For instance, on WeChat, one user wrote, "The Shanghai Local Consumer Committee reveals 4806 complains about the online travel agency in 2014, and 7806 complains in 2015. As a local resident, I would prefer to buy a ticket directly from airline companies, rather than by an online travel agency (OTA). How do we trust these OTAs?"[37] This user's post is symptomatic of a larger societal-wide issue of internet ethics in China where customers have been swindled into buying fake products or unqualified services and having a difficult time getting their money back from dishonest companies.[38] And so, in the pulse of convergence in contemporary China we find online customers taking up social media channels to voice their anger about internet business administrators and dishonest online travel agencies.

In terms of the relationship between traditional media and social media outlets, we find the pulse of convergence starts from Weibo and then spreads out into other internet media channels (both internet forums and online traditional state media news outlets). Moreover, we found that the stories that were first posted on Weibo resembled the stories that were subsequently posted in other internet media platforms (traditional state media online versions). In both the Baidu and Ctrip crises, our analysis revealed that the initial wave of social media posts strongly influenced later stages of public deliberation, even those that occurred in traditional state media outlets. This conclusion suggests that the posts from the "explosion" stage bear a potential agenda-setting function, as the posts released during the spreading and regression stages either confirm those initial messages or are forced to engage with them, hence reproducing much of the language first aired in the explosion stage.

Concluding Thoughts on Communication Trends, Convergence Periods, and Crisis

Our chapter examined convergence periods and influential factors in two Chinese crisis communication cases in 2016. In terms of communication trends and convergence periods, we found that the Baidu and Ctrip cases showed similarity across three periods of a crisis: explosion, spreading, and regression. We found that the first three stages of Fink's four stages theory, prodromal, acute, and chronic, were condensed in what we conceptualize as the periods of explosion and spreading, in both the Baidu and Ctrip crises. In both instances, we found that Weibo was the crucial generator/platform of traffic, with WeChat and state-run media playing lesser roles during the spreading and regression phases of the crises.

The implications of our examples suggest a few characteristics of crisis communication. First, the speed and spread of information going viral was extremely quick, quicker even than other cases noted before 2016. According to Wang and Shen and Lan and Zhen, crisis trends in Chinese contexts usually peak after ninety-six hours.[39] However, in the Baidu and Ctrip crises, Weibo posts peaked in just twenty-four hours—the explosion period—followed by WeChat and internet trends. Next, we found that when a second "trigger" was introduced, as was the case when Miao Li posted his second scathing article criticizing Ctrip, it generated a second pulse of convergence, thus restarting the pattern of explosion, spreading, and regression. Third, in terms of the quantity of hits in our examples, Weibo was the most-used social media platform during both crises. This runs contrary to some claims that WeChat has overtaken Weibo to become the most used and most influential social media platform in China.[40] Finally, the Baidu and Ctrip examples show unique convergence trends starting on Weibo and moving over to the internet and WeChat. This is reflective of the trend of Chinese netizens turning to Weibo as an outlet to post stories, especially when voicing anger about the unethical business practices and calls for more accountability and social justice.

And so we conclude here with a few points of insight. First, we believe that Chinese IT enterprises must do the hard work of adhering to ethical business practices and confirming their commitment to serving the public as socially responsible entities. Second, the government needs to step up its oversight of such entities and hold them accountable for their misdeeds. For instance, Baidu and Ctrip did not work to reduce potential harm at individual and societal levels. Baidu only made an official statement near the end of the crisis, during the regression period, and Ctrip lied publicly by claiming that fake tickets are sold only in a "two to ten thousand" ratio. These inappropriate responses further damaged the public image of these companies and prolonged their respective crisis periods. At the same time, the government's slow and lax responses to both crises further fueled suspicions. These two cases show the importance of the need for strong ethical grounding and accountability if the companies and the government hope to win back trust.

Third, in the Baidu crisis, working under the constraints that the Baidu system imposes upon consumers, users were not able obtain complete and credible search results, meaning that even as netizens sought to respond to the crisis, they were forced to do so while working under Baidu's Party-imposed monopoly on information. Netizens seeking medical information not only empathized with dismissed forum administrators, but also shared similar experiences of being wronged. Rather than solely criticizing the Party, netizens took to critiquing Baidu in their calls for internet policy change and reform. Thus, social media platforms provided netizens an outlet to speak out, and to advocate for accountability, fair practices, and the protection of their online legal and medical rights—even while these same users noted that they were doing so without access to open and fair information. The online crisis communication we have analyzed here thus speaks, sometimes directly and oftentimes obliquely, to the hopes and dreams of netizens in contemporary China. Indeed, our research shows how China's netizens long to access the information and open participatory platforms that enhance civic engagement and political participation. In this sense, our study of crisis communication points to a deep and abiding hope in contemporary China.

We want to underscore this point regarding the role the Chinese government should play in crisis events such as the ones examined in this chapter. Our research shows that a lack of governance and regulation were major factors contributing to the crisis in both events. Early in 2008, Baidu was profiting from the illegal use of a search results ranking-system. Its unethical business practices were revealed over several occasions, yet each time such charges were raised, the government was inadequate in responses to accountability or reform.[41] Likewise, in early 2015, netizens revealed similar experiences with Ctrip and fake air tickets, yet the government imposed neither consequences nor accountability upon the company.[42] Surprisingly, yet tellingly, on March 15, 2016, on International Consumers' Day, the Chinese National Tourism Administration (国家旅游局) awarded Ctrip the Advanced Unit of National Civilized Traveling Award (全国文明旅游先进单位).[43] It was ironic that a company that had cheated customers was being hailed as the national example of online business practices. Although the Baidu and Ctrip crises have passed, the commercial factors, social environment, and political system in China that produced these crises have not yet changed. If enterprises, internet businesses, and public sectors continue on the same path, then the same communication crises are likely to occur in the future—hence putting any sense of internet ethics and government credibility at risk.

NOTES

1. See Guobin Yang, *The Power of the Internet in China: Citizen Activism Online* (New York: Columbia University Press, 2011); Zhengzhi Shi and Guobin Yang, "New Media Empowerment and State-Society Relations in China," in *The Internet, Social Media, and a Changing China*, ed. Jacques deLisle, Avery Goldstein, and Guobin Yang (Philadelphia: University of Pennsylvania Press, 2015), 71–85; Sally Xiaojin Chen, "Collective Action in Digital China: A Case Study of the 2013 Southern Weekly Incident," in *China's Contested Internet*, ed. Guobin Yang (Copenhagen: NIAS Press, 2015), 283–304.

2. Ryan Kilpatrick, "'Toxic' Running Tracks at Chinese Schools Threaten to Leave Students Infertile," *Hong Kong Free Press*, October 14, 2015, https://www.hongkongfp.com/2015/10/14/

toxic-running-tracks-at-chinese-schools-threaten-to-leave-students-infertile/; Fan Liya, "Children Sick from Another Toxic Running Track, Say Parents," *Sixth Tone*, September 20, 2017, http://www.sixthtone.com/news/1000881/children-sick-from-another-toxic-running-track%2C-say-parents.

3. Zhuo Ban, "Her Milk Is Inferior: Breastfeeding, Risk, and Imagining Maternal Identities in Chinese Cyberspace," in *Imagining China: Rhetorics of Nationalism in an Age of Globalization*, ed. Stephen J. Hartnett, Lisa B. Keränen, and Donovan Conley (East Lansing: Michigan State University Press, 2017), 205–234.

4. See "South China Doctor Killed by Former Patient," *China Radio International*, May 7, 2016, http://english.cri.cn/12394/2016/05/07/3521s926839.htm.

5. Didi Kirsten Tatlow, "Chinese Man's Death in Custody Prompts Suspicion of Police Brutality," *New York Times*, May 12, 2016.

6. For instance, see Shan Phillips, "Mobile Internet More Popular in China Than in U.S.," *Nielsen*, August 4, 2010, http://www.nielsen.com/us/en/insights/news/2010/mobile-internet-more-popular-in-china-than-in-u-s.html.

7. Chen Xieyuan, "Chinese Mobile Internet Population Hits 780 Mln: Report," *CRI English*, December 7, 2017, http://english.cri.cn/12394/2016/05/18/4161s928014.htm.

8. The introduction in this book lists the Party media's six basic responsibilities. See also Xi Jinping, *The Governance of China*, vol. 2 (Beijing: Foreign Languages Press, 2017), 360, speech delivered on February 19, 2016, "Improve All Aspects of Party Media Leadership."

9. For instance, in the following months officials from the Cyberspace Administration of China, the National Health and Family Planning Commission, and the State Administration for Industry and Commerce opened an investigation into Baidu after the student, Zexi Wei, died of cancer, allegedly because of the faulty information found on Baidu that led him to a fraudulent cancer treatment. See Austin Ramzy, "China Investigates Baidu after Student's Death from Cancer," *New York Times*, May 3, 2016; Anthony Kuhn, "China Investigates Search Engine Baidu after Student Dies of Cancer," *NPR*, May 3, 2016; and Shan Juan, "Baidu Faces Probe after Outcry over Cancer Treatment," *China Daily*, May 3, 2016.

10. See "央视批百度多个疾病贴吧被出售：卖的是钱，要的可能是命！" [CCTV Criticized Multiple Baidu Illness Forums Being Sold: The Trade Might Bring Financial Returns, but at the Expense of Lives!], *The Paper*, January 12, 2016, https://www.thepaper.cn/newsDetail_forward_1419808.

11. See "Baidu under Fire for Profiting from Medical Forums," *China.org.cn*, January 14, 2016.

12. Liu Wei 刘巍 and Fu Ming 傅明, "百度迷途：藏在财报里的卖贴吧真相" [Baidu's Lost Future: The Truth Hidden behind Selling Baidu Forums], *Time-Weekly*, January 19,

2016, http://www.time-weekly.com/html/20160119/32395_1.html.

13. For a detailed story covering the various perspectives involved see Sui-Lee Wee, "Scandals Catch Up to Private Chinese Hospitals, after Fortunes Are Made," *New York Times*, November 15, 2018.

14. See "携程去哪儿都出事，在哪里能买到便宜靠谱的机票？(附攻略)" [Both Ctrip and Qunaer Had Crises; Where Do We Find Cheap and Reliable Tickets? (Tips Attached)], *CCTV News*, January 14, 2016, https://mp.weixin.qq.com/s?__biz=MTI0MDU3NDYwMQ==&mid=406737792&idx=1&sn=459fb5ba4ec9a2c033075985fc060bfd&3rd=MzA3MDU4NTYzMw==&scene=6#rd.

15. For instance, see "Chinese Online Travel Giant Ctrip Caught in Stolen Miles Scandal," *China Global Television Network* (*CGTN*), January 12, 2016, https://america.cgtn.com.

16. See Patrick Shaou-Whea Dodge, "Imagining Dissent: Contesting the Façade of Harmony Through Art and the Internet in China," in Hartnett, Keränen, and Conley, *Imagining China*, 311–338.

17. See Uriel Rosenthal, Michael T. Charles, and Paul T. Hart, *Coping with Crises: The Management of Disaster, Riots, and Terrorism* (Springfield, IL: Charles C. Thomas, 1989). See also Uriel Rosenthal, R. Arjen Boin, and Louise K. Comfort, *Managing Crises: Threats, Dilemmas, Opportunities* (Springfield, IL: Charles C. Thomas, 2001).

18. George W. Bush used the term "war on terror" on September 16, 2001, in his "Address to a Joint Session of Congress and the American People." For the full text of that speech check the whitehouse.gov web link at https://georgewbush-whitehouse.archives.gov/news/releases/2001/09/20010920-8.html. For a critique of post-9/11 rhetoric, see Stephen J. Hartnett, *Globalization and Empire: The U.S. Invasion of Iraq, Free Markets, and the Twilight of Democracy* (Tuscaloosa: University of Alabama Press, 2019).

19. For example, in the context of the 7/7 terrorist attacks in London and the discourse of resilience, see Hamilton Bean, Lisa Keränen, and Margaret Durfy, "'This Is London': Cosmopolitan Nationalism and the Discourse of Resilience in the Case of the 7/7 Terrorist Attacks," *Rhetoric & Public Affairs* 14, no. 3 (2011): 427–464.

20. Steven Fink, *Sticky Fingers: Managing the Global Risk of Economic Espionage* (iUniverse, 2003).

21. Steven Fink, *Crisis Management: Planning for the Inevitable* (New York: American Management Association, 1986).

22. For Mitroff's five stages of crisis management, see Alexandros Paraskevas, "Mitroff's Five Stages of Crisis Management," in *Encyclopedia of Crisis Management*, ed. K. Bradley Penuel, Matt Statler, and Ryan Hagen (Thousand Oaks, CA: Sage Publications, 2013).

23. See Changrui Li 李昌瑞, "风险社会的政治挑战" [Political Challenge of Crisis Society],

in 公共传播视野下的社会风险与危机传播 [Crisis Society and Communication from a Public Communication Angle], ed. Ning Zhang 张宁 and Jie Zhang 张洁 (Guangzhou: Sun Yat-sen University Publishing House, 2015), 13–22. See Li Huajun 李华军 and Chen Xianhong 陈先红, 中国危机公关案例研究报告 [Research Reports on Chinese Crisis Public Relations Cases] (Wuhan: Huazhong University of Science and Technology Publishing House, 2014). See also Yang Kui 杨魁 and Liu Xiaochen 刘晓程, 危机传播研究新论 [The New Research on Crisis Communication] (Beijing: Chinese Social Science Publishing House, 2011).

24. Lan Yuexing 兰月新 and Zeng Yunxi 曾润喜, "突发事件网络舆情传播规律与预警阶段研究" [A Study on Emergency Communication Trends and Alerts], 情报杂志 *Journal of Information* 5 (2013): 16–20.

25. Wang Haiyan 王海燕 and Yang Shen 沈阳, "媒体监督与企业公关的博弈" [The Competition between Media Surveillance and Enterprise Advertisement] 新闻记者 *Journalist* 6 (2013): 52–57.

26. Melissa W. Graham, Elizabeth J. Avery, and Sejin Park, "The Role of Social Media in Local Government Crisis Communications," *Public Relations Review* 41, no. 3 (2015): 386–394; Clark F. Greer and Kurt D. Moreland, "United Airlines' and American Airlines' Online Crisis Communication Following the September 11 Terrorist Attacks," *Public Relations Review* 29, no. 4 (2003): 427–441.

27. Brooke Fisher Liu, Lucinda Austin, and Yan Jin, "How Publics Respond to Crisis Communication Strategies: The Interplay of Information Form and Source," *Public Relations Review* 37, no. 4 (2011): 345–353.

28. Ibid. See also Yan Jin, Brooke Fisher Liu, and Lucinda L. Austin, "Examining the Role of Social Media in Effective Crisis Management: The Effects of Crisis Origin, Information Form, and Source on Publics' Crisis Responses," *Communication Research* 41, no. 1 (2014): 74–94.

29. For data sets in Beijing, we turned to the data service company Hong Bo Zhi Wei. Hong Bo Zhi Wei 宏博知微 can be accessed at www.zhiweidata.com.

30. We used the following Chinese characters when searching our data sets: 百度、贴吧 and 携程、假机票.

31. Zheng He Dao 正和岛, "盘点BAT反腐6大事件！也许唯一能阻挡他们前进的就是内部腐败" [Summarizing Six Anticorruption Cases from BAT! Maybe the Best Way to Prevent Corruption Is the Force Coming from Intrainstitutional Corruption], *ChinaVenture.com.cn*, September 22, 2016, https://www.chinaventure.com.cn/cmsmodel/news/detail/302701.html.

32. For more on the president's anticorruption campaign, see the *South China Morning Post*'s

"Topic Page" at https://www.scmp.com/topics/xi-jinpings-anti-corruption-campaign. See also "Visualizing China's Anti-corruption Campaign," *China File*, August 15, 2018, http://www.chinafile.com/infographics/visualizing-chinas-anti-corruption-campaign.

33. See "百度出售地区吧：'郑州吧'一年承包费200万" [Baidu Sells Local Forums: Zhengzhou Forum Marks 20,000 RMB Rental Fee], *ifeng.com*, January 14, 2016, http://hn.ifeng.com/a/20160114/4191543_0.shtml.

34. "Chinese Online Travel Giant Ctrip Caught in Stolen Miles Scandal," *China Global Television Network* (*CGTN*), January 12, 2016.

35. Li Miao 李淼, "携程在手，说走就走不了" [With Ctrip in Hand, You Cannot Leave Whenever You Want], January 13, 2016, https://zhuanlan.zhihu.com/p/20487446.

36. For Ctrip's PR statement see "Ctrip Involved in Fake Flight Tickets Row," 中*Times* [GB Times], January 13, 2016, https://gbtimes.com/ctrip-involved-fake-flight-tickets-row.

37. Li Miao, "With Ctrip in Hand."

38. For recent examples see the Huxiu website at https://m.huxiu.com/article/136946.

39. Wang and Shen, "Competition between Media Surveillance and Enterprise Advertisement." Lan and Zeng, "Emergency Communication Trends."

40. For a report that WeChat has now taken over Weibo as the most influential social media platform in China, see Xin Chen, "陈鑫 ["Zimeiti de fazhan jihui yu tiaozhan"] 自媒体的发展机会与挑战" [Challenges and Opportunities for the Development of WeMedia], 中国传媒科技 [Media Technology in China] 14 (2013): 40–41, http://www.labour-daily.cn/ldb/node41/node2151/20140315/n35379/n35382/u1ai183461.html.

41. For instance, see Xue Qingyuan 薛庆元, "百度涉嫌侵害消费者个人信息安全被起诉 法庭已立案" [Baidu Being Sued for Allegedly Violating Users' Personal Information; the Court Has Established the Case], *finance.sina.com.cn*, January 5, 2018, https://finance.sina.com.cn/chanjing/gsnews/2018-01-05/doc-ifyqkarr7365143.shtml.

42. See "携程骗钱黑幕—亲身经历携程机票诈骗" [Inside Stories of Ctrip Frauds— Personal Experiences of Under-the-Table Scam on Ctrip], *tianya.cn*, March 25, 2015, http://bbs.tianya.cn/post-travel-686954-1.shtml.

43. It was widely reported by the Chinese news media. For example, see *The Chinese Consumers Web* at http://www.ccn.com.cn/419/566270.html.

PART 3

Case Studies in the Changing Mediascape of China

Rebuilding in Unity

The 2015 Tianjin Explosions and Renewal Discourses in Chinese Social Media

Lisa B. Keränen and Yimeng Li

O n August 12, 2015, global news services announced a series of explosions in Tianjin "so strong that they shook homes on the other side of the city and sent flaming debris arching over nearby high-rise buildings."[1] Residents reported being awakened before midnight by what felt like an earthquake that ripped the facades from nearby buildings, producing convulsions that registered as seismic shockwaves on nearby geological survey monitors.[2] Images of a dramatic fireball in the night sky circulated on social media, with early reports claiming seven dead and an estimated three to four hundred injured. Authorities later identified the source of the explosions as 800 tons of improperly handled ammonium nitrite at the Tianjin Dongjiang Port's Ruihai International Logistics, a licensed hazardous chemical storage site. According to official reports, the 2015 Tianjin explosions killed 173 people, including 104 firefighters and 11 police first-responders; they injured nearly 800 people and damaged more than 304 buildings, 12,428 cars, 17,000 housing units, and 7,533 intermodal containers, causing more than $9 billion in damages.[3] The ensuing investigation revealed a network of corruption involving more than 700 tons of illegally stored sodium cyanide among 129 other improperly contained hazardous chemicals that "exploded, combusted, leaked, or diffused."[4] In February 2016, the Chinese government concluded an investigation of the incident, naming 123 persons responsible, including the son of a local police officer who was a secret co-owner of Ruihai International Logistics.[5] More than forty-nine people were sentenced to prison, including government officials, Ruihai's leaders, and port workers in "one of China's worst-ever industrial tragedies."[6]

The Tianjin explosions provide an occasion to examine the interconnected nature of crisis, identity, and discourses of renewal as they appear in response to a human-caused crisis in China.[7] Illuminating the creative potential of calamity, Kevin Rozario explains that crises are attention-getting because they "present opportunities for processing, intellectually and emotionally, the experience of living in a world of systematic ruin and renewal, destruction and reconstruction, where technological and environmental disasters always loom."[8] In such a time, the *epideictic* rhetoric of praise and blame intertwines with narratives of national identity and can fuel discourses of recovery, resilience, and renewal.[9] *Renewal discourses*, which project prospective visions of recovery and rejuvenation, appeared publicly after the Tianjin explosions, as seen in a prominent banner "Rebuild in Unity," which was erected above the port's gate and was still visible on the explosion's one-year anniversary.[10] Appearing amid construction signs facing rows of shipping containers, and appearing hopeful and forward looking even while referencing a tragedy, the sign crystallized key elements of renewal discourse—it offered a future-focused call to citizens to create a shared community, one that promised to transform a devastating and painful loss into a positive outcome.

In exploring discourses of renewal in response to the Tianjin explosions, this chapter offers three main contributions. First, it extends research concerned with how renewal discourses function in postcrisis times, offering a non-Western case study to a body of predominately Western-focused analyses.[11] One of several notable exceptions is Cotton et al.'s analysis of organization communication following Japan's Fukushima disaster, but a major difference in our case is that the government (and not a corporate leader) assumed responsibility for postcrisis communication after the port explosions.[12] Most existing analyses examine cases wherein "the discourse of renewal reaffirms the CEO or leader's role as the interpreter or framer of meaning following a crisis."[13] By contrast, our study examines how the government, instead of corporate spokespersons, took command of postcrisis communication. As Yi-Hui Christine Huang, Fang Wu, and Yang Cheng explain of the People's Republic of China, the government "often assumes the principal acting role in conjunction with or instead of other institutions involved in a crisis."[14] Thus, the Tianjin explosion offers the opportunity to examine the extent to which renewal discourses appear during a non-Western government's response to crisis.

Second, this chapter extends our understanding of the complex communicative, social, and material responses to the Tianjin explosions themselves. The overwhelming majority of English-language academic publications about the Tianjin explosions address hazardous materials, critical care, and environmental remediation and disaster response.[15] The smaller share of communication-related scholarship investigating the Tianjin explosions has examined the roles of trust in local authorities' press conferences and the ways rumor-policing techniques stimulated Weibo discourse. Addressing the first topic, Xueyu Wang has found that the first six press conferences lacked transparency, noting that even the Party-sponsored *People's Daily* called them "not satisfactory."[16] The Communist Party's official news organ remarked that the press conferences had been "criticized by quite a lot of people," marking what was perhaps an effort to situate blame away from national toward local governance.[17] Wang's detailed investigation of the process and content of the local press conferences found a second series of press conferences improved in terms of open information-sharing, largely because of local officials' hard-won attempts to restore trust through the use of evidence. Improvements in real-time communication responded to public need.

Addressing the second topic, the roles of rumor-related Weibo posts, Jing Zeng, Chung-hong Chan, and King-wa Fu tallied sources to find that "more than 50 websites were shut down, more than 300 social media accounts in China were suspended, and 12 people were arrested for circulating rumors online" in the aftermath of the Tianjin explosions.[18] Their analysis offers clues about the remarkable and productive convergence of rumor-related messaging across websites and social media. Zeng et al.'s analysis of more than one hundred thousand rumor-sharing and rumor-related posts, rumor-rebuttal posts, and deleted posts found that "for almost all analyzed topics, after Weibo began to openly refute the related rumors, more posts discussing this topic were published by Weibo users." They concluded that "there is insufficient evidence to show that *rumor removal* consistently leads to a chilling effect on the Weibo platform," despite pervasive claims from Western media sources that censorship was actively quashing citizen critique.[19] Such a finding raises interesting questions about the roles that rumor-removal plays in generating conversation in online formats. Clearly, more work can be done to understand the types of responses citizens and officials produced in the aftermath of these dramatic explosions, to track the information flows that emerge during crisis events.

Finally, this chapter contributes to conversations about how China as a nation-state is configured in official and publicly circulating social media discourses, particularly when media converge on a particular incident.[20] Extending the work of Benedict Anderson, Hartnett and colleagues explain that "the rhetorical work of imagining communities is always relational: any sense of an emerging new Chinese national identity is being formed, in part, in contrast."[21] In the case of the Tianjin explosions, representations of postcrisis renewal bear on constructions of China as a nation-state because of the government's lead role in response and recovery. Since, as Yi-Hui Christine Huang and Sora Kim note, "the government [of China] has the power and requisite access to interrupt and intervene in a crisis event," the Tianjin explosions provide a unique opportunity to examine how crisis, renewal, and national identity converge.[22]

In this chapter, we explore if, how, and with what effect renewal discourses are mobilized in official and citizen social media discussion of the Tianjin explosions in contrast to international-facing Chinese news stories. In the twenty-four hours following the blasts, more than 590 million Weibo users viewed content about the explosions, making Weibo a significant site of official and citizen expression and opinion formation.[23] Although the early posts about Tianjin were censored, with a number of rumor-mongering accounts deleted, online content continued to proliferate, posted by citizens, corporations, and official government sources alike.[24] By comparing internally focused official, state-sanctioned Weibo posts, and uncensored citizen posts with the outward face of the crisis presented in the English-language news *China Daily*, we offer an analysis of how leaders and citizens made sense of the Tianjin crisis and to what extent renewal discourses figured in the responses. Ultimately, we find that while renewal discourses were muted in the immediate aftermath of the Tianjin explosions, the government projected strength and unity in its response.

Our chapter proceeds in three parts. First, we offer a brief review of the literature on crisis and renewal. Then, we outline our method before offering an analysis of our findings. We close by suggesting an agenda for future research on discourses of renewal in China's mediated public sphere. Methodologically, our analysis merges rhetorically informed qualitative and quantitative analysis to show how partnerships between rhetorical scholars (first author) and social science media scholars (second author) can provide promising avenues for future collaboration between scholars working in the United States and China.[25] Such collaborations can offer in-depth texture to quantitative or big data analyses. In this way, our chapter relates to the central themes of this volume by examining a case of postcrisis media convergence in which the government played an active role in responding to disaster in the "3.0 era of digital governance."[26]

Crisis, Renewal, and the Prospects for Building Identity

By all accounts, with their "deadly blasts," which "felt like an 'atomic bomb,'" the Tianjin explosions constituted a crisis requiring swift action.[27] According to Matthew Seeger and Robert Ulmer, crises are "often framed as devastating events evoking a sense of severe urgency, serious threat, and devastating loss."[28] Seeger and Ulmer, along with Timothy Sellnow and their colleagues and graduate students, among other researchers, have spent decades studying how organizations and groups respond to crisis.[29] Their analyses of postcrisis communication have identified a typical set of communication responses to crisis, including the rhetoric of image restoration and apologia, with their attendant discourses of praise and blame.[30]

By now, it is commonplace to observe that apologia, a form of *epideictic* rhetoric that includes defensive rhetoric, often follows a crisis.[31] Organizational spokespeople frequently respond to crises with apologetic discourse that consists of a combination of "simple denial of the act, evasion of responsibility, reduction of the offensiveness, compensation, corrective action, and mortification designed to repair or restore image."[32] In the case of the Tianjin explosions, both the Ruihai corporation in charge of chemical storage in Tianjin and the government that regulates such storage facilities faced challenges because of the scale of the explosions and the ensuing death, damage, and injury. While many existing studies of corporate crisis responses focus on the speech acts of the corporate spokesperson's responses, Ruihai Logistics and its public relations team remained silent about the incident. Their lack of response presumably occurred because the organization's key members were quickly placed in police custody and because the government and its media outlets typically assume leading roles in responding to crises and disasters in the mainland, a feature that allows us to examine the institutionalization of public relations at the government level.[33]

In addition to finding that crises elicit apologetic discourses, Seeger and Ulmer, among others, have advanced the "discourse of renewal theory," which builds on earlier work about organizational renewal.[34] The theory is based on the observation that crises create opportunities for positive outcomes and can therefore generate language about rebuilding and renewal. According to Seeger and Griffin Padgett, discourses of renewal "address the communication exigencies associated with rebuilding, recovery and revitalization."[35] By contrast to the discourses of blame and responsibility, which look to the past, discourses of renewal look to the future, featuring "ways to move forward in constructing or reconstructing new, and better organizational forms."[36] In the West, renewal discourses have become a staple organizational and governmental response to crisis.[37]

Seeger and others have identified several recurrent renewal discourse patterns. As Seeger and Griffin Padgett explain, "A postcrisis discourse of renewal is characterized by four dominant features: prospective focus; the opportunities inherent in the crisis; provisional rather than strategic responses; and ethical communication grounded in core values."[38] While renewal discourses may emerge from official, leadership organizations and from communication professionals and public relations firms, we observe that governments, citizens, and the media, too, can play a role in creating, circulating, resisting, cultivating, and shaping renewal discourses. The Tianjin port explosions provided a discursive opening for government, media, and citizens to look beyond the crisis to envision new future ways of doing and being. Given the absence of research on renewal discourses in the Chinese public sphere and the potential of the crisis for producing such rhetorics, we compare discourses of renewal originating from government officials, mediated sources, and citizens in order to begin to understand how these discourses played out postcrisis in the Chinese public sphere in the weeks and months immediately following the explosions.

Because crises can produce challenges to an existing system, renewal discourses often evoke shared values and, presumably, identities.[39] A large and growing body of interdisciplinary literature examines how crises can serve as occasions for identity work. Much of this work builds from Benedict Anderson's notion of *imagined communities*, the idea that peoples and nation-states are not innate or given but rather produced discursively as part of an ongoing processes of identity work.[40] In communication studies, Maurice Charland extended this idea through the concept of *constitutive rhetoric*, language that calls a people into being.[41] More recently, Kevin Rozario observed that calamities supply the exigence for an "extraordinary" amount of cultural work, while Hamilton Bean and his coauthors explored how a sense of British nationalism was activated in response to the London 7/7 bombings, which killed people from a wide range of nationalities but became associated with a uniquely "British resilience."[42] Bean et al. focused on how the discourse of "resilience," as an organizing metaphor, structured official and policy responses to the bombings. In these cases, responses to crisis or tragedy, whether natural or human induced, occurred during occasions when national identity was also challenged, extended, or reasserted. Across this emerging literature, then, renewal discourse is characterized as providing means of asserting community and invoking national identity in the face of crisis and loss.

With more than 810 million (and growing) netizens, 92 percent of whom are mobile internet users, and a 52 percent total national internet penetration, China's digital public sphere supplies a vibrant and growing site for examining postcrisis communication.[43] Weibo uniquely offers a significant set of official and public responses to crises. In the immediate aftermath of the Tianjin explosions, more than one million posters took to Weibo to comment on the crisis, generating a rich snapshot of discourse.[44] We investigate how official government, official media, influential bloggers, and everyday citizens responded to the Tianjin explosions in the wake of the crisis by examining the uncensored Weibo posts and news articles. To gather Chinese social media posts about the Tianjin explosions, we gathered "hot" Weibo posts representing government, media, big V (verified, influential posters), and citizen content. We coded them for the presence or absence of the four characteristics of renewal discourse. Meanwhile, we gathered English-language *China Daily* news reports of the Tianjin explosions to determine whether renewal discourses were being projected to international audiences and coded them for renewal elements, while tracking their dynamics via rhetorical analysis.

Renewal Discourses on Weibo after the Tianjin Explosions

The first part of the chapter examines the "hot" Weibo posts, those that were reposted and circulated the most. We identified and cataloged the hot Weibo posts in the six-month period following the explosion, from August 12, 2015, to February, 12, 2016, when the public inquiry concluded, using the key words *Tianjin* and *explosion*. Of 440 hot posts during this time, 90 minimally met the characteristics of renewal discourse. Figure 1 reveals the overall dynamics of renewal discourse in the hot posts, showing the ebb and flow of renewal discourse over time.

Predictably, hot posts about Tianjin declined over time, with several outlying peaks. One peak occurred around one week after the accident, during a period of high discussion and media convergence, covering topics such as the firefighters'

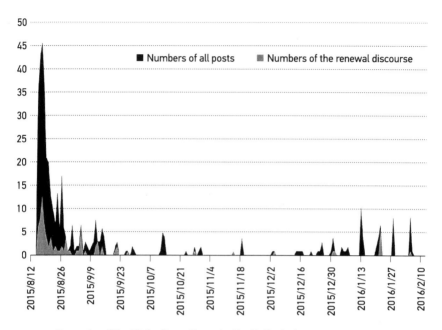

FIGURE 1. Dynamics of Hot Weibo Posts About the Tianjin Explosion

bravery, blame discourse, rumors and clarification of rumors, and large informational messages. During this initial period, features of renewal discourses appeared, as posters looked to a future where such accidents could be prevented. A second peak occurred on October 13, 2015, when another explosion happened in Tianjin, but renewal discourses were not prominent in these posts that linked to the earlier Tianjin explosions. What follows is a period of lesser volume, with several tiny fluctuations. The third noteworthy peak—or rather sets of peaks—occurred between January 13 and February 10, when the government released its investigation findings. During this final period, a news story of a dead firefighter's mother who got pregnant again generated much attention and reposting, synecdochally standing in for rebirth and renewal.

The "hottest" post, reposted and commented on the most, appeared August 17, 2015, and belonged to Weibo ID "People's Daily."[45] Prompting 16,610 reposts and garnering 5,569 comments, the hot post read:

> #Tianjin explosion accident# Six days before, at this moment, the fire sparked and the bang came, it smashed the peaceful night. Up to now, 114 people are dead, 70 are

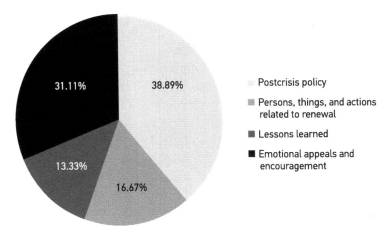

FIGURE 2. The Hottest Post on the Tianjin Explosions. This image appeared on the People's Daily Weibo account on November 23, 2017.

still out of touch. Tomorrow is the first 7th night. Tonight, no matter where you are, let's light the candles together. May the investigations be thorough, bring comfort and rest to the dead and truth to the living. May such accidents never happen again!

Because this post mentions the investigation and to some extent references the past—characterizing blame and a forensic orientation, it only minimally satisfies the four criteria of renewal discourse outlined by Seeger and Griffin Padgett: it is (partially) future-oriented, it focuses (superficially) on the opportunity to come together inherent in the crisis, it offers a provisional rather than a strategic vision (may such accidents never happen again), and it is grounded in the ethical response of the community (to remember the dead on the seventh day after death, a cultural norm). While appropriate for generic expectations of the seventh day, it missed the chance to promote renewal more broadly in terms of rebuilding, and therefore might fall under the umbrella of what we term a "muted" renewal discourse, one that makes only vague and superficial references to community healing and a better future. As we see in the post, amid the memorial lights, masked-clad spectators gathered, protecting themselves from pollution and illness while taking photos and sharing images on social media.

Similar "muted" renewal discourses appeared sporadically across the ninety hot posts, which emanated from three types of Weibo IDs: the media, the response organizations, and the "big V" microbloggers whose "verified" or "V" accounts signify their status as celebrity thought influencers; their accounts can boast millions of followers.[46] The media's use of renewal elements occurred in 64.44 percent of their posts, while nonmedia organizations included future references 18.89 percent of the time, and big Vs appeared in 16.67 percent of their posts. This disparity suggests the influential role of the media in rebuilding a sense of social cohesion in the aftermath of a crisis. Elements of renewal discourse raised by citizens were not detected significantly in hot posts during the six-month period, owing perhaps to the low probability that a citizen post would be picked up and reposted en masse.

We divided all the renewal discourse into four types, coding for postcrisis policies and future-related changes; people, things, and actions related to renewal; lessons learned; and emotional appeals and encouragement. As figure 2 shows, the postcrisis policy content occupied the biggest share of the posts, emotional appeals and the encouragement came close after, and the lessons learned appeared the least.

In terms of media discourses, more than half of the posts focused on the after-crisis policies presented by the government and related enterprises. Premiere Li Keqiang's speech was widely cited in the posts, including his promise to publish all the investigation results and give an explanation to the relatives of the dead, to the Tianjin citizens, to the whole nation, and to the historical record. Tianjin officials also made similar promises during their press conferences.[47] Such discourse is not fully grounded in renewal because of its focus on investigating the past, but in this case the look to the future was clear, as the government announced its intention to build an eco-park and set up a monument, while compensating victims.[48] Because of the investigation, Ruihai Logistics did not make any posts about this explosion, but real-estate and service-related enterprises stepped up posts intended to help victims relocate in the aftermath of the explosion.

Appeals to ending human-manufactured disasters, wishes that the dead may rest in peace, and sentiments urging the living to "stay strong" collectively appeared in 17.24 percent of the renewal posts. Such sentiments occurred especially on the seventh day after the explosion. Comforting emotional encouragement figured strongly in the posts on this day, such as "The storm will pass," "The light will eventually come," "May all the people, who went through the 8/12 Tianjin explosion move toward the dawn with hope," and "Wait for dawn." When considered against what we can presume was the critical commentary of many disappeared posts (along with misinformation and rumors), these platitudes substituted critique with a campaign of Party-approved good tidings.

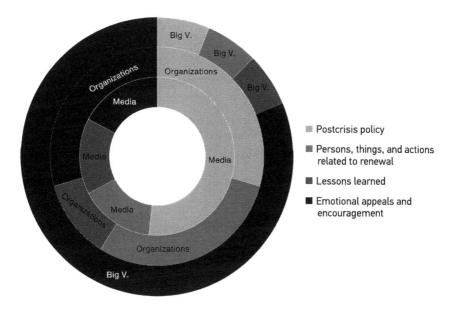

Postcrisis policy

Persons, things, and actions related to renewal

Lessons learned

Emotional appeals and encouragement

FIGURE 3. Fragmented Portions of Media, Government, and Big V. Weibo Posts by Major Themes

Posts featuring people and objects associated with renewal and the lessons learned from this explosion occupied the same share of the discourse, at 29.41 percent. What differs from the media discourses was that the emotional appeals and encouragement messages were raised through an individual perspective. For instance, such content might feature a letter written by a Tianjin citizen to the firefighters or repeat encouraging words from Japanese netizens. Other posts about how a brave, dead firefighter's mother got pregnant again, how a comatose firefighter revived one month after the blasts, how a puppy survived the blast, and so on, sought to emphasize the faces of bravery and create an emotional bond with victims, while stressing resilience and renewal themes. Still other posts focused on lessons learned from the Tianjin explosion, emphasizing how the government encouraged all the provinces to remove dangerous chemical enterprises from populated districts. After the Tianjin explosion, many provinces reported their chemical removal plans in quick succession; more than one thousand chemical enterprises needed to be removed across China at a total estimated cost of $400 billion yuan.[49] That the Tianjin explosions created an opening to acknowledge and fix the precarity of China's chemical storage, revealing hundreds of potentially deadly sites, is significant, but so, too, is the government's central staging as the paternal hero urging localities to clean up their toxins.

The renewal discourses of the big V posters emphasized encouragement, with 86.67 percent of their discourses geared toward positive, affirming messages for the future. Similar to the media discourses, renewal discourses peaked on the seventh day after the explosion. As Cotton et al. note, "as a prospective strategy," renewal "focuses on healing the organization [or community] by looking to the future, avoiding blame, and realigning the culture of the organization or community with foundational values."[50] Here, for both media and big V posters, encouragement and healing occupied a prominent share of the media posts, framing the crisis as an opportunity for coming together. Overall, elements of renewal appeared in a portion of the hot posts, but fewer than expected, revealing a missed opportunity for collective renewal work.

The Outward-Facing Discourses: The Tianjin Explosion on the World Stage

If the Weibo posts communicated content primarily, although not exclusively, in China, to the Chinese diaspora, and among Chinese speakers, *China Daily* supplied the outward-facing English-language content for global public consumption, which raises the question: to what extent did renewal discourses pervade international news coverage to this face-threatening event?[51] Past analyses have found that Chinese post-SARS media coverage of crisis and disaster tends to project a vision of strength and competence, suggesting that renewal discourses might be a rhetorically ready resource for government leaders in times of crisis.[52] By contrast, earlier post-crisis analyses of the government's response to SARS and the 2007 "Made in China" controversy revealed ineffective strategies of denial, silence, and minimization.[53] The present rhetorical and content analysis suggests that renewal discourses were not a prominent feature of English-language news coverage in *China Daily*. And while the silence and denial were not primary strategies of crisis management in this case compared to, say, SARS and earlier crises, there was room to improve in terms of offering a comprehensive look at the economic, cultural, and regulatory conditions that led to the explosions.

Using the online search database Lexis-Nexis, we identified fifty-one news stories about the Tianjin explosions between August 12, 2015, and the end of February 2016 across *China Daily*'s various versions (Hong Kong, Europe, United States, etc.)

TABLE 1. Major Themes in *China Daily* Coverage of the Tianjin Explosions

Information, damage, and casualties	15	60%
secne, damage, casualty	7	
eyewitness accounts	3	
victim assistance	3	
environmental impacts	2	
Emotion	6	24%
praise for heroism	3	
grief/sympathy	2	
blame	1	
Policies, effects, and consequences	4	16%
safety regulations	2	
information disclosure	1	
punishment	1	
	n = 25	100%

using the search terms *Tianjin* and *explosion*. Eliminating duplicate stories with verbatim or nearly verbatim content produced a list of twenty-five news stories about the Tianjin explosions, revealing the high degree of convergence in media reports of the case. These were read in their entirety several times and inductively coded into major themes with an eye toward renewal discourses.[54] Perhaps owing to the genre of the news report, none included any substantial features of renewal discourse, although occasional statements appeared hinting at renewal (but these did not satisfy the full criteria for renewal discourse). For instance, here and there, an article included a statement that gestured toward building a better future out of the explosions, such as reporting on the memorial park that would be built at the site.[55]

Overall, renewal discourse did not appear as a prominent feature of *China Daily*'s English-language news coverage, prompting thematic coding to identify topical patterns of response. The major inductively coded themes in this news coverage included information sharing about the scene, including damage and casualty information; emotion; and policy, aftereffects, and consequences. Consistent with inductive coding, each article was read twice and categorized in terms of its most prominent theme, which coincided with the headline and leading paragraphs.[56] Emergent themes were then collapsed into broader categories. For instance, the emotion theme contained stories that extolled the heroism of the firefighters, expressed grief and sympathy for victims, or detailed the condolences of foreign officials, while the policy, aftereffects, and consequences category contained subthemes about proposed safety regulations and information disclosure alongside environmental clean-up plans.

Across these categories the coverage overall worked to project the sense of a government in control. Although the word *corruption* was not apparent in the archived news reports in mainland China, by contrast to international news, which heavily used the term, government actions to ensure safety and reduce contamination were recurrent.[57] Indeed, the only place the term *corruption* appeared was as part of the word *anticorruption*, an article noting that an "anti-corruption body did not identify links between the probe and the Tianjin blasts."[58] Stories about mobilization of the PLA's biochemical experts and environmental monitors, by contrast, sought to assuage concerned readers and highlight the efficacy of China's rapid response. For instance, statements such as "Zong Guoying, top official of the Tianjin Binhai New Area, said at a news conference that the area's government has set up a service center to coordinate issues related to compensating for damaged homes and property" and "Chinese military orders arsenal safety check after Tianjin blast" worked to cement the picture of a government in firm charge of the crisis.[59] Here again, this Party-approved staging of the government as hero and problem-solver obscures the broader governance issues that led to the accident in the first place.

Another noticeable feature of the *China Daily* news coverage was the invocation of praise for firefighters, a number of whom died during response efforts.[60] As early as three days after the explosions, the *New York Times* observed the focus on heroism, stating that "the state media on Saturday featured moving tales of heroism and survival—including the rescue of a 50-year-old man found in a battered shipping container—while censors worked to delete social media posts criticizing the paucity of information or suggesting an official cover-up."[61] *China Daily* coverage featured statements such as that of President Li:

> All the firefighters on active or inactive duty participating in the rescue are well-trained. They knew well about the danger, and chose to risk their own lives. We are very sorry and sad for their sacrifice. They are all heroes. There is no difference between active or inactive duty for heroes.[62]

While such coverage may typify postdisaster communication, it does bear noting that instead of focusing on corruption and environmental communication, the media converged on tales of heroism and sacrifice.

One article stood out from the rest in terms of quantity and content, a reprinted blog posting about information disclosure running four thousand words—about four times the length of even the longest of other articles in the corpus. Ostensibly written by a Hong Kong journalist whose perseverance garnered an impromptu interview with Premier Li during his visit to Tianjin during the immediate aftermath of the explosions, the article advanced an argument for media transparency in responding to crises and disasters in China, while praising Premier Li's forward-thinking vision of transparency. After establishing the scene, the article establishes Li's bravery, observing his tour of the scene without protective gear, which projected strength, resilience, and the perceived safety of the crisis response:

> Premier Li was in a white shirt without a chemical splash suit or mask. "The scene was like in a Hollywood disaster film when we came here." A field staff member said: "We were worried about the safety of Premier Li. At the beginning, the wind flowed towards the sea but suddenly it changed direction towards us. The smell was pungent."

"It was not the first time Premier Li appeared tough at the scene of the disaster," the author noted.[63]

After establishing Li's hardiness as a proxy for his fitness to lead during crisis, the article spent multiple paragraphs emphasizing both Li's insistence on transparency and the importance of transparency in China overall:

> The first thing Premier Li did was to promote information disclosure about the Tianjin explosions. "If authoritative information cannot reach the public, rumors will spread widely," said Premier Li.
>
> "Whether it is safe or not must be confirmed by statistics rather than guarantees without evidence," Li said: "It's important to be clear in telling the truth: What is the gas? In what situation and at what range could it have what kind of effect? Make sure that information disclosure is in time and accurate, as well as open and truthful."

Elsewhere, statements such as "Disclosure has been the primary premise of governance under Li Keqiang," "Earlier, when Li was vice-premier of China, he made great efforts to promote disclosure," and "Public opinion was solicited before the fuel tax reform was implemented in 2008 as requested by Li" worked as government public relations to reinforce the putatively open response to the crisis, as well as to establish the importance of transparency in future crisis response. Together, these statements reveal efforts to counter the perception that censorship and information control were strong features of the Tianjin response, which had been alleged at the local level and which can be seen in the continued blocking of Western news sites like the *New York Times*.[64] Instead, the government sought to project its strength, leadership, and transparency in responding to crisis. While not a discourse of renewal, this portrayal projects the image of a competent and assured national identity, even while tightly controlling informational flows. As we can see here, the Party was determined for readers to conclude that it was firmly in command of the response and recovery, going so far as to publicly speak of "transparency" and being "open and truthful," all while engaging in another round of censorship and information control.

Overall, our comparison of the presence and dynamics of internally focused renewal discourses in social media and outward-looking renewal discourses in *China Daily* found that renewal discourses were muted in hot social media posts and nearly absent from English-language newspaper discourses. We found that renewal discourse did not predominate in the early coverage of the incident in any platform by any user subgroup, even when platforms converged across highly salient coverage. Features of renewal discourse were more present on social media at the beginning of the crisis and during key news moments over time.

We can only speculate on the material and discursive factors that may have limited renewal discourses in response to the Tianjin explosions. Scholarship on the discourse of renewal has identified five conditions that limit its use, several of which apply in this case. Benoit, for instance, has noted that natural disasters might be more apt for renewal discourses, while Kevin Wombacher and coauthors observe that "destruction of infrastructure also allows for the application of commonly understood metaphors, such as 'rising from the ashes' or 'a fresh start.'"[65] Although not a natural disaster, the clearing of infrastructure in the explosion created ample material and rhetorical opportunities for renewal discourse, as the "Rebuilding in Unity" banner outside of Tianjin port declared. Second and third, the levels of "support of organizational stakeholders" and "degree of observable correctable action" are factors that enable or constrain renewal discourses, with the Tianjin case offering a complicated relationship between citizens and the government, which took ownership of the crisis response, and a high degree of observable corrective action.[66] The fourth factor affecting renewal discourses is the "ownership or control of the organization," with private organizations seeming more likely to use renewal, a factor that may partially explain its limited appearance in Tianjin.[67] Additionally, place can serve as a salient factor for renewal discourses, with the particular places of some crises serving as a rhetorical resource. Wombacher and colleagues explain:

> Space and place are important symbolic and rhetorical aspects of a postcrisis context. In some cases, such as explosions (intentional or unintentional) and natural disasters, the structures in place prior to the crisis are gone and leave communities with no other options than to rebuild in the same space, rebuild the structure in a new place, or forego whatever activities were previously hosted by the structures.[68]

Finally, the fact that a company, Ruihai Logistics, was in charge of the hazardous chemicals storage that exploded created opportunities for discourses of blame that focused on removing the offenders from society, while preserving the image of the government working diligently on behalf of citizens. This feature likely encouraged the focus on fact-finding about the past.

That the English-language *China Daily* reportage did not feature renewal discourse prominently reveals a missed opportunity for national identity work in the face of a crisis. In China, renewal discourses resonate with broader "road to rejuvenation" narratives, those seen in official state narratives at the National Museum in Beijing and elsewhere across contemporary political discourse.[69] Such narratives position China as having emerged from its century of humiliation as a global economic and cultural leader; as Ian Johnson describes it, this narrative tells "the story of how China was laid low by foreign countries in the 19th and 20th centuries but is now on the path back to glory."[70] We posit that the relative absence of renewal discourses in this case is due to the nature of the crisis, the nature of the government's rhetorical constraints or reluctance to use renewal discourses in such contexts in China, a cultural pattern or set of genre-based expectations, or to a combination of factors, including factors not mentioned above.

Regardless of the reasons for the lack of renewal discourse in these platforms, our analysis confirms the government's public relations role in projecting strength and command over the Tianjin crisis, a pattern previously identified in case studies of Sichuan earthquake responses and avian influenza news reports.[71] In the case of the Tianjin explosions, this projection of strength and command over the crisis converged in social media and in English-language news reports. To project control, the government stressed its sending PLA chemical experts to the scene, its thorough investigation, and its punishment of wrongdoers. And so one of China's worst industrial disasters, an event rife with lax oversight, both corporate and government corruption, and enough intrigue to fill novels of speculation, was miraculously turned in the pages of *China Daily* into a testament to the Party's competence, kindness, strength, and forward-looking vision. Such are the workings of propaganda in the age of convergence, where, in this case, the government controls the levers of public communication.

Understanding Renewal Discourses in China's Digital Communication Environment

We have brought the concept of *renewal discourses* to an investigation of Chinese media, convergence, and governance in the immediate aftermath of a human-manufactured crisis. By tracking how renewal discourses were utilized—or, in this case, not utilized—by various parties in response to the 2015 Tianjin explosions, we examined the dynamics of postcrisis communication in the Chinese public sphere, providing insight into how government sources, media outlets, and citizens made sense of the disaster.

This chapter extends the literature on renewal discourse and on rhetorical/media constructions of China in several ways. First, it adds a non-Western analysis to a predominately Western-focused set of existing studies to show a case where renewal discourses were moderately employed after a crisis. Second, it examines renewal discourse as something that can be dispersed through various organs of society and taken up by government as an institutional public relations and governance mechanism and not one exclusively generated by a corporation and its spokespeople responding to a crisis. Our study further emphasizes the role that social media can play in disseminating renewal discourse throughout society. Third, it combines the sensitivities of rhetorical analysis (first author) with social media content analysis (second author) to uncover the dynamics—and missed opportunities—of renewal discourses across converging media in a postcrisis environment. Thus, it illuminates how studies of Chinese media can be enriched by rhetorical analysis and theories, which can add a qualitative dimension and texture to analysis.[72]

Despite the relative scarcity of renewal discourses in this case, we suggest that examination of renewal discourses can shed light on China's changing communication patterns overall. As Huang and Xu observe:

> Disasters and accidents are different from everyday large-scale activities, so most government departments are usually caught off guard. A steady flow of information usually has to be sent to the commanders and then exported after analyzing and processing. The traditional way is to release the news that the government wants to spread preferentially. However, this outdated pattern is likely to become completely invalid in the mobile Internet era, and, if used, may even have an opposite effect to that intended.[73]

Our analysis confirms that the command-and-control mode of communication was not solely at work during the aftermath of the Tianjin explosions, which generated a rich tapestry of expressions from government, media, and citizens alike. Although rumor and panic-inducing posts were eliminated, the 440 hot posts and *China Daily* coverage testify to widespread efforts to disseminate useful information, as do the *China Daily* stories, which nevertheless projected a government firmly in command of the situation and advocating for open information sharing, even while tightly containing certain topics and types of information.

Our analysis is limited by several factors. First, the limited nature of the data set and the cross-cultural analysis constrain the generalizability of our findings. Second, we acknowledge the ethical dilemmas of using Western theories like discourse of renewal theory to analyze Chinese discourses. Third, we caution that studies of a broader swath of renewal discourses in China are warranted.

To extend this preliminary work, we suggest that mediated renewal discourses and their capacity for identity formation and solidification deserve additional research attention in China. Given the near certainty of large-scale, human-induced future crises, a need exists to explore how official discourses of blame and renewal operate in the evolving landscape of China's era of 3.0 digital communication. As innovations prompt changes in public communication strategies, scholars can track how and with what effect renewal discourses converge across media platforms. China's rise in the twentieth and twenty-first centuries supplies a story of renewal that is continually retold across various forms of converging media, and scholars would do well to analyze renewal discourses across numerous genres, crises, and platforms.

NOTES

This chapter was created in cross-continental partnership. Both authors narrowed the focus, scope, and research question and found secondary literature. Li did the hard work of gathering, categorizing, coding, and translating Weibo posts and drafting a description of her findings, while Keränen supplied the theoretical background, collected and analyzed the *China Daily* English-language news coverage, and drafted the bulk of the text. Li generated figures 1–3, while Keränen created table 1. The authors thank Claire Shannon, Stephanie Tolbert, and Rudong Zhang for their research assistance.

1. Claire Phipps and Matthew Weaver, "China Blasts," *The Guardian*, August 13, 2015, online at https://www.theguardian.com/world/live/2015/aug/13/tianjin-explosion-hundreds-injured-killed-china-blasts-latest-updates. See also "'At Least' 7 Dead, 300 Hurt in China Warehouse Blast," *Belfast Telegraph*, August 12, 2015, https://www.belfasttelegraph.co.uk/news/world-news/at-least-7-dead-300-hurt-in-china-warehouse-blast-31447740.html.

2. Tang Yue, "Two Foreigners Describe the Tianjin Explosions, *China Daily*, August 13, 2015, http://www.chinadaily.com.cn/china/2015-08/13/content_21591389_2.htm.

3. "Tianjin Explosion: China Sets Final Death Toll at 173, Ending Search for Survivors," *Guardian*, September 12, 2015, https://www.theguardian.com/world/2015/sep/12/tianjin-explosion-china-sets-final-death-toll-at-173-ending-search-for-survivors.

4. Bin Zhao, "Facts and Lessons Related to the Explosion Accident in Tianjin Port, China," *Natural Hazards* 84 (2016): 708.

5. See Song Miou, "Tianjin Blast Probe Suggests Action against 123 People," *Xinhua*, February 5, 2016, http://www.xinhuanet.com/english/2016-02/05/c_135078801.htm; and Ben Chu, "China's Flawed Corruption Crusade: How the Tianjin Disaster Was the Latest Consequence of a System That Places Profit before Public Safety," *The Independent* (London), August 22, 2015, http://www.independent.co.uk/news/world/asia/corruption-in-china-the-tianjin-explosion-offers-a-glimpse-of-how-the-country-really-works-10466255.html. The quotation is from Chu.

6. Merrit Kennedy, "China Jails 49 over Deadly Tianjin Warehouse Explosions," *NPR*, November 29, 2016, https://www.npr.org/sections/thetwo-way/2016/11/09/501441138/china-jails-49-over-deadly-tianjin-warehouse-explosions. The company's chairperson was eventually fined about US$100,000 and received a "suspended" death sentence, which was expected to be commuted to life in prison. See "Chinese Chemical Factory Boss Given Suspended Death Sentence," *The Telegraph*, November 10, 2016, https://www.telegraph.co.uk/news/2016/11/10/chinese-chemical-factory-boss-handed-suspended-death-sentence-as/.

7. For exposition on renewal discourses, see Matthew W. Seeger and Donayle R. Griffin Padgett, "From Image Restoration to Renewal: Approaches to Understanding Postcrisis Communication," *Review of Communication* 10, no. 2 (2010): 127–141. Also see Robert R. Ulmer and Timothy L. Sellnow, "Crisis Management and the Discourse of Renewal: Understanding the Potential for Positive Outcomes of Crisis," *Public Relations Review* 28 (2002): 361–365; Blair Thompson, Angela M. Jerome, Holly J. Payne, Joseph P. Mazer, E. Gail Kirby, and William Pfohl, "Analyzing Postcrisis Challenges and Strategies Associated with School Shootings: An Application of Discourse of Renewal Theory," *Communication Studies* 68, no. 5 (2017): 533–551; Alfred J. Cotton III, Shari R. Veil, and Nicholas T. Iannarino, "Contaminated Communication: TEPCO and Organizational Renewal at the Fukushima Daiichi Nuclear Power Plant, *Communication Studies* 66, no. 1 (2015): 27–44; and Matthew W. Seeger, Robert R. Ulmer, Julie M. Novak, and Timothy Sellnow, "Post-crisis Discourse and Organizational Change, Failure and Renewal," *Journal of Organizational Change Management* 18, no. 1 (2005): 78–95.

8. Kevin Rozario, *Culture of Calamity: Disaster and the Making of Modern America* (Chicago: University of Chicago Press, 2007), 6.

9. For more information about epideictic rhetoric, see Aristotle, *Rhetoric*, trans. W. R. Roberts and I. Bywater (New York: Modern Library, 1984). Rozario, *Culture of Calamity*, discusses the connection between crisis and national identity.

10. The image comes from Wang Tao, "Tianjin Explosions: 1-Year Later," *The Diplomat*, August 13, 2016, https://thediplomat.com/2016/08/tianjin-explosions-1-year-later/.

11. Several exceptions do exist, such as Juyan Zhang, "Public Diplomacy as Symbolic Interactions: A Case Study of Asian Tsunami Relief Campaigns," *Public Relations Review* 32 (2006): 26–32; Juyan Zhang and William L. Benoit, "Message Strategies of Saudi Arabia's Image Restoration Campaign after 9/11," *Public Relations Review* 30, no. 3 (2006): 161–167; and Cotton, Veil, and Iannarino, "Contaminated Communication." For other postcrisis work, see, in particular, Seeger et al., "Post-crisis Discourse"; Ulmer and Sellnow, "Crisis Management"; and Seeger and Griffin Padgett, "From Image Restoration."

12. Cotton, Veil, and Iannarino, "Contaminated Communication."

13. Seeger et al., "Post-crisis Discourse," 84.

14. Yi-Hui Christine Huang, Fang Wu, and Yang Cheng, "Crisis Communication in Context: Cultural and Political Influences Underpinning Chinese Public Relations Practice," *Public Relations Review* 42 (2015): 209.

15. For representative works, see Gui Fu, Jianhao Wang, and Mingwei Yan, "Anatomy of Tianjin Port Fire and Explosion: Process and Causes," *Process Safety Progress* 35 (2016): 216–220; Guo-qiang Li, Shi-ke Hou, Xin Yu, Xiang-Tao Meng, Liang-liang Liu, Peng-bo

Yan, Min Tian, Shao-Lei Chen, and Hui-juan Han, "A Descriptive Analysis of Injury Triage, Surge of Medical Demand, and Resource Use in an [sic] University Hospital after 8.12 Tianjin Port Explosion, China," *Chinese Journal of Traumatology* 18 (2015): 314–319; Hong-Yu Wang and Hai Yan Wu, "Problems in the Management of Mass Casualties in the Tianjin Explosion," *Critical Care* 20 (2016): 47; Hui Zhang, Huabo Duan, Jian Zuo, MingWei Song, Yukui Zhang, Bo Yang, and Yongning Niu, "Characterization of Post-disaster Environmental Management for Hazardous Materials Incidents: Lessons Learnt from the Tianjin Warehouse Explosion, China," *Journal of Environmental Management* 199 (2017): 21–30.

16. Xuyue Wang, "A Struggle for Trustworthiness: Local Officials' Discursive Behaviour in Press Conferences Handling Tianjin Blasts in China," *Discourse and Communication* 10 (2016): 412–426.

17. Wang, "A Struggle for Trustworthiness."

18. Zeng, Chan, and Fu, "How Social Media Construct."

19. Ibid., 314.

20. Stephen John Hartnett, Lisa B. Keränen, and Donovan Conley, "Introduction: A Gathering Storm or a New Chapter?," in *Imagining China: Rhetorics of Nationalism in an Age of Globalization*, ed. Stephen John Hartnett, Lisa B. Keränen, and Donovan Conley (East Lansing: Michigan State University Press, 2017), 1–13.

21. Benedict Anderson, *Imagined Communities: Reflections on the Origin and Spread of Nationalism* (London: Verso, 1983).

22. Yi-Hui Christine Huang and Sora Kim, "Cultures of Crisis Response: Chinese Public Relations Practices in Context," *Chinese Journal of Communication* 11, no. 1 (2018): 2.

23. This figure comes from "China Silences Netizens Critical of 'Disgraceful' Blast Coverage," *BBC News*, August 13, 2015, https://www.bbc.com/news/world-asia-china-33908168.

24. Ibid.; Jing Zeng, Chung-hong Chan, and King-wa Fu, "How Social Media Construct 'Truth' around Crisis Events: Weibo's Rumor Management Strategies after the 2015 Tianjin Blasts," *Policy and Internet* 9, no. 3 (2017): 297–332.

25. Cai Peijuan, Lee Pei Ting, and Augustine Pang, "Managing a Nation's Image during Crisis: A Study of the Chinese Government's Image Repair Efforts in the 'Made in China' Controversy," *Public Relations Review* 35 (2009): 213–218. For a primer on rhetorical analysis, see Sonja K. Foss, *Rhetorical Criticism: Exploration and Practice*, 5th ed. (Long Grove, IL, Waveland Press, 2018).

26. Media and journalism professor Shen Yang as cited in Minmin Huang and Oulu Xu, "Premier Li's Promotion of Information Disclosure," *China Daily*, September 18, 2015, http://www.chinadaily.com.cn/china/2015-09/18/content_21920258.htm.

27. Hao Zhang and Xuejie Zhao, "Facts You Need to Know about Deadly Blasts in Tianjin," *China Daily,* August 13, 2015, http://www.chinadaily.com.cn/china/2015-08/13/content_21591958.htm; the atomic bomb quotation is from Caroline Mortimer, "Tianjin Explosion: Gigantic Crater Left by Chinese Factory Accident Revealed, *The Independent,* August 19, 2016, https://www.independent.co.uk/news/world/asia/tianjin-explosion-photos-china-chemical-factory-accident-crater-revealed-a7199591.html.

28. Matthew W. Seeger and Robert R. Ulmer, "A Post-crisis Discourse of Renewal: The Case of Malden Mills and Cole Hardwoods," *Journal of Applied Communication Research* 30, no. 2 (2002): 126.

29. See, for example, Matthew W. Seeger and Robert R. Ulmer, "Virtuous Responses to Organizational Crisis: Aaron Feuerstein and Milt Cole," *Journal of Business Ethics* 31 (2001): 369–376; Matthew W. Seeger, Timothy L. Sellnow, and Robert R. Ulmer, "Communication, Organization, and Crisis," *Communication Yearbook*, vol. 21 (Thousand Oaks, CA: Sage, 1988), 231–275; Gary A. Kreps, "Sociological Inquiry and Disaster Research," in *Annual Review of Sociology*, ed. R. E. Turner and J. F. Short Jr. (Palo Alto, CA: Annual Reviews, 1988), 309–330; Keith M. Hearit, "'Mistakes Were Made': Organizations, Apologia, and Crises of Social Legitimacy," *Communication Studies* 46 (1995): 1–17; and William L. Benoit, "Image Repair Discourse and Crisis Communication," *Public Relations Review* 23 (1997): 177–186.

30. Benoit, "Image Repair Discourse"; Hearit, "Mistakes Were Made"; Seeger and Ulmer, "Virtuous Responses."

31. Aristotle, *Rhetoric*; Benoit, "Image Repair Discourse"; William L. Benoit, *Accounts, Excuses and Apologies* (Albany: State University of New York Press, 1995). For a classic and early take on apologia in the field, see B. L. Ware and Wil A. Linkugel, "They Spoke in Defense of Themselves: On the Generic Criticism of Apologia," *Quarterly Journal of Speech* 59 (1973): 273–283.

32. Ulmer and Sellnow, "Crisis Management," 362.

33. "China Silences Netizens"; Zhang and Zhao, "Facts You Need"; Ni Chen, "Institutionalizing Public Relations: A Case Study of Chinese Government Crisis Communication on the 2008 Sichuan Earthquake," *Public Relations Review* 35 (2009): 187–198.

34. Seeger et al., "Post-crisis Discourse"; Ulmer and Sellnow, "Crisis Management"; Seeger and Griffin Padgett, "From Image Restoration"; Cotton, Veil, and Iannarino, "Contaminated Communication." Their work builds on Gordon L. Lippitt, *Organization Renewal: A Holistic Approach to Organization Development*, 2nd ed. (Englewood Cliffs, NJ: Prentice-Hall, 1982).

35. Seeger and Griffin Padgett, "From Image Restoration," 132–133.

36. Ibid., 136.
37. Shari R. Veil, Timothy L. Sellnow, and Megan Heald, "Memorializing Crisis: The Oklahoma City National Memorial as Renewal Discourse," *Journal of Applied Communication Research* 39, no. 2 (2011): 164–183; Marita Sturken, "The Objects That Lived: The 9/11 Museum and Material Transformation," *Memory Studies* 9, no. 1 (2015): 13–26.
38. Ibid.
39. Ulmer and Sellnow, "Crisis Management."
40. Anderson, *Imagined Communities*.
41. Maurice Charland, "Constitutive Rhetoric: The Case of the *Peuple Québécois*," *Quarterly Journal of Speech* (1987): 73, 133–150.
42. Rozario, *Culture of Calamity*; Hamilton Bean, Lisa Keränen, and Margaret Durfy, "'This Is London': Cosmopolitan Nationalism and the Discourse of Resilience in the '7/7' Terrorist Attacks," *Rhetoric & Public Affairs* 14 (2011): 427–464.
43. "Chinese Internet Users Surge to 802 Million in Test of Government's Ability to Manage World's Biggest Online Community," *South China Morning Post*, August 21, 2018, https://www.scmp.com/tech/china-tech/article/2160609/chinese-internet-users-surge-802-million-test-governments-ability.
44. "China Silences Netizens."
45. The second author verified the source on November 23, 2017, as from https://weibo.com/2803301701/CwiqPzcOT?refer_flag=1001030103_&type=comment#_rnd1511447524757.
46. Florian Schneider, "China's 'Big V' Bloggers: How Celebrities Intervene in Digital Sino-Japanese Relations," *Celebrity Studies* 8, no. 2 (2017): 331–336.
47. Huang and Xu, "Premier Li's Promotion."
48. Huang and Xu, "Premier Li's Promotion."
49. Jennifer Duggan, "China to Relocate Almost 1,000 Chemical Plants in Wake of Tianjin Blasts," *The Guardian*, August 30, 2015, https://www.theguardian.com/world/2015/aug/30/china-relocate-chemical-plants-tianjin-blasts-miao-wei-pollution.
50. Cotton, Veil, and Iannarino, "Contaminated Communication," 28.
51. Lisa B. Keränen, Kirsten N. Lindholm, and Jared Woolly, "Imagining the People's Risk: Projecting National Strength in China's English-Language News About Avian Influenza," in Hartnett, Keränen, and Conley, *Imagining China*, 271–300.
52. Chen, "Institutionalizing Public Relations"; Keränen, Lindholm, and Woolly, "Imagining the People's Risk"; and Claire Heffernan, Federica Misturelli, and Kim Thompson, "The Representation of Highly Pathogenic Influenza in the Chinese Media," *Health, Risk, and*

Society 13 (2011): 603–620. See Bean, Keränen, and Durfy, "This Is London," on the limits of resilience discourse.

53. Peijuan, Ting, and Pang, "Managing a Nation's Image."

54. Thomas R. Lindlof and Bryan C. Taylor, *Qualitative Methods in Communication*, 2nd ed. (Thousand Oaks, CA: Sage, 2002).

55. Xinhua, "Monument to Be Built on Tianjin Blast Site," *China Daily*, September 5, 2015, http://www.chinadaily.com.cn/china/2015tianjinblasts/2015-09/05/content_21791743.htm.

56. Lindlof and Taylor, *Qualitative Methods in Communication*.

57. See Chu, "China's Flawed Corruption Crusade."

58. See, for example, Yue Tang and Yinan Zhao, "Moment of Silence Honors Tianjin's Dead," *China Daily*, August 19, 2015, http://www.chinadaily.com.cn/china/2015-08/19/content_21643393.htm.

59. Tang and Zhao, "Moment of Silence."

60. Michael J. Hyde, "The Rhetor as Hero and the Pursuit of Truth: The Case of 9/11," *Rhetoric & Public Affairs* 8 (2005): 1–30.

61. Andrew Jacobs, "Tianjin Officials Struggle to Contain Fallout as Angry Relatives Demand Answers," *New York Times*, August 15, 2015, https://www.nytimes.com/2015/08/16/world/asia/china-tianjin-blasts-chemical-containment.html.

62. Huang and Xu, "Premier Li's Promotion."

63. Huang and Xu, "Premier Li's Promotion."

64. Wang, "A Struggle for Trustworthiness."

65. Benoit, *Accounts, Excuses, Apologies*; Robert R. Ulmer, Matthew W. Seeger, and Timothy L. Sellnow, "Post-crisis Communication and Renewal: Expanding the Parameters of Post-crisis Discourse," *Public Relations Review* 33, no, 2 (2007): 130–134. The quotation is from Kevin Wombacher, Emina Herovic, Timothy L. Sellnow, and Matthew W. Seeger, "The Complexities of Place in Crisis Renewal Discourse: A Case Study of the Sandy Hook Elementary School Shooting," *Journal of Contingencies and Crisis Management* 26 (2018): 165.

66. Wombacher et al., "Complexities of Place," 166.

67. Ibid.

68. Ibid., 170.

69. Ian Johnson, "At China's New Museum, History Toes Party Line," *New York Times*, April 3, 2011, https://www.nytimes.com/2011/04/04/world/asia/04museum.html.

70. Ian Johnson, "Xi Jinping and China's New Era of Glory," *New York Times*, October 13, 2017,

https://www.nytimes.com/2017/10/13/sunday-review/xi-jinping-china.html?_r=0.

71. Chen, "Institutionalizing Public Relations"; Keränen et al., "Imagining the People's Risk"; Heffernan, Misturelli, and Thompson, "Representation."

72. Foss, *Rhetorical Criticism.*

73. Huang and Xu, "Premier Li's Promotion."

Code Switching and Language Games in Contemporary China; or, Convergence and Identity Construction on WeChat

Todd L. Sandel and Peimin Qiu

China has been described by some scholars as an undifferentiated whole, held together by a unified culture and language. Jared Diamond, for example, claimed that when challenged by European powers in the nineteenth century, China "lost" because it was encumbered by its "single writing system" and "substantial cultural unity."[1] On the other hand, when the linguist John McWhorter described China, he wrestled with how to describe a place where people speak a range of mutually unintelligible codes: "What are called the dialects of Chinese are as different from one another as are the Romance languages, and speakers of one must learn the others as foreign tongues." Yet because Chinese is written using "symbols" and not an alphabet, McWhorter argued, this "means that all of the Chinese varieties can be written with the same script." This feature of written language, combined with the "unifying effect of Chinese culture," means that Chinese varieties should be counted as dialects and not distinct languages.[2] A vision of China as a "unified whole," however, may look different when considering everyday speaking practices. When meeting someone from China for the first time, it is commonplace to ask: Where are you from? What is your hometown? What "*fangyan* is spoken there"?[3] This can then lead to an interesting discussion about differences between how words and phrases are uttered in that person's *fangyan* (dialect/local language) and how they are pronounced in Standard Chinese (also called Mandarin or *putonghua*). The picture that emerges from a local point of view is that China is not a unified whole but an amazingly diverse patchwork of regional dialects, local language norms, and overlapping cultures.

Beginning from this understanding of the rich complexity of languages, this chapter examines how China is both unified and diverse, and how the languages used within China are both being brought together and diversified in new ways as they mix and evolve in the new world of communication convergence. To unpack this topic, we look at online communication shared among China's youth, members of the so-called post-1980s generation born after the implementation of the one-child policy.[4] Most are well educated, have ready access to media, and, as we demonstrate, use a variety of linguistic forms to communicate online, notably when using WeChat, China's most popular smartphone application.[5] The context for this study is Macao and those who interact regularly with people in the adjacent city of Zhuhai. This is a rapidly modernizing region of China where Cantonese is the most commonly spoken *fangyan* and, similar to how youth in Shanghai use mixed online communication,[6] youth of this region mix Cantonese with Standard Chinese, English, and other representational (including especially visual) forms, thus making for a remarkably rich stew of communicative practices.

Before proceeding we must first address the question: What is a Chinese *fangyan*? In Chinese, *fang* 方 is the character for place, as in *difang* 地方, and *yan* 言 is the character for language, as in *yuyan* 语言. The two characters, *fang* 方 and *yan* 言, when combined, may be understood as the language (*yuyan*) of a place (*difang*). In a comprehensive study of the Chinese language, Norman (1988) claimed that "there are literally scores of mutually non-intelligible varieties of Chinese . . . [and] [n]o comprehensive dialect survey for the whole of China has ever been carried out."[7] This may be due not only to China's size and population, but also because China is a linguistically rich and diverse place, where regional differences abound. Take, for instance, the common Chinese greeting, "Have you eaten yet?" In Standard Chinese (Mandarin) it is pronounced as "Ni chi bao le mei?" Yet in Hoklo (also known as Taiwanese) it is "Li jia ba boe?" and in Cantonese "Lei [or nei] sik bao mei?" Likewise, the phrase "Have you eaten your rice yet?" in Mandarin is "Ni chi fan le mei?" in Shanghainese "Nong chet vah leh va?" and Hunanese "N chah fan le mou?"[8] These local ways of speaking index regional variations that may map onto differences of culture and language. Considered within this book about communication and convergence in the contemporary China, then, our chapter dives to the very foundation of human understanding by asking: How are daily communication practices in contemporary China enriched, complicated, and rendered more cosmopolitan as youth in Macao play with representation on WeChat? As these online communication practices evolve, what kinds of code switching are taking place, and how does this network of language games in turn drive identity construction in contemporary China?

To frame our questions in a larger context, we wonder how such linguistically diverse communication practices can give rise to a single "imagined community."[9] As noted above, scholars point to China's writing system as a unifying symbolic system. Throughout the dynastic period, for example, "literary Chinese" was the written form used for official and most scholarly documents: "In the Qing dynasty, the ordinary written administrative language was a late form of literary Chinese."[10] Learning to write literary Chinese was acquired through years of rigorous study, primarily by those who prepared to take examinations to join China's bureaucracy.[11] Another feature of literary Chinese was that it could could be read and pronounced in different ways.[12] Written messages could be communicated among people who pronounced characters differently, a convergence point that served to bridge linguistic differences. In the modern period, China's official written and spoken language transformed dramatically. As the Qing Dynasty (1644–1912) came to an end, and as Western missionaries established schools across China, the purpose of education changed.[13] Instead of serving as the primary vehicle for training scholars in classical Chinese and Confucian texts to pass civil service examinations, a new, mixed Sino-Western curriculum promoted science, nationalism, and modernism. Then, following the establishment of the Republic of China (ROC) in 1912, the Chinese Nationalist (Kuomintang or KMT) government made efforts to create a national language based upon vernacular forms that could be used in modern media and education of the masses. Hence, in 1926, the already tottering Nationalist government sought to unify the nation by creating a National Language based upon Beijing's *fangyan*.[14]

Following the end of war with Japan in 1945 and the removal of the KMT government to Taiwan in 1949, this National Language system, using standardized, traditional characters and a pronunciation system consisting of "Mandarin phonetic symbols," was imposed on Taiwan.[15] In mainland China under the administration of the People's Republic of China (PRC), scholars developed a separate simplified writing system and a Romanized pronunciation scheme, Pinyin, in 1955 named *putonghua*, or the "common language," with the goals of overcoming illiteracy and "nation-building."[16] For the Communists, then, like the Nationalists before them, the struggle to unify China as a coherent postcolonial nation, an "imagined community" with a shared vision, hinged in no small part on bringing the culture's many *fangyan* into one linguistic camp: a strong and unified China, Mao believed, needed one language and one writing system, not a melange of local customs that hindered communication.

Despite Mao's efforts to create a unified Chinese language, today's Standard Chinese consists of two forms that differ in a number of ways: one difference is the use of traditional (in Taiwan, Hong Kong, and Macao) or simplified characters (in most of the mainland); a second difference is that hundreds of words and phrases are both spelled and pronounced differently. For instance, the way to call something "authentic" in Taiwan is *daodi*; in China this same word is *didao*. The verb "to copy" in Taiwan is *dayin*; in China this verb is *fuyin*. Yet despite differences in vocabulary and differences in pronunciation, these two versions of Standard Chinese are similar and usually mutually intelligible—hence the almost daily feature of Chinese life where friends check each other's pronunciation to make sure they are understanding each other.[17] Furthermore, as Standard Chinese has been adopted for use in formal education and promoted via media, it has spread and is now spoken and/or written across all regions of greater China. The use of Standard Chinese is perhaps greatest among China's post-1980s generation youth and has thus become the lingua franca of greater China.[18] But does this mean that the rise of Standard Chinese is signaling the end of China's nonstandard *fangyan*? Does the age of communication convergence mean that Mao's dream of a unified nation held together by a unified language is finally coming true?

To answer this question broadly is beyond the scope of this study. However, it is possible to answer it in part. First, consider where this study is situated, the Macao-Zhuhai region of the Pearl River Delta. This is one of the wealthiest parts of China, where new ideas and communication technologies are available and adopted readily, especially among youth.[19] Furthermore, Hong Kong and Macao—both special administrative regions of China—are places where Cantonese is the lingua franca, even for well-educated youth.[20]

Second as we shift our focus to messages shared in an online context, consider that China's internet is a platform for the emergence of new and mixed linguistic forms.[21] Studies conducted in Hong Kong and in Shanghai show that new forms of online discourse and code switching have emerged, marked by the mixing of English, Standard Chinese, and a local *fangyan* (i.e., Cantonese or Shanghainese).[22]

As demonstrated below, we find youth in Macao/Zhuhai similarly using mixed linguistic forms and creatively incorporating other symbolic systems, such as emoji, as afforded by the social media app WeChat.[23]

In this backdrop of language mixing and communication convergence, we continue with a brief overview of the historical and modern development of written vernacular Cantonese, highlighting practices in both Hong Kong and Macao. Next, we present our findings and discuss implications for how WeChat serves as a platform for the ongoing flows and creation of new linguistic forms, code switching, and identity expressions.

Written Vernacular Cantonese in Hong Kong

Snow, in a comprehensive study, examined vernacular Cantonese in Hong Kong, one of the most linguistically special placees in the Chinese-speaking world. It is important to note that Hong Kong and Macao—which Snow failed to mention—are the only places in China where educators have the option to instruct schoolchildren in written Chinese through a spoken *fangyan*—Cantonese.[24] They are also places where a written vernacular Cantonese that incorporates nonstandard Chinese characters—that are not formally taught—are widely used; these occur in a variety of texts, both public and private, such as advertisements, newspapers and magazines, emails, text messages, and social media.

Written vernacular Cantonese has a history stretching back centuries: earliest written vernacular forms, including Cantonese and Southern Min (Taiwanese), were used in such folk performances as opera, songs, poems, or religious liturgies.[25] Prior to 1949, places like Hong Kong and Guangzhou experienced an active "dialect literature movement," when the Communist Party—in an effort to spread literacy to the masses—encouraged the development and use of dialect forms in a variety of publications, such as newspapers, books, novels.[26] Following the establishment of the PRC, however, the dialect movement ceased in Guangzhou and other areas of China. Whereas in Mao's China there were strengthened efforts to fortify Standardize Chinese into one language and writing system, in colonial Hong Kong written vernacular Cantonese did not cease, but grew in use.

Both before and after the handover to the PRC in 1997, Hong Kong was diglossic: Standard Chinese (and English) existed alongside spoken and written vernacular Cantonese. In contrast with nearby mainland cities such as Guangzhou, the number of articles written in vernacular Cantonese, as opposed to standard Chinese, increased across time; this varied, however, according to the political leanings of a publication, with Cantonese appearing more often in popular and left-leaning publications than right-leaning conservative ones.[27] Cantonese was used prominently in magazines, comic books, "pocketbooks"—short works that could be read while riding on the bus or train—and advertising. Before 1997, vernacular Cantonese was a "low" code (i.e., informal communication, the uneducated and lower classes of people) and Standard Chinese a "high" code. However, after 1997 Cantonese gained prominence as a marker of Hong Kong identity, and was even promoted among academics, who produced Cantonese dictionaries and grammars. Hence, Cantonese, as a key element of a "Hong Kong identity," has come to elicit the embedded dynamics of culture and communication; language and identity converge to further enrich Chinese diversity.

Written vernacular Cantonese differs from standard, Mandarin-based Chinese in two ways: syntax and the use of nonstandard characters. This is apparent in the example below.[28] Consider the sentence, "I give you a book." In Standard Chinese, using traditional characters, it is written as

S	+V	+IO	+MW	+DO
我	給	你	一本	書
Wo	gei	ni	yiben	shu
I	give	you	one (+ measure word)	book

In this sentence, the syntax is Subject 我 + Verb給 + Indirect Object你 + Measure Word Phrase一本 + Direct Object書.

The same sentence written in Cantonese:

S	+V	+MW	+DO	+ IO
我	畀	一本	書	你
Ngo	bei	yatbun	syu	nei (lei)
I	give	one (+ measure word)	book	[to] you

There are two noteworthy differences. One is the second character in the sentence, the verb 畀 for "give," pronounced *bei*. While it has the same meaning as the Standard Chinese character 給 (*gei*), it is both pronounced and written differently. This is an exclusively Cantonese character. The second difference is the syntax. Whereas in Standard Chinese the indirect object precedes the direct object, in Cantonese the positions are reversed: the direct object precedes the indirect object.

Macao's Vernacular Cantonese Practices

Starting in 1557, Macao was administered by a European power, Portugal. The Portuguese administrators paid little attention to Macao's educational system, resulting in what Bray and Koo call a "poly-centred collection of education systems."[29] After the handover to the PRC in 1999, Macao was granted a high degree of autonomy as one of China's two "Special Administrative Regions" (SAR). In addition to designing its own local currency and legal system, Macao has control over, and a distinct, language policy that includes two official languages: Portuguese and Chinese. Local law requires official communication in both languages. Schools provide instruction in one of these languages, although, importantly, "the law does not explicitly state which variety of Chinese (Cantonese and Putonghua) should be used as medium of instruction."[30] Most students attend schools where Cantonese is the primary language of instruction, and a minority offer instruction in Portuguese, Mandarin, or English—supplemented with Mandarin Chinese language instruction. Furthermore, the Macao government does not take an official stand on the use of simplified or traditional characters, with traditional characters favored in most schools and society at large.[31] While local media are influenced by the mainland's policies, they are not directly censored by Chinese authorities.[32] Local news broadcasts on "Macau TDM" (Teledifusão de Macau) are delivered primarily in Cantonese (there is also a Portuguese language channel); the internet is uncensored, and media produced in Hong Kong and Taiwan are available.

When looking at language practices in Macao, we find that Cantonese is the first and/or prefered language of most residents in Macao, with written vernacular Cantonese used regularly.[33] For instance, the characters for "taxi" are written as 的士, pronounced in Cantonese as "dik si"; an underground "car park" is written as 地庫 (*dei fu*), and one often sees the possessive character written in nonstandard form as 嘅 (*ge*), not 的 (*de*), as it is in Standard Chinese. We see this nonstandard character in the image in figure 1. The phrase positioned directly above "Your Catering Professional" is written in vernacular Cantonese, 您嘅外賣專家, pronounced as "Nei ge ngoi maai zyun gaa." The second character, 嘅 (*ge*), is a possessive particle that is nonstandard.

FIGURE 1. Vernacular Cantonese in Commercial Signage

FIGURE 2. Vernacular Cantonese in Official Signage

While most official public signs are written in Standard Chinese, there are exceptions. The photograph in figure 2 was taken in December 2014 at a government office in Macao. Most of it is in Standard Chinese. However, the text displayed most prominently in the center is a vernacular Cantonese expression (using standard characters): 及早續期 *kap zou zuk kei*, or in English, "apply early." In Standard Chinese this same phrase would be written as 提早續期 (*tizao xuqi*), as the standard phrase for "early" is *tizao*. Yet the Cantonese phrase here is 及早 (*kap zou*).

These are but two examples of vernacular Cantonese writing that are often seen in Macao. An analysis of newspapers, which is beyond the focus of this chapter, would also show that like Hong Kong, local Macao newspapers that cater to "popular" audiences (i.e., a tabloid, akin to the *New York Post* or *The Sun*) use more vernacular Cantonese writing.[34] In the backdrop of the Chinese government's policies and Macao's local laws, we highlight the prominent use of Cantonese while also noting that Portuguese, English, and Mandarin are foregrounded in the vernacular in different contexts. We now turn to online communication practices to explore the kinds of language mixing that showcase the ever-evolving world of communication convergence, and that are driving identity construction in contemporary China.

Macao Youth's Online Communication

Anecodotal evidence indicates that the use of vernacular Cantonese has increased among Macao's youth, notably their online and social media communication. This is perhaps not surprising, when considering findings from studies of youth in other contexts. For instance, in a study of colloquial Arabic in Saudi Arabia, Azmi and Aljafari found that young people are most adept at reading colloquial Arabic, as they use it regularly in social media messages.[35] In China, where internet use and penetration is greatest among youth, the internet is a context where creative expression is most prolific, where online writing occurs that some may call "deviant," and the social norms that happen in face-to-face communication, such as deference to elders or social superiors, are less likely to be observed among youth.[36]

The creativity of expression seen among China's youth comes during a time of rapid growth of online communication, and most notably, the social media app WeChat (*Weixin* 微信) that was created in 2011. By 2018 there were an estimated one billion monthly active users on WeChat, with most in China, spurred in part by WeChat's excellent design.[37] Unlike other social media apps like Facebook or Instagram, WeChat is not blocked by China's internet censors, making it readily available as a social media platform in China and Macao.[38] According to data collected by the Macao Association for Internet Research, WeChat ranks highest in usage as a social media app among mobile phone users in Macao. Data also show that 99 percent of fifteen- to twenty-four-year-olds and 97 percent of twenty-five to thirty-four-year-olds use the internet. Among all internet users, 92 percent use a cell phone daily, and the most popular app (78 percent) is WeChat.[39]

Methods and Data Collection

This study began with a personal observation by the second author. She grew up in Zhuhai, a city adjacent to Macao. Qiu would often cross the border to visit her aunt and cousin who live in Macao. Then, after completing an undergraduate degree in China, she moved from Zhuhai to Macao and worked at a company for two years. During an initial period of adjustment she noticed differences in communicative practices, and how people would code-switch and code-mix.[40]

In Macao, Qiu noticed that people would often code-switch or mix Cantonese and English, whereas in Zhuhai people would mix Cantonese and Standard Chinese. Another difference was that when exchanging messages on WeChat, her colleagues and friends—most of whom were young like herself—told her she did not use enough emoji. These observations motivated this study.

Our data consist of two parts: (1) twenty-one WeChat screenshots—collected over a six-month period from 2014 to 2015, and (2) interviews about code-switching in WeChat messages. Qiu collected screenshots from people she knew personally, including friends and/or colleagues at the company in Macao where she worked prior to this study. Attention was paid to collecting messages that demonstrated the creative use of emoji, the mixing and appropriations of other languages, and repairs, such as when a word or phrase was misspelled. Twenty-one screenshots surfaced with one or more of these features.

For the second stage of research Qiu developed a list of questions for interviews with thirteen participants. Some were conducted individually and others with two or three participants jointly. Locations varied, with some conducted at the University of Macau, others at a hotel lobby, coffee shop, or restaurant. The initial questions of each interview probed demographic questions, such as age, occupation, frequency of use of WeChat, years spent in Macao, and primary friendship groups; this was followed by open-ended questions about code switching or code mixing. Participants talked about their experiences in code switching on WeChat, how they used emoji, and the impact of code switching on everyday conversations and interpersonal relationships. For the last part, participants were presented with preselected screenshots and asked to comment on each. They were asked to guess the identity of the people who composed the messages (e.g., a local Macao person, or someone from mainland China) and whether they would post similar messages. They also made interpretive comments about images and texts that they were shown.

Participants ranged in age from twenty-two to thirty years old; they were informed that their messages were being used for this study, and provided written consent to use their messages. For the second phase of this study, Qiu conducted thirteen interviews with Cantonese-speaking young adults. All gave written consent; approximately half (six) were born and raised in Macao. The rest (seven) lived in Macao but grew up in Zhuhai or other parts of Guangdong province. All interviewees spoke Cantonese as their first language; they were also fluent or conversant in Mandarin (Standard Chinese) and English. Interviews were conducted in Cantonese and transcribed into Standard Chinese. The authors jointly analyzed transcripts. All personal identifying information has been removed to protect participants' identities.

From these data, we looked for emergent rules, interpretations, meanings, and identities. In the following section, we present, interpret, and comment on seven screenshots. We chose these because they display different types of code mixing involving different languages (e.g., Standard Chinese and Cantonese), mistakes, and/or the creative use of emoji or other images. In our discussion we draw upon the interpretive comments participants made about these screenshots during interviews.

WeChat Screenshots: Language Mixing

This first excerpt is the shortest. It was a message exchanged with Qiu's cousin, a lifelong resident of Macao. The opening is a mix of vernacular Cantonese and English: 聽朝 10:30 去 body check (*teng ciu* 10:30 *heoi* body check; English translation: morning 10:30 go body check). Qiu replied, 好 *hou* (good). This is followed with a question, 在哪吃 (Where [go] eat?).

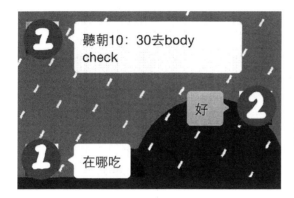

FIGURE 3. English-Cantonese-Chinese Language Mixing

Note the mixing of three codes: vernacular Cantonese, Standard Chinese, and English; singly they would be unintelligible to a monolingual speaker. The opening, 聽朝 (*teng ciu*) is vernacular Cantonese. The next phrase, "body check" is English; yet for the monolingual English speaker the meaning would be unclear: "body check" is a direct translation of the Cantonese term 體檢 (*tai gim*), or health checkup. Thus, the first message, translated into English, could be rendered as "[I] have to go to a checkup at 10:30 this morning." The response, 好, means "good" or "okay." The character 好 is the same in both Cantonese and Standard Chinese. However, the reply 在哪吃 is not Cantonese, but rather Standard Chinese. In Pinyin, pronounced as "zai nar chi," it means, "Where [go] eat?" If it were written in vernacular Cantonese, it would read as 去邊度食 (*heoi bin dou sik*).

In a follow-up interview Qiu asked her cousin why she wrote 在哪吃 and not the Cantonese phrase, 去邊度食. Her cousin explained that it was because of the input method she used to write Chinese, Cangjie, and that she could write 在哪吃 with fewer keys than are required to write 去邊度食. Chinese characters can be typed on a phone or computer with a number of different methods. Most users in Macao use Cangjie, a system developed in Taiwan that is based upon "building" characters with the keyboard; the other is to use a phonetic system, such as Pinyin, or a Cantonese phonetic that is similar to Jyutping. Therefore, the choice of this phrase seems influenced more by how to input a character, or time-use efficiency, rather than a linguistic decision.

Qiu asked other participants to comment on this screenshot. All readily understood the meaning of the first two turns, as they understood vernacular Cantonese and the meaning of "body check." However, they found the phrase 在哪吃 confusing. That is, while the meaning was clear, the identity of the speaker—whether a "local" from Macao or an "outsider" from Guangdong—was not. Most thought this person was an "outside" person from another province of China, who had only recently learned to write in vernacular Cantonese. Thus, we see that in online communication the perceived identity of participants can blur, as messages are impacted by technology, character input behavior, and user choice.

Cantonese-English Message

This next screenshot is similar to the first. It starts with vernacular Cantonese, marked by use of the character 唔, pronounced as "m," meaning "no" or negation. 我可能去唔到啦，要等11月份 (*Ngo ho nang heoi m̱ dou laa, jiu dang 11 jyut ban*), literally translated as "I maybe cannot go, have to wait until November." Then there is a code-switch and response in English, "I see." The reply is in mixed

FIGURE 4. Cantonese-to-English Messages

English-Cantonese: "sorry" 呀. The final character 呀 (pronounced as "aa"), is a tag particle that comes at the end of an utterance and does not convey referential meaning. Instead, it changes the key of the utterance, making it sound like speech: final particles such as *aa* or *la* are common in everyday spoken Cantonese.[41] The closing utterance is in English: "Never mind."

When this image was presented to interview participants, they said two things. One was that people usually follow the language of the preceding utterance. This we see from examining the order of languages/codes:

Turn 1: Cantonese
Turn 2: English
Turn 3: Mixed English/Cantonese
Turn 4: English

Another point is that the type of code-switching observed in these utterances also occurs in everyday speech. Participants who moved to Macao from nearby cities said that when they first arrived, they noticed how local Macao residents inserted English words and phrases into their speech. This impacted their own speaking practices. One interviewee commented:

> After working for two years [in Macao], just as you say, I really started to unconsciously change. But when going back to Zhuhai, your friends who have never worked in Macao, and you're chatting, you start to randomly add English. . . . Then they'll say, "How come you always say so many English words?"

This participant was not aware how her speaking habits had changed until she went to Zhuhai and chatted with friends who had "never worked in Macao." These friends noticed a linguistic mixing similar to that displayed in figure 4.

Character Switch

Code switching (or mixing) may involve not only a switch from one language to another, but a character switch, as in the following. The opening two messages (by poster 1) are in vernacular Cantonese and written in *simplified* characters. 原来我记错左; 今个星期都系朝早去补 *Jyun lai ngo gei co zo; gam go sing kei dou hai*

FIGURE 5. Simplified-Traditional Chinese Character Switch

ciu zou heoi bou [Originally I remembered wrong. This week the tutoring class is in the morning]. The response is also in vernacular Cantonese, but in *traditional* Chinese characters: 死啦 咁你來5來得切去啊一家? *sei laa gam nei lai m lai dak cai heoi aa jat gaa* [Dead. Do you think you can make it this time?]. Following this switch, poster 1 responded, also in traditional characters: 黎唔切, 所以今日唔洗去 *Lai m cit, so ji gam jat m sai heoi* [Can't make it. So today I won't go]. The chat closes with poster 2's response, again in traditional characters, 咁都得 *gam dou dak* [That's all right].

While Macao's official language policy is to use traditional characters, simplified characters are not sanctioned. In commercial districts that appeal to Chinese tourists, such as in and around casinos, many signs and business advertisements are written in simplified characters. Furthermore, people who cross the border from Macao to China for work and/or school are exposed to and use both kinds of characters. Furthermore, when inputting characters on a mobile phone, the user can easily switch between simplified and traditional character sets. Hence, this may explain how and why the messages we have been discussing, written in vernacular Cantonese, display a switch from simplified to traditional characters.

When interview participants commented on this screenshot they noticed the character switch, but did not find it remarkable. Rather, their attention was drawn to the use of the number 5, in the form of an emoji (discussed later): 來 5 來. The meaning of the phrase was clear, as the number 5, *m* in Cantonese, is pronounced the same as the word for no or a negation, also *m*. The phrase literally means "come not come?"; it is a way to formulate a question. The usual way to write the question, based upon spoken vernacular Cantonese, is 黎唔切 (*lai m cit*); this is how poster 1 replied. Why did poster 2 write the phrase as來 5 來? The person who wrote this explained that she thought it was a "cute" and playful way to phrase the question. She also explained that it was easy to insert this emoji when typing on her phone.

Message Repairs

As studies in conversation analysis and ethnomethodology demonstrate, during workplace interaction participants develop ad hoc rules for how to respond to each other, as "context is both a project and a product of the participants' actions."[42] Such rules may be created and/or invoked when an apparent rule violation occurs. The following is one example of institutional talk. The participants were three friends who worked at the same company in Macao. Participant 1 opened with a question in English, "What's your plan these two days *kwan*"? Both participant 2 and participant 3 responded, using a style of English that may reflect an underlying Cantonese structure: "Don't actually have plans," dropping the implied initial pronoun "I" and the adjective "any." Likewise, participant 3 responded, "So u need party," a Cantonese-style construction, transforming the "to" infinitive "need [to] party" into a zero infinitive "need party." This exchange of messages apparently flowed smoothly, even with such phrases as "The interviews are on those three English paper owners." However, the last word of the final turn was marked as a mistake, when participant 1 wrote "bou." He then self-corrected and wrote "boy*," showing that the word was misspelled and that he knew how to spell it correctly.

When participants viewed this excerpt, they discussed a number of strategies for addressing mistakes. One tool that a number of them mentioned is the ability to "recall" a problematic message. If a message is sent to people who are not relationally close, or if the message is a job-related task, they will be more careful with message construction, and read it before sending it out. But if they send out a poorly worded message, or one with an obvious mistake, such as in this example, they will

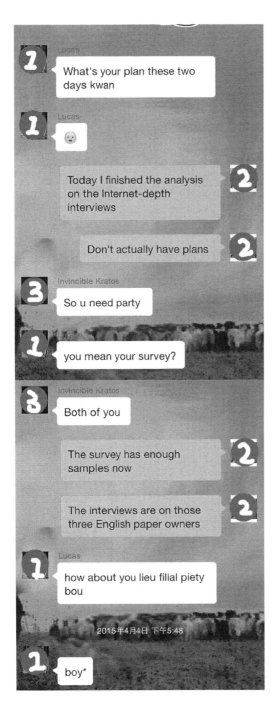

FIGURE 6. English Language Repair

try to recall it. Or, another tactic, as in this message, was to repair the message with an asterisk, thereby marking the correction.[43] This we see in the last turn: "boy*." But, participants explained, if they are chatting with close friends, they usually do not correct mistakes such as misspellings, wrong characters, or inappropriate emoji. Instead mistakes may be overlooked or left unmarked, because friends would be more likely to understand the intent and meaning of such messages. Friends who want a clarification can ask for it, just as a repair could be made in face-to-face conversation.

Emoji, Rules, Generational Differences

Perhaps one of the most interesting features of WeChat messages is the use of emoji and stickers. In early text-based computer-mediated communication, users would "accent" messages with pictorial images called "emoticons," such as the well-known smiley face :).[44] With the development of online technologies, especially the smartphone, a greater array of "emotion" accents have been created, most notably in Japan, where such images were first called "emoji."[45]

Figure 7 is a short message shared between two colleagues at a company in Macao. It is comprised of mixed codes: vernacular Cantonese, English, and emoji. An English translation is provided in order to show meaning and word order.

1 Ha ha. Good news, helen and bond bond this week both did confirm to do one event, since [the time] they came into the company, it is for them the first real time that they have done one by themselves, using their own hands and feet.

　We give them a little encouragement with our applause

2 [Emoji indicating "Thumbs up"]

This is a series of complex, mixed-language messages; monolingual speakers of Cantonese and/or English would find them difficult to decipher. Note, for example, the second message: 我地比d. The first two characters, 我地 (*ngo dei*), are Cantonese for the plural pronoun "we." Next is a combined form 比d, pronounced in Cantonese as "bei + d." The character 比 in Standard Chinese means "to compare." However, here it signifies the verb "to give," based upon the Cantonese pronunciation of the character *bei*. In Standard Chinese this verb would be written as 給, and in the model Cantonese sentence shown above, this verb was written using

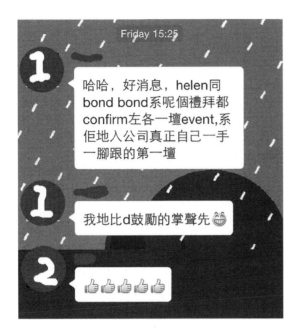

FIGURE 7. Emoji Rules and Cantonese Characters

the nonstandard character 畀. Likewise, the letter *d* is used for its sound qualities. The adjective meaning "a little" is pronounced "di" in Cantonese, but written as 點 in Standard Chinese.

This novel use of characters and Latin letters to represent vernacular Cantonese and English is common in messages shared among Macao's young adults. Perhaps because they are ubiquitous, other interviewees did not comment on this aspect of the message. The emoji, however, were remarked upon and discussed by interview participants:

> н: My friend said [my] messages were "too serious." So I forced myself to add emoji.
>
> н: If you add some relaxed expressions for them, . . . and they send you relaxed expressions, then you have a different language . . . and I feel there is better communication.
>
> ı: If [the emoji] is big, then you need only one. But if it is small, normally I will always put three together in a row.

H's friend said her messages were "too serious." Emoji were added to change the key of the message, to make it seem "relaxed" and less serious. This pattern of communication among youth who use WeChat is one that we have found else-where.[46] The emergent rule of putting three emoji together points to the emergence of a syntax that bridges China's youth across regions and linguistic fangyan.

In another interview, a participant spoke about the differences between "language" (文字 *man zi*) and emoji:

> Emoji is a picture. . . . And these pictures can express into language that feeling, that meaning that sometimes words cannot express. And sometimes you want to be vague; and sometimes words are a very explicit thing. And if you want to have a vague section of words, you can use these pictures that will allow for a vague expression of feeling. And it's also code switching, that lets you have different kinds of interpretations to come out.

For this participant, emoji and language, or written Chinese characters, were perceived differently. Written characters were sometimes believed to be "very explicit"—perhaps implicating the referrential function of language to name things or actions. Emoji, however, were described as "vague" and conveyed feelings and emotions, much as would be communicated nonverbally in face-to-face interaction. This allowed for the possibility of a code switch, a change in mood, and opening the message to multiple interpretations.

Later in this same interview Qiu asked participants about perceived genera-tional differences, if they used WeChat or other social media to communicate with their parents, and if they did, how their expressions and use of languages were similar or different. In response S said, "Every morning my mom gets up and plays on her iPad. Friends in her group will share new information. So she will slowly accept this, and she will also use these new expressions." This participant's mother apparently was learning "new expressions" while using her iPad and communicating with friends—peers of the same age—giving evidence to technological and communicative convergence. D and E, however, responded differently:

> D: If I send emoji to my mom, she doesn't understand what I'm sending her.
> E: Yeah. I'm the same. She will say, "What are you sending [me]? Don't play these things with me!"

These young people said that their mothers did not readily adopt the use of emoji in messages. For D's and E's elders, the meaning of emoji was unclear. E's mother saw it as a form of "play" and not suitable for conversation. Thus, while the emoji and new expressions were apparently adopted by some older folk, others did not adopt them; this indicates that language innovation may begin with younger people and then is adopted later by older folk.

Superior-Subordinate

The message in figure 8 was shared between Qiu and the boss at her former company. It has both code mixing and a code switch from Cantonese to English. We also see emoji and a repair. Yet it differs from others in tone, arguably because, as a form of institutional talk, it involved an exchange of messages between a superior (boss) and subordinate (employee).[47]

FIGURE 8. Superior-Subordinate Messages

QIU: *Zou san aa* Macy, *ming tin soeng ng lei wui hai gung si maa*

[Good morning *Macy*, will you be at the company tomorrow morning?]

MACY: *ngo daai koi zung ng sin faan* [smiley face emoji]

[I will probably be back at noon (smiley face emoji)]

MACY: *Yiqi (jat chhai)* lunch?

[Together lunch?]

QIU: *Hou aa* [smiley face emoji]

Yes aa [smiley face emoji]

MACY: [winking face emoji] see u than

MACY: then

Qiu opened with a formal greeting, "Good morning Macy." It was written not in Standard Chinese (早上好 *zaoshang hao*), but in Cantonese (早晨阿Macy). This was followed by the request "Will you be at the company tomorrow morning?" While written in vernacular Cantonese, it did not include emoji, which may indicate a more formal tone. In reply, the boss answered the question, "I will probably be back at noon." The adverb, probably (大概*daai koi*), appears to be a hedge, indicating politeness. Yet the message was closed with the addition of a single, small emoji, a smiley face, softening the message. Macy then added a tag question, written in mixed Chinese-English, 一起 "lunch?" This indexed the conversational implication that Qiu wished to meet her boss for lunch. In the third turn, Qiu accepted the request, replying with a mixed-code message, 好阿 (*hou-aa*), where the final particle *aa* 阿 indexes both a Cantonese, colloquial expression, and a phatic expression of agreement.[48] The text is followed by an emoji, a smiley face, reciprocating her boss's use of an Emoji.

For the final turn the boss switched from vernacular Cantonese and mixed Cantonese-English to English. The turn began with the "sly face" emoji, indicating agreement. This was followed by the English phrase "see u than." The word "than," however, was misspelled. Macy sent the word again with the corrected spelling, "then," in a repair.

When reflecting upon these messages, Qiu commented:

Based on the whole conversation, we are more like friends than [people in a] working relationship, which is hugely different from the stereotype [of] conversation between superordinate and subordinate. The addition of emoji eases the tension between each other during the communication. The emoji faces reflect senders' feelings, which makes emotions visible, [even though WeChat is] not face-to-face communication. For people with high-ranking position in workplace, [an] emoji makes them feel more approachable toward their employees.

The perception that WeChat is a platform that facilitates the lessening of social and power distance echoes what we found earlier: a person in a subordinate position, such as an employee or student, over the course of time may become less conscious of power and focus more on the content of a message and less on the social status of the sender.[49] These online practices may lessen relational and social distance.

Mixing and Voicing

The last screenshot, figure 9, is arguably the most complex. It combines the creative use of emoji, Cantonese, English, Chinese (simplified and traditional characters), and the picture of a famous Korean actor. The occasion for this message was the upcoming sixth anniversary of Sina, a media company in Macao. The Korean actor, Kim Soo-hyun, was well known in Macao, as he was named a winner in the Fifteenth Huading Awards for his role in the Korean drama *My Destiny* (the award is based upon viewers' survey of the top one hundred television series broadcast in China). Kim Soo-hyun was contacted by Sina employees who attended the Huading Awards ceremony. He consented to having his picture taken while holding the sign. On the upper left-hand corner of the sign there appears in English "To Sina Weibo." Underneath, in large letters, is the handwritten message in simplified Chinese characters, 新年快乐 (*Xinnian kuaile*), or "Happy New Year." Beneath is the same phrase written in Korean Hangul. At the bottom is the actor's signature. The image was then posted to Weibo (China's version of Twitter).

An employee who saw the actor's picture resent it to colleagues at Sina. Poster 2 posted a penguin emoji, followed by "Sina"—the name of the company. Poster 1 replied, in colloquial Cantonese (marked by 啦 *la*), "今天 bond bond 靠你啦" ("Today bond bond is depending upon you *la*"). Poster 2 replied: "嘟敏俊 xi." The three characters 嘟敏俊 are Do Min Joon, the actor's screen name written in Chinese; poster 2 made the name sound more "Korean" by adding *xi*, Korean

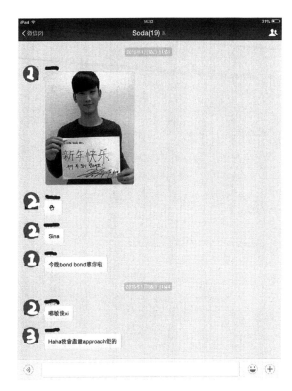

FIGURE 9. Voicing and Ventriloquizing a New Year's Greeting

for "Mr." The message closed as poster 3, writing in Cantonese—marked by the Cantonese character 佢 *keoi* (third-person pronoun): "Haha 我會盡量 approach 佢的" ("I will do my best to approach his [fame/achievement]").

1 *Korean actor Kim Soo-hyun*
  新年快乐
  Happy New Year
2 Penguin emoji
2 Sina [addressee, company in Macao]
1 今天 bond bond 靠你啦
  Today bond bond is depending upon you la
2 嘟敏俊 xi
  Do Min Joon xi [Kim's character on show, *My Destiny*]
3 Haha 我會盡量 approach 佢的
  I will do my best to approach his [fame/achievement]

This exchange shows a way to creatively insert images to create different personas. The three participants engaged with the Korean actor's picture, speaking for and through it. In the last turn, poster 3 responded to "him" by promising to work hard and "approach" his accomplishment. Here we see what Bakhtin would call "voicing," showing how language has the "taste" of a context and is populated by intentions.[50] That is, the participants animated and responded to the actor as though he were speaking to them, manipulating him like a puppet—a kind of discourse that Cooren and Sandler would call "ventriloquated."[51]

From this we see how WeChat users could do more than simply share propositional content. They creatively used a variety of linguistic forms—Cantonese, Standard Chinese, traditional and simplified characters, English, emoji—to create messages that are humorous, build social rapport, and cut across social barriers. In other words, while their spoken and written Cantonese may originate in the speech and writings of previous generations, they are creating new mixed forms, new vocabularies, and new rules. And this may lead to a new identity, one that is not limited to one side of the Macao-Zhuhai border, but in an online medium that can be shared across all of China, and beyond.

Conclusion

We began this chapter with the observation that some scholars have failed to acknowledge China's linguistic diversity. In the modern period and since the fall of the Qing Dynasty, both the ROC and PRC governments have supported a single, national language (or common language, *putonghua*). Yet, as we have argued, the data presented illuminate a different and more diverse side of "China," one that uses a local *fangyan*, Cantonese, English, Mandarin, and emoji to create new message forms. These may symbolically index and construct imagined communities linked to a place (e.g., Hong Kong/Macau), or a generation (i.e., youth conversant in online communicative practices). We have shown how new communication technologies and platforms such as the app WeChat allow for the space and context where novel and creative communication practices can emerge and converge. The mixed, online communication codes developed by youth in the Macao-Zhuhai region incorporate a variety of languages and registers—including Standard Chinese, a *fangyan*, English, and other forms—a conclusion that coincides with earlier observations in Taiwan, Hong Kong, Shanghai, and other regions of China.[52]

We draw two implications from this study. The first is that online forms of communication, especially the kinds of short chats and messages shared on WeChat, may afford the creation of novel words and expressions. Macao's multilingual young adults communicate on their mobile phones using WeChat, with processes of code switching, code mixing, and a wide range of linguistic codes, including Cantonese, English, Standard Chinese, emoji, and even Korean. While some members of older generations found the creation and use of new words and expressions unintelligible, and/or too "playful" to count as serious communication, all these converging factors produced the unique cultural context for modes of expression that this generation of youth interpreted as lessening social distance and creating relational closeness.

A point of interest is how young adults are embracing the use of emoji. These representational and highly visualized symbols are used to accent messages, impart affect, and change the relational quality of exchanges. Perhaps one appeal of emoji is that they work socio-pragmatically as "nonreferential indexes" and derive their meaning by pointing to some dimension of interactional and cultural context.[53] That is, an Emoji symbol is attractive because it is "vague" and "open" to multiple interpretations, and not "limited" or "closed" in meaning, as Chinese characters might be perceived. While modes of communication increasingly converge on and between WeChat and other social media platforms, meanings cannot be fully closed; new mixed linguistic forms and terms, emoji, images, and others, facilitate greater polysemy just as in the offline world, where ritual objects can have multiple meanings.[54] And thus, online language games show us how languages come together and fragment apart at the same time, how China is complexly both unified and diverse, and how identity is continually evolving.

Our second implication is a critique of an argument made by McWhorter, who saw in Chinese culture the power to unify China's many unintelligible *fangyan*, or "dialects."[55] While it may be that dialect writing was severely sanctioned and in decline during the second half of the twentieth century, it has not died out entirely.[56] We find, and regularly encounter, vernacular Cantonese writing in both Hong Kong and Macao. Recent studies conducted both in Hong Kong and in Guangdong province indicate high regard for Cantonese.[57] With new communication technologies and online platforms, vernacular Cantonese is oftentimes used in an even more mixed manner as young adults create new characters, expressions, and forms, during diglossic situations.[58] This may foretell of possible convergences in the communicative practices of youth across greater China, with the sharing of new terms, expressions, and ways to embed emoji and images into their chats. At the same time, we do not foresee dialect forms of writing and speaking being erased by standard *putonghua*.[59] Rather, we argue that Cantonese and other nonstandard varieties will continue on, albeit in supplemental new forms, for instance, their use by youth to highlight or animate their voices and intentions.

We argue that a better way of understanding the appearance of a unified cultural China is to see it as the imposition of the Party, state, and government—or in the premodern period, the empire. When the power of the state was strong in the twentieth century and mass media (e.g., newspapers, radio, television) grew to reach all parts of China, there was a movement toward greater linguistic and cultural unity. This arguably is true of China's post-1980s generation, who were educated in *putonghua* and standard written Chinese. However, movement toward a cultural standard is perhaps countered by the development of new and evolving forms of communication, namely via social media and online communication. Converging factors produce this unique and culturally diverse context for more open modes of expression and inclusiveness, yet they also empower Chinese *fangyan* to develop in alternative and nonunitary fashion. This is not unique to Macao and has been observed in the online communication of youth in other regions of China.[60]

Young people, who are ready adopters of new technologies and the generation most likely to participate in and create novel linguistic forms, are finding avenues along the communication supply chain to develop and express new voices. This does not necessarily mean that all will write or speak using the same vernacular *fangyan* of previous generations, or that a particular *fangyan* will spread across China. Rather, young people are incorporating a mix of words, images, codes, and texts that they understand. Online platforms and new technological tools provide them with more access and power to construct new iterations and unique identity expressions that may in turn be shared globally.

NOTES

1. Jared Diamond, *Guns, Germs, and Steel: The Fates of Human Societies* (New York: Norton, 1999); Jared Diamond, *Collapse: How Societies Choose to Fail or Survive* (New York: Penguin, 2005).

2. John McWhorter, *Word on the Street: Debunking the Myth of "Pure" Standard English* (Cambridge, MA: Perseus Publishing, 1998), 178.

3. *Fangyan* is most often translated as "dialect," but can also be translated as "local

language" or "topolect." See Victor H. Mair, "What Is a Chinese 'Dialect/Topolect'? Reflections on Some Key Sino-English Linguistic Terms," *Sino-Platonic Papers* 29 (1991): 1–31.

4. Stanley Rosen, "Contemporary Chinese Youth and the State," *Journal of Asian Studies* 68, no. 2 (2009): 359–369.

5. Todd L. Sandel and Bei Ju, "The Code of WeChat: Chinese Students' Cell Phone Social Media Practices," in *Communicating User Experience: Applying Local Strategies to Digital Media Design*, ed. Trudy Milburn (Lanham, MD: Lexington Books, 2015), 103–126.

6. Wei Zhang, "Multilingual Creativity on China's Internet," *World Englishes* 34 (2015): 231–246.

7. Jerry Norman, *Chinese* (Cambridge: Cambridge University Press, 1988), 187–188.

8. Todd L. Sandel, "Dialects," in *The International Encyclopedia of Language and Social Interaction*, ed. Karen Tracy, Todd L. Sandel, and Cornelia Ilie (Boston: John Wiley & Sons, 2015), 351–364.

9. See Benedict Anderson, *Imagined Communities: Reflections on the Origin and Spread of Nationalism*, rev. ed. (New York: Verso, 1991); for a study using Anderson's concept to make sense of contemporary China see Stephen J. Hartnett, Lisa B. Keränen, and Donovan Conley, eds., *Imagining China: Rhetorics of Nationalism in an Age of Globalization* (East Lansing: Michigan State University Press, 2017).

10. Literary Chinese, also called "Classical Chinese," is a translation of the term *Wenyanwen*. Norman, *Chinese*, 133.

11. David C. S. Li, "Chinese as a Lingua Franca in Greater China," *Annual Review of Applied Linguistics* 26 (2006): 149–176.

12. Donald B. Snow, *Cantonese as Written Language: The Growth of a Written Chinese Vernacular* (Hong Kong: Hong Kong University Press, 2004).

13. John K. Fairbanks and Edwin O. Reischauer, *China: Tradition and Transformation* (Boston: Houghton Mifflin, 1989).

14. Chris Wen-Chao Li, "Conflicting Notions of Language Purity: The Interplay of Archaising, Ethnographic, Reformist, Elitist and Xenophobic Purism in the Perception of Standard Chinese," *Language & Communication* 24 (2004): 97–133.

15. Mandarin phonetic symbols are colloquially known as *BoPoMoFo*, named after the first four characters of this pronunciation system. Li, "Conflicting Notions"; Norman, *Chinese*; Todd L. Sandel, "Linguistic Capital in Taiwan: The KMT's Mandarin Language Policy and Its Perceived Impact upon the Language Practices of Bilingual Mandarin and Tai-gi Speakers," *Language in Society* 32, no. 4 (2003): 523–551.

16. Li, "Conflicting Notions." Li, "Chinese as a Lingua Franca," 155.

17. Todd L. Sandel, Hsin-I Sydney Yueh, and Peih-ying Lu, "Some Distinctive Taiwanese

Communication Practices and Their Cultural Meanings," in *The Handbook of Communication in Cross-Cultural Perspective*, ed. Donal A. Carbaugh (New York: Routledge, 2017), 118–128.

18. David Bradley, "Introduction: Language Policy and Language Endangerment in China," *International Journal of the Sociology of Language* 173 (2005): 1–21; Lau Chun Fat, "A Dialect Murders Another Dialect: The Case of Hakka in Hong Kong," *International Journal of the Sociology of Language* 173 (2005): 23–35; Li, "Chinese as a Lingua Franca."

19. Michael J. Enright, Edith E. Scott, and Ka-mun Chang, *Regional Powerhouse: The Greater Pearl River Delta and the Rise of China* (New York: John Wiley & Sons, 2005).

20. Li, "Chinese as a Lingua Franca."

21. Guobin Yang, *The Power of the Internet in China* (New York: Columbia University Press, 2009).

22. Loretta Fung and Ronald Carter, "New Varieties, New Creativities: ICQ and English-Cantonese E Discourse," *Language and Literature* 16, no. 4 (2007): 345–366; Loretta Fung and Ronald Carter, "Cantonese E-Discourse: A New Hybrid Variety of English," *Multilingua* 26, no. 1 (2007): 35–66. Zhang, "Multilingual Creativity."

23. Sandel and Ju, "The Code of WeChat."

24. Snow, *Cantonese as Written Language.*

25. Donald B. Snow, "Chinese Dialect as Written Language: The Cases of Taiwanese and Cantonese," *Journal of Asian Pacific Communication* 4, no. 1 (1993): 15–30; Snow, *Cantonese as Written Language.*

26. Snow, *Cantonese as Written Language.*

27. Ibid.

28. Adapted from Gisela Bruche Schulz, "'Fuzzy' Chinese: The Status of Cantonese in Hong Kong," *Journal of Pragmatics* 27 (1997): 295–314. Cantonese words and phrases are written in *Jyutping*, without tonal marks, in accord with a system developed by the Linguistic Society of Hong Kong; Standard, Mandarin Chinese is written in Pinyin.

29. Mark Bray and Ramsey Koo, "Postcolonial Patterns and Paradoxes: Language and Education in Hong Kong and Macao," *Comparative Education* 40, no. 2 (2004): 224.

30. Ming Yee Carissa Young, "Multilingual Education in Macao," *International Journal of Multilingualism* 6, no. 4 (2009): 416.

31. Bray and Koo, "Postcolonial Patterns and Paradoxes"; see also Xi Yan and Andrew Moody, "Language and Society in Macao: A Review of Sociolinguistic Studies on Macao in the Past Three Decades," *Chinese Language and Discourse* 1, no. 2 (2010): 293–324.

32. Bill Chou, "Local Autonomy in Action: Beijing's Hong Kong and Macau Policies," *Journal of Current Chinese Affairs* 42, no. 3 (2013): 29–54.

33. Xin Guan and Todd L. Sandel, "The Acculturation and Identity of New Immigrant Youth in Macao," *China Media Research* 11, no. 1 (2015): 112–124.

34. Yan and Moody, "Language and Society."

35. Aqil M. Azmi and Eman A. Aljafari, "Modern Information Retrieval in Arabic: Catering to Standard and Colloquial Arabic," *Journal of Information Science* 41, no. 4 (2014): 506–517.

36. Zhang, "Multilingual Creativity." Jin Liu, "Deviant Writing and Youth Identity: Representation of Dialects with Chinese Characters on the Internet," *Chinese Language and Discourse* 2, no. 1 (2011): 58–79. Sandel and Ju, "The Code of WeChat."

37. Simon Atkinson, "WeChat Hits One Billion Monthly Users—Are You One of Them?," *BBC News*, March 6, 2018, http://www.bbc.com/news/business-43283690. Sandel and Ju, "The Code of WeChat."

38. Sandel and Ju, "The Code of WeChat."

39. "2014 Nian Aomen Hulian Wang Shiyong Zhuangkuang Diaocha Fangfa Ji Zhuyao Jieguo" [Year 2014 Major Findings from a Survey of the Uses, and Situation of Macao Internet Users], *The Internet Is Changing our Lives Socially, Politically, Economically and Culturally*, 2015, http://www.macaoInternetproject.net/index.php/blog/2014/08/20140704a/3/澳門互聯網調查結果 (accessed November 13, 2015).

40. See Barbara E. Bullock and Almeida Jacqueline Toribio, "Themes in the Study of Code-Switching," in *The Cambridge Handbook of Linguistic Code-Switching*, ed. Barbara E. Bullock and Almeida Jacqueline Toribio (Cambridge: Cambridge University Press, 2009), 1–17. Following from their work, we claim that in a code switch a speaker alternates languages at the sentence or phrase level, keeping each separate, as the following: "How are you doing? *Wo hen hao* [I am well]." In a code mix languages are not kept separate; syntax and morphology are mixed such that a monolingual speaker of either would find an expression unintelligible, for example: "*Wo mingtian yao* go home [Tomorrow I will go home]."

41. Fung and Carter, "Cantonese E-Discourse"; Rint Sybesma and Boya Li, "The Dissection and Structural Mapping of Cantonese Sentence Final Particles," *Lingua* 117, no. 10 (2007): 1739–1783.

42. Paul Drew and John Heritage, "Analyzing Talk at Work: An Introduction," in *Talk at Work: Interaction in Institutional Settings* ed. Paul Drew and John Heritage (Cambridge: Cambridge University Press, 1992), 3–65. Carly W. Butler and Richard Fitzgerald, "'My F***ing Personality': Swearing as Slips and Gaffes in Live Television Broadcasts," *Text & Talk* 31, no. 5 (2011): 525–551. John Heritage, "Conversation Analysis and Institutional Talk," in *Handbook of Language and Social Interaction*, ed. Kristine L Fitch and Robert E. Sanders (Mahwah, NJ: Lawrence Erlbaum, 2005), 105.

43. See Lauren Brittany Collister, "*-Repair in Online Discourse," *Journal of Pragmatics* 43 (2011): 918–921.

44. Eli Dresner and Susan C. Herring, "Functions of the Nonverbal in CMC: Emoticons and Illocutionary Force," *Communication Theory* 20, no. 3 (2010): 249–268; Joseph B. Walther and Kyle P. D'Addario, "The Impacts of Emoticons on Message Interpretation in Computer-Mediated Communication," *Social Science Computer Review* 19, no. 3 (2001): 324–347.

45. Sandel and Ju, "The Code of WeChat."

46. Ibid.

47. Heritage, "Conversational Analysis."

48. See Sybesma and Li, "Dissection and Structural Mapping."

49. Sandel and Ju, "The Code of WeChat."

50. Mikhail Bakhtin, *The Dialogic Imagination: Four Essays*, ed. Michael Holquist, trans. Caryl Emerson and Michael Holquist (Austin: University of Texas Press, 1981), 293.

51. François Cooren and Sergeiy Sandler, "Polyphony, Ventriloquism, and Constitution: In Dialogue with Bakhtin," *Communication Theory* 24, no. 3 (2014): 225–244.

52. Hsi-Yao Su, "Reconstructing Taiwanese and Taiwan Guoyu on the Taiwan-Based Internet," *Journal of Asian Pacific Communication* 19, no. 2 (2009): 313–335. Fung and Carter, "New Varieties." Zhang, "Multilingual Creativity." Liu, "Deviant Writing."

53. Michael Silverstein, "Shifters, Linguistic Categories, and Cultural Description," in *Language, Culture, and Society: A Book of Readings*, ed. Benjamin Blount (Prospect Heights, IL: Waveland Press, 1995), 187–221.

54. Wendy Leeds-Hurwitz, *Wedding as Text: Communicating Cultural Identities through Ritual* (New York: Routledge, 2002).

55. McWhorter, *Word on the Street.*

56. See Sandel, "Linguistic Capital in Taiwan," for a description of Taiwan's past strict "dialect" suppression policies.

57. Julie May Groves, "Language or Dialect, Topolect or Regiolect? A Comparative Study of the Language Attitudes towards the Status of Cantonese in Hong Kong," *Journal of Multilingual and Multicultural Development* 31, no. 6 (2010): 531–551. Dana Funywe Ng and Juanjuan Zhao, "Investigating Cantonese Speakers' Language Attitudes in Mainland China," *Journal of Multilingual and Multicultural Development* 36, no. 4 (2015): 357–371.

58. See Fung and Carter, "Cantonese E-Discourse."

59. Liu, "Deviant Writing."

60. Ibid.

"Plowing Fortunes," or Fine Wine with Chinese Characteristics

US and UK Media Representations of the Chinese Wine Industry

David R. Gruber

A mountain of books and news articles over the past five years have anxiously pronounced the so-called rise of China.[1] The body of research in rhetorical studies likewise expands, focusing on social and political discourses about China and the foreign media frames regarding China.[2] Amid the broader conversation around China's influence resides a striking number of news reports focusing on China's engagement with Western cultural practices signifying power and elitism, including China's new "thirst for fine wine."[3]

The Telegraph recently reported "wine mania," as Chinese businessmen have purchased up to one hundred Bordeaux vineyards.[4] The *New Republic* employed militaristic terms, stating that China "conquered France's wine country."[5] Likewise, the *International Business Times* recently declared China "a wine power," referring not only to China's mass consumption of wine—estimated at two billion bottles per year—but also referring to its desire to cultivate world-leading fine wine, a move seemingly aligned with the CPC's (Communist Party of China, or Party hereafter) aspirations to exert "soft power" as it aims to become a "world superpower."[6]

Describing the attention to wine through a geopolitical lens, Maguire and Lim propose that media representations associate wine with "cultural legitimacy, savoir faire, sophistication, and high culture," yet British and American media rhetorically

2

7

position China as indelibly lacking in cultural capital. Maguire and Lim accuse the media of perpetuating a one-sided "geopolitics of consumption." The result, they argue, is a paradox: "Despite China's economic power, its legitimacy on a global scale remains low with regard to global hierarchies of taste and distribution of prestige." Put simply, Maguire and Lim account for negative representations of Chinese wine drinkers through appeals to an unsettling shift in the global power balance. Wine culture is one place, they argue, where scholars can see Western media "defending their style of life as superior or more civilized" such that when "ascendant groups" move to adopt those styles, they are rejected and new styles then forge new unattainable paths for legitimacy.[7] In terms of cultural convergence, Maguire and Lim point to the ways that geopolitics, the exercise of soft power, the consumption of elite products, the media narratives surrounding them, and the legitimacy of "taste" all come crashing together in complex and interactional ways.

Accounting for negative representations of the rise of China by setting Western media outlets in the role of mouthpiece for political interests threatened by China has now become somewhat commonplace. A bevy of recent scholarship draws strong connections between geopolitical concerns and Western media representations, lambasting news conglomerates for harboring anti-Chinese colonial attitudes rooted ultimately in regional insecurity or cultural prejudice. Mawdsley, for instance, investigates media reports about Chinese interests in Africa, arguing that UK newspapers "tend toward the simplistic binary between well-intentioned West and amoral, greedy and coldly indifferent Chinese" in an effort to delegitimize Chinese development.[8] Likewise, Suspitsyna asserts that the *Chronicle of Higher Education* routinely positions China as "culturally inferior Other" by negatively portraying its education system and setting up unfair comparisons with the United States, effectively positioning US universities within a frame of "global governmentality" even amid a "rhetoric of well-intentioned proclamations about building the US-China friendship."[9] Naduvath suggests that contemporary "geopolitical anxieties" as well as an "anti-communist motivation" account for distortions of Chinese identities and cultures prevalent in Western media, where values of democratic pluralism are privileged and where any shift in the "global power architecture" produces immediate resistance.[10] The overarching conclusion from such research may be that "media scripts can (re)produce and circulate geopolitical understandings as well as unsettle them."[11] The media are undoubtedly capable of investing geopolitical anxieties into interpretations of news events; as Paterson and Nothias note, the news is a cultural text imbued with colonial attitudes and may tend to produce "representations that sustain colonial ideologies."[12] Even so, it remains an open question as to whether present geopolitics or colonial remnants are a sufficient explanation for negative representations of China when examined in the context of specific social conversations.

This chapter focuses on recent US and UK media coverage about the development of China's own homegrown wine industry, investigating within that circumscribed sphere the extent to which Chinese economic and cultural developments remain tethered to global geopolitics as a basis for explaining the presence of any unflattering or damaging representations. This chapter also explores the extent to which Chinese wine cultivation is rhetorically compared with and against Western wine cultures to understand if and when the media govern ideas about the wine industry in China through the reproduction of colonial or Western narratives. Looking across twenty-five articles published by major media outlets in the United States and United Kingdom between 2013 and 2016 (CNN, the *New York Times*, *The Guardian*, BBC, *The Telegraph*), the study confirms the presence of negative, even politically suppressive, representations of China and the palpable imposition of geopolitical discourses as frameworks for interpretation. However, this study also complicates past scholarship by suggesting that negative comparisons to Western wine cultures are not forwarded *solely* with reference to anxious geopolitical realignments but *also* with persistent reference to the problems of capitalism and the need for a set of viticultural ideals—ones specific to wine agriculture, usually encompassed by the word "terroir"—to mitigate those problems. Put another way, convergence among politics and media discourses about wine in China necessarily encounter economic structures as well as cultural and subcultural impositions alongside the material limitations of farming.

The sampled texts, I argue, expose more of the story about why Chinese farmers' (lack of) attention to lifestyle and land management exists as a salient point of discussion in Western media representations and why such representations serve as seemingly valid critiques of China's fine-wine industry. That is, I advance a thesis that fast-moving capitalist development, as evident in China's wine industry, is perceived in Western media as disadvantageous to winemakers; this perception opens up the room to critique the CPC's exercise of capital and heightens the rhetorical appeal of terroir—a predominantly Western glorification of how the soil and climate of a region mesh with grape varietals over long periods of time to produce an expression fitting local preferences in a region, something itself cultivated over several generations.[13] The slow development of land, the meticulous selection of the varietal, the careful choice of the vintner in cutting growth, the measured pace of vine maturation, and the declaration that generations are needed to understand how to operate a high-quality vineyard all converge within Western media representations and are worth investigating, especially when the taste of a glass of Chinese wine can so easily serve as a synecdoche for feelings about China and be a vehicle for critiques of fast-moving development under "capitalism with Chinese characteristics."[14] This is not to suggest that media discourses raising questions about vineyard management or land management are not overlapping with geopolitics; they are. Rather, this is to say that in the world of communication convergence, discussions about China's wine, in particular, are complex formations, sets of intermeshed ideas about capitalism, government control, viticulture planning, wine characteristics, food culture, and politics.

Of course, any celebration of terroir in the relevant news texts likely foregrounds and benefits an elite subcultural group of winemakers and seems, almost inescapably, saturated with the privilege of a dominant class able to give the time and resources to a lifestyle of wine.[15] Accordingly, any attention to terroir—or more generally to the celebration of slow farming—cannot be considered completely independent from colonial histories or present geopolitical anxieties. These are inherently entangled insofar as economic realities, trade agreements, ownership rights, technological solutions, pest control, and so on, together forging agriculture methods and ideas about how to best cultivate products. Nevertheless, taking notice of such references in conjunction with economic and geopolitical anxieties in popular news discourses proves useful to mapping and unpacking the media landscape, to developing alternative rhetorical responses for Chinese wine growers, and to suggesting new ways of reporting for news agencies. Overall, I plan to make more evident converging trends across geopolitics, economics, material infrastructures, and cultural ideals in media discourses.

In particular, better understanding how "terroir" converges with geopolitical frameworks aids in evaluating why the Chinese wine industry is represented as a distasteful product, literally, of China's rapid industrialization. Such portrayals, judging Chinese land developers as moving too fast and hyperconcerned with profit at the expense of product and planning, constructs an image of capitalism as a wild tangle that must be trimmed and managed, like the operations of the vineyard, to create good wine. This analysis adds complexity to past media scholarship on negative representations of China's wine industry, demonstrating how geopolitics can and does surface within discourses of state power under threat *as well as* within subtle cultural expressions at the nexus of agriculture and economics.

The analysis also stages a positive challenge to those overseeing and working within the Chinese wine industry to think specific situations and locales through the perspective of convergence. The goal, as oft repeated in China, to ensure the harmonious balance between people and nature indeed foregrounds convergence because the pursuit necessarily aims to regard all of the varied discourses and materialities that occur jointly around things like making wine. State-guided "harmonization" cannot become a reality without analyzing how people nurture wine, how they fund it, how they actually encounter it, how they talk about it, where they send it, how they use it, and then, of course, whether it appeals to foreigners, and what it tastes like to locals when paired with distinctive Chinese foods. Harmony and balance is itself *of and about convergence.* Although I start with Western media texts, I hope to show that these are useful toward discovering latent rhetorical potentials and themselves point toward interesting convergences worth consideration.

In like manner, I also offer a challenge to Western media outlets. Calling attention to unfair or easy metaphors in prominent news texts foregrounds an inordinate focus on Western habits, expectations, and routine forms of communication; the intellectual effort implies the need for a greater emphasis on Chinese situations, habits, and specific local discourses. In fact, if media outlets necessarily generate new rhetorical capacities when granting coverage to any topic, then avoiding simplistic or dualistic discussions about complex issues has built-in positive implications. Here, in this particular case, the question for the media when considering the realities of what this volume describes as "convergence" is probably not how much China's homegrown wine tastes like France's or America's nor how far ahead or behind Chinese wine producers might appear to be, but why wine is interesting in China, what the wine does for China, and what makes this or that wine look and feel "Chinese" to different audiences; the engagement, at that point, must go far beyond well-wrought Western metaphors. In fact, wine development imposes material conditions that can ultimately and should—it seems fair to assert—serve Chinese people and palates from within their own descriptions and points of view. The aim, of course, is not to give over coverage to those being covered but, rather, to turn the rhetorical realities of convergence back on one's self to realize that we are all caught up in social-historical-material-symbolic machinations that often require foregrounding another's perspective or writing a story without the good-bad, right-wrong, tasteful-tasteless, state-versus-state invocations that breed ruptures where bridges are needed.

Methods Overview

The Guardian recently described China's rapid development of vineyards as a new "gold rush," offering a particularly potent metaphor within the context of media representations of China's wine industry.[16] Using the "gold rush" as an entry point, I build a qualitative examination drawing from rhetorical scholarship about the discourses of China as well as from metaphoric criticism in rhetorical studies, interrogating the social and political undercurrents articulated across several media reports of China's wine region.[17] After a discussion of text selection and a review of metaphoric criticism, I detail several characteristic examples.

Moving from the "gold rush" metaphor to several related "frontier" metaphors in the data set, I argue that the sampled texts infuse historical anxieties about the boom-and-bust patterns of capitalism into viticultural arenas even as they advance the centrality of terroir to support critiques of Chinese development, demonstrating convergence across these arenas. Yet I suggest that these frontier metaphors also expose positive, alternative rhetorical strategies for those invested in the Chinese wine industry. The conclusion outlines new metaphoric strategies, following Marita Gronnvoll and Jamie Landau's (2010) recommendation that rhetoricians can consider how an existing metaphor might be positively reconfigured.[18] The result is a suggestion for redirecting the "frontier" toward an emphasis on Chinese inventiveness; further, I argue for the reclamation of terroir in (re)presenting the land through a Chinese lens, a terroir with *Chinese characteristics*, advancing a rhetoric of the people's affective investment in Chinese land and the distinctiveness of Chinese food and palates in conjunction with addressing economic factors that might undermine the ability of Chinese vintners to manufacture and market a specifically local production.

On Text Selection

To facilitate the study, archive searches of specific news databases were conducted. Investigation of news archives ensured total coverage across specific US and UK news outlets, including CNN, the *New York Times*, BBC, *The Guardian*, and *The Telegraph*. These five media outlets were chosen due to their global, wide-ranging impact. They also proved pertinent because they were the foundation for other studies examining China's wine industry.[19]

Text selection within each news archive followed a criterion-based sampling method adhering to three criteria: (1) results must be fairly recent—between November 2012 and November 2015, (2) results must be published as news or as lifestyles articles, not explicitly marked as political opinion pieces or advertisements, and so on, and (3) results must have both headlines and text related specifically to China's wine industry.[20] The search relied upon the search term "China wine," sorted by relevance.

In total, twenty-five articles fit the criteria. Eight derived from US news outlets, four from CNN, and four from the *New York Times*. Seventeen derived from UK media outlets, four from the BBC, five from *The Guardian*, and eight from *The Telegraph*. Upon dividing them into two groups—(A) those that focused specifically on new wines being grown in China versus (B) those focusing on China's interest in purchasing foreign wines—a total of nine articles fell into Group A. Focusing only on Group A allowed the study to remain centered on media representations of China's burgeoning wine region, allowing comparisons to prove more targeted and, thus, more illuminating with respect to China's domestic production and development.

On Metaphoric Criticism

Because metaphoric criticism is not a single, defined methodology in the field of rhetoric, this chapter follows the approach laid out by Stern and subsequently adopted by Condit et al. in their analysis of genes in scientific discourse.[21] The analysis hinges on identifying key metaphors and then analyzing them in terms of the "tenor" and the "vehicle," critically adhering to an interactionist view presuming that "metaphors are active together" such that comparing two things/ideas creates new potentials when employed in a new context.[22] In this respect, Stern's approach examines possibilities for interpretation only inside of a particular context. Supporting this mode of analysis, Stern argues that one thing/idea is metaphorically elucidated through another but that the context determines the presuppositions and beliefs swimming within the interpretation such that some interpretive possibilities become more plausible than others without one single idea necessarily cognitively dominating independent of context.[23] The approach is generally aligned with rhetorical scholars who recognize the importance of attending to specific environments, audiences, and affects when examining texts, situating metaphors as much more than conceptual enhancement.[24]

In a mode familiar to rhetorical inquiry, metaphors do not merely serve an "illuminary function" intended to embellish or make "matters more intelligible to an audience."[25] They are "modes of perception."[26] The role of the scholar in conducting metaphoric criticism, then, is to elicit and elucidate "the perceptions and inferences that follow from it and the actions that are sanctioned by it."[27] Following this rhetorical position, I do not assume that any metaphors "have innate, monosemic meanings that determine the mindsets of those who use them" but, rather, entail "a set of diverse potential meanings."[28] In brief, I take context and audience to matter substantively when analyzing metaphors.

I proceed by examining a range of popular US and UK news texts to call attention to similarities in conceptual relationships, that is, repeated imagery used to describe the Chinese wine industry, often similar in tone or history. I then argue for the relevance of specific interpretations drawing from historical and cultural sources and the aforementioned rhetorical scholarship on China.[29] Following Stern in this respect, I identify metaphors to elicit and elucidate "those particular properties that are in fact M-associated [creatively linked] with those expressions in that context."[30] To this end, I set the stage with a brief discussion of headlines appearing in the data set and then move to interpret the metaphoric depictions, arguing that critiques of China's terroir emerge from these depictions and prove salient for Western readers precisely because of the way that geopolitical anxieties converge with economic worries and the material limitations or difficulties of growing wine.

Geopolitical Headlines on China's Wine Industry

Antagonistic geopolitical metaphors, perhaps unavoidably, abound in Western news reports about China, even within the most mundane topic areas. Reports about China's burgeoning wine industry are no exception; war and conquer metaphors are peppered throughout. In the sampled texts, headlines range from "China Overtakes France for Red Wine" to "Red Dawn for Chinese Wine."[31] Such headlines imply geopolitical invasion and reek of an existential threat to Western empire.

The "red dawn" metaphor is especially interesting in this regard, as it likely refers to a 1980s film where the United States is invaded by the Soviet Union. In *Red Dawn*, US citizens must resist occupation to preserve their national identity and ideals, fighting against a red Communist sun rising. Likewise, the metaphor could recall the mariner's folktale about seeing a "red dawn" and predicting good weather due to an effect produced by light passing through air particles preceding a high-pressure system, a metaphor that tellingly implies change—as well as good fortune for China and, perhaps in ironic juxtaposition, the thick presence of industrial smog—while drawing on the official color of the Communist Party.[32]

Threatening war and conquer metaphors demonstrate the persistence of geopolitical frameworks of interpretation in discussions of China's expanding wine industry, as confirmed by other scholars.[33] However, metaphors appealing to an international rat race for wealth and power also remain prominent, raising the question of how they are incorporated into texts, and to what ends. Looking first to the "gold rush" metaphor as a prominent example allows investigation into the assumptions and presumptions swimming within the body of sampled texts. To explore the data set, three characteristic examples are discussed and analyzed, starting with *The Guardian's* depiction of a new Chinese "gold rush."

The Gold Rush Metaphor

A June 2016 edition of *The Guardian* features an article with the title "China's Bordeaux: Winemakers in 'Gold Rush' to Turn Deserts into Vineyards: International Wine Giants and the Super Rich Are Plowing Their Fortunes into an Arid Corner of Ningxia Region."[34] Treating the title (and subtitle) as critically informative, three overarching implications, indeed themes, become immediately evident. The first is the time-dependent nature of the enterprise, that is, associating growth in the wine industry with the frenzy of the famous gold rushes of the 1800s in both the United States and Australasia. The second theme is a concern about the climatic and geological fitness for viticulture in China, evidenced within descriptions like "arid region," which can indicate an ability to grow concentrated wines or a difficulty in making wine. The third theme is the attention to the actors involved. In this case, the author makes clear that "plowing fortunes" does not refer to poor people working hard jobs to earn well-deserved money; it refers to rich people getting richer on the backs of the poor. The "plowing" is both a plowing over as well as a plowing through.

Thinking these themes together results in a complicated image of China's new industry, implying winners and losers, booms and busts. At the very least, the article expresses doubt about the industry's conditions for success. Stories of "migrant workers" toughing out "punishing" winters in China and carving up "rocky soils" play with the multiplicities and vagaries of language to imply future potentials while keeping optimism on a short leash. The agricultural context for the gold rush metaphor—hard labor and tough lands—is presented in tandem with the observation that China already endured a "Great Leap Forward" and a "Great Famine" with serious consequences; all of this context sits like a heavy stone amid any lighter depictions of a wine region now glittering with gold.[35] Insofar as the author wields the gold rush metaphor to organize discussion of the region's growth around resource challenges, industrial hazards and labor pitfalls, the upward boost of any new "gold rush" for wine falls flat on the present dangers of agro-capitalism as much as any anxious reordering of geopolitics.

The dualism of risk and reward inherent in the gold rush metaphor is aptly detailed by economists Beaudry, Collard, and Portier when they describe a gold rush as a period of time attracting "large increases in expenditures" but where the "external effect on productivity" is often unclear because the return on investment tends to be mitigated by one market player eventually taking a "dominant position in the market." The result, they argue, is a boom that fizzles or busts. Although some individuals may see profit, "The social [i.e., macro-level societal] gains may be small or nil." As they note, in 1898, the population of Dawson City in Yukon Territory exploded to thirty thousand and then fell to only nine thousand by 1910. Many digging for gold, in contrast to wealthy entrepreneurs, were nomadic cowboys and hardscrabble treasure hunters living in makeshift tents along rivers in North America. When the land stopped giving up its gold or when dominant players emerged, nearly everyone went home empty-handed.[36] Noting that numerous Chinese laborers immigrated to the United States in the 1800s without much financial benefit while confronting harsh conditions and fierce prejudice inculcates the gold rush metaphor with an undeniable tenor of economic trouble and failure.[37]

Another way of putting this might be to say that the gold rush, as metaphor, conjures images in a Western context of overly exuberant dreams of great wealth as well as inevitable destitution and disappointment. *The Guardian* article plays with this dualism. Leading with the story of Gao, a bright young farmer who borrowed three hundred thousand yuan from her parents to start the winery called

Silver Heights, the reader learns of an "award winning boutique winery." However, the article then stresses that the "biggest wine producers" are now billion-dollar Chinese firms. Subsequently, the author highlights the massive, growing scope of the competition: "There are 207 registered wineries in Ningxia compared with just one in 1983." The attendant observation that Moët Hennessy opened a winery in 2013 foreshadows a coming bust and, in fact, leads into the second half of the article, which emphasizes the challenges now facing the region, namely, the struggle to produce a competitive wine. Within two paragraphs, the reader hears the director of a wine consulting firm comparing China's wine to a child's painting; another "wine critic" declares that the wine tastes like "dirty sweat socks" and "cleaning fluid."[38] Such dramatic juxtapositions—dreams and disgust, taste and distaste—construct a "geopolitics of consumption," as Maguire and Lim note; yet these representations also compose an economic critique about the harsh risk-reward structure of an agricultural "gold rush," foreshadowing a bust.[39]

The gold rush metaphor echoes a much longer critical analysis of capitalism after the California gold rush. As literary and cultural critic George Henderson (1999) notes in a history of California's gold rush period, capitalist development can be viewed, in retrospect, as operating with three tendencies and perpetuating three related fictions inside of the discourses about that period. In terms of tendencies: the first is "for capitalist development to be expressed through cycles of boom and bust." The second tendency is toward development that makes some people much more likely than others to reap "the 'benefits' of capitalism." The third is the tendency for spatial extension or the need for "the perpetuation of its own [profit-driven] operations." Accordingly, as Henderson argues, three fictions emerge. Capitalist development in rural contexts perpetuates the belief that all inhabitants of agricultural land will benefit, that all will benefit equally, and finally, that the benefit will last and produce sustainable industries. Henderson here outlines a history of discourse about capitalism as historical comment, noting how literature about the gold rush period expresses the felt struggles of the age. "Agriculture was a site that capital could not fully make its own and was yet that site which capital intently strove to capture."[40] In stories of the time, the family farmer was forced to flee, forced to suffer, or forced to find his or her own way after inevitable disappointment.

These themes swimming within *The Guardian* article, intentionally or not, recycle period-specific capitalist criticisms, composing a tension between the hopeful excitement of gold rush mania, on the one hand, and the denigrating state of capitalist expansion in the agricultural sector on the other. Amid the presence of small bouts of positivity within quotations from Chinese farmers—where, for instance, the successful Gao from the Silver Heights Winery is quoted as saying, "We hope [for fine wine and growth]"—*The Guardian* article concludes with a striking judgment about the possibility of Chinese wines ever tasting as if produced in Bordeaux: "'[Perhaps in] a thousand years,' she [Gao] laughed." The article then states, "In some ways, the winemaker says her home in China's harsh interior reminds her of France: 'We have sunshine like Avignon.'" As a final line, the appeal to "sunshine" reads, perhaps optimistically, as an expression of hope in the confirmation of best climatic conditions for fine wines; yet, juxtaposed against the previous phrase—"in a thousand years"—the audience might, rather, read the ending as a superficial appeal to one factor among many, composing something similar to a depressing mid-twentieth-century realist novel where the lead character, desperate to find peace in the troubled environment, draws a simple comparison that the audience knows will not resolve the conflict.

Overall, the gold rush metaphor warns Chinese farmers about the disasters of capital and acts as an expression of concern for those who must not only "tackle prejudice" against their product but "might not have enough water to support the industry" as it expands beyond sustainability.[41] Conversely, the metaphor engages broader "geopolitical anxieties" by implying that China, through state-controlled planning, rides shortsighted economic expansion in an effort to reorganize a cultural hierarchy dominated by the West. In this way, the metaphor functions as a critique of hope-laden nationalism within China's own version of "capitalism with Chinese characteristics," warning of potential economic problems long familiar to Western agricultural contexts.

Of course, any Western media outlet criticizing the conditions of Chinese farming and highlighting its endeavors as unrealistic may be another example of colonialism, the pompous declaration that the West knows best. Likewise, these kinds of news stories might indicate the psychological depths of experience specific to Western agriculture through the twentieth century. Looking across other news texts from the sample, one sees is a persistent capitalist cynicism that functions to solidify the need for vintners to embrace self-possessed economic interest, as articulated in the concept of terroir. Put another way: to care for the farmer's own interests, to preserve one's own land, and to protect against corporate profiteering is to resist the "fictions of capital" because if farmers do not, then—so the story goes—they risk losing everything.[42]

The "Stampede" Metaphor

Similar to the "gold rush," the "stampede" metaphor recalls the Old West and carries many of the same overtones. The reader imagines cattle charging across an open plain, kicking up dust and trampling everything in their path. In the metaphor, the reader can assume one of three different perspectives—that of the animal charging amid heaving masses, that of a rugged cowboy watching the chaos in awe from a distance, or that of a rancher spooking the cattle, whether on purpose or accidentally, who knows? The truth of what sent them running and how this stampede might end remains uncertain. In this case, any positive ending for the people running with the bulls in China's wine industry has been consumed by a dust cloud of media negativity.

The first use of the stampede metaphor appeared in a 2015 *New York Times* article titled "China's Winemakers Seek Their Own Napa Valley"; the subtitle read: "A Sudden Stampede." Interestingly, the same Mrs. Gao and the same Silver Heights vineyard are highlighted for readers, who hear about her can-do spirit, as in *The Guardian* piece. The structural pattern of the narrative is also the same. First, the story highlights Mrs. Gao's early entrance into the wine industry in China, recognizing her success. Then the story takes a bad turn, just as in *The Guardian* piece, calling attention to the onslaught of wine profiteers, questioning the industry's sustainability. Then the author states, "Suddenly, what had been a slow buildup turned into a stampede."[43] The image is quickly directed toward economics—not coincidentally, a bull market, or an extension of the stampede metaphor—as the author cites prices "taking off." The question beneath the text, then, is who or what gets trampled and whether the bulls are still running.

Subsequent pages quickly spill the answer. Initial positivity about "signs of prosperity" and the rise of "middle-class Chinese" in the Ningxia wine region are accompanied by the strange tale of an investor parceling off a huge chunk of quality land at one hundred times the purchase price; tales of "Disneyesque" chateaus and Ningxia officials encouraging "the willy-nilly planting of grapes without understanding which varietals" leads to an invariably blunt conclusion: "Much of the explosion in wine consumption was driven by government officials and executives at state-owned companies buying expensive vintages for banquets and gifts."[44] In brief, in this sampled text, the Chinese government fills the role of the rancher who spurs the cattle to charge and then later fences them in. The stampede of the bull market winds down to an unsteady halt; who or what profits, outside of mass conglomerates, is left unknown but implied. The future success of wine in China sits unresolved in the text and largely situated as the CPC's problem to solve, since the government itself is clearly positioned as pushing the industry onto the region. At this juncture, Chinese government policy converges with what feels like specifically American imagery about economics, risk-taking, and agricultural life.

The rush to build a market—or to "stampede"—as a competitive impulse, and equally as rhetorical construction, establishes the means for a future disaster (or economic default). In emphasizing the extent of the global competition, the "stampede" metaphor then allows the author to discuss who or what gets trampled—and by whom. For example, a 2014 CNN story adds a comment by Simon Zhou, a wine distributor, who says, "Many wine companies, especially those state-owned companies, are run by people not in the wine business or have little knowledge of winemaking and grape growing," suggesting both the elitism of those who have the capability to benefit from the wine industry and the embedded skepticism that anyone involved will ultimate see a profit.[45] Another sampled text from *The Guardian* (2013) titled "China's Wine Boom of Little Profit to Pandas and Small Farmers" notes that much of the vineyard land is state owned; the author of that article quotes a farmer saying, "Farmers like us never drink wine."[46] In that small comment, the article inculcates a division between those who benefit and those who do not while highlighting the various parties involved as relatively naive about wine. The implication being: How can they produce wine if they don't know anything about it and don't even like drinking it? Overall, then, the stampede metaphor emphases how economics, when driving decision-making where specialist expertise is needed, introduces the possibility for insinuating crippling naivete and ultimate failure; yet, more basically, the metaphor suggests that capitalism, even with "Chinese characteristics," cannot be a reliable guide to agricultural success in the wine industry because viticulture is one arena where the bulls and their wranglers must be equally experienced to survive the run.

The economics of the frontier imagery are particularly evident in the 2014 CNN article, which introduces yet another related frontier metaphor, calling China's winemakers "pioneers." Implicit in this metaphor is a blend of heroism, adventurism, and risk-taking. As Leah Ceccarelli notes, frontier imagery tends to imply "adventurous loners, separated from a public that both envies and distrusts them, but that nonetheless comes to rely on the profitable discoveries that they bring back from the frontier of research." Ceccarelli treats frontier metaphors as a category, and although she examines scientific contexts, her overarching conclusion is that such metaphors serve to establish a "wilderness" context that rhetorically positions a rhetor as the rightful claimant over new lands or wealth.[47] Alternatively, the metaphor also leaves open the possibility that the pioneer might be the victim of the uncontrollable wilds and the native inhabitants of the land. This embedded dualism not only mirrors the positive-negative structure of many of the news articles in the sample but, perhaps, allows the news writer to take on the role of the (metaphoric) cowboy watching from a distance, shaking his head while standing in awe of the "stampede."

Seen from a different angle, the attempt to share two sides of a story, as many Western news writers are trained to do, results in commonplaces, the production of manufactured, easy tropes having both a positive and negative dimensions that can be played out.[48] A different explanation positions persistent use of North American tropes of communication as indicative of the tendency to conceptualize foreign practices in familiar terms.[49] Alternatively, such tropes might indicate a tendency to see the American history of Western frontierism being repeated in China, to some extent an indication of both an underlying respect and a derision for ruthless expansion. Still another possibility is that these popular metaphoric "frontier" tropes frame China within "simplistic binaries" that are, essentially, unfair and biased—that is, they depict Chinese as rushing to absorb Western elite cultures and yet failing, desperately hoping to be like Westerners but not succeeding; such simplistic representations set Western interests in a dominant position and frame advice from Western interests as needed for success.[50]

Whatever the case, frontier metaphors may have rhetorical benefits. They provide the opportunity for China to claim success should the so-called risk-taking venture prove successful. Conversely, they allow China to blame any defeat on Western-dominated contexts or the uncontrollable wild lands of desert regions. In either case, the state-run industry may appear favorable. Thus, the frontier metaphors, as far as metaphors go, may not be so bad. Then again, heavy perpetuation of such metaphors, as the next section demonstrates, resists an image of China as technologically advanced or working to ensure the prosperity of its people.

The "Red Planet" Metaphor

The title of a 2016 news article sampled from *The Guardian* reinforces yet more frontierism messages with respect to China's new state-powered industry. The title reads: "The Red Planet: China Sends Vines into Space in Quest for Perfect Wine." The reader is told that "a selection of cabernet sauvignon, merlot and pinot noir vines" were sent into space to help scientists decipher how to genetically manipulate vines to survive "the sun-scorched Gobi desert," which lies inside "an impoverished region at the heart of China's nascent wine industry with punishing –25C winters."[51]

What immediately stands out in these visceral descriptions is the juxtaposition between a "quest for perfect wine" and the need to develop stronger strains for "impoverished regions." On the one hand, the textual appeal to "perfection" justifies the multi-million-dollar space venture and communicates the unbridled enthusiasm of China's state-sponsored activity. The Communist nation-state is presented as willing to go to any lengths—even to outer space!—to craft a fine Chinese wine, more "perfect" than all others. On the other hand, the detail that the region is impoverished communicates disconnect between investment in wine and the needs of local people. Indeed, mixing the idea of a "perfect" wine with a search for "suitable" vines results in at least two possible interpretations.[52]

The first is that the Chinese government uses the space program in propagandistic ways for unrealistic and ultimately antipragmatic endeavors. The appeal to "perfection" in wine, in other words, contrasts with the image of the farmer focused on making a barely acceptable product without losing the vines to cold weather. Equally, the image of "space wine" sounds so far out and expansive that it presents China as going to absurd lengths to extend its "soft power" and to force a viable wine region onto the world's stage. The second possible interpretation is that China demonstrates provident thinking, well beyond its current position, setting long-term goals, despite present realities. This interpretation allows for China's vast expenditure on space wine to be seen as an investment in farmers now being goaded by the state to plant vineyards for the future.

Whatever way the reader chooses to interpret the passage, the "red planet" functions as an enthymeme, or a textual place where the reader intuitively understands that China itself is the red planet both because the ruling Communist Party associates with the color red and because much of the wine production in China focuses on red varietals. This viticulture detail crafts yet another enthymeme for wine connoisseurs. The color red is not merely a political signification but a gastronomic one, that is, an obsession with red wine.

Those familiar with viticulture in China may tend to see an elaborate scientific experiment in space as yet another way to organize Chinese wine consumption around the red varietals (and hence "red planet"), ignoring white wine varietals that may be suited to the landscape. Several high-profile wine commentators have noted that people in China associate the color white with death and the color red with luck, leading to a glut of red wines, putting farmers in difficult positions when the land may better fit varietals like Riesling and Chenin Blanc.[53] One sampled text puts it this way, "With such variety of both climate and soil, generalisations [about which varietals are being planted] ought to be impossible. But it remains the case that most Chinese wine is red."[54] The observation emphasizes the role of market pressures unique to wine agriculture in China. The enthymeme, then, insinuates that local preference has not balanced with the land's performance. Thus, the "red planet intuits a soon-to-be-alien landscape resulting from an economy unsuited to profit-driven expansion over viticulture. Put bluntly: China's obsession with red wine at whatever the cost, the article seems to say, risks making it into a "Mars" in the wine industry, the "alien" and "outsider."

Mars, of course, is already within the metaphor; however, the question is how the reader implicitly understands China as a Mars-like planet. At the conservative end of an interpretive spectrum, China may be positioned geologically within the metaphor, being like Mars insofar as having a "cold," "impoverished," and "harsh" landscape, as noted in the text.[55] At the expansive end of the scale, China may be conceptualized sociologically or nationally, as a place where vast sums of money and new scientific breakthroughs will be needed to launch sustainable industry. Alternatively, China may be a planet of the future, what Hartnett calls a "post-colonial colonizer" working to reconfigure Western impositions to its benefit and wield a history of oppression as fuel for a rabid nationalism.[56]

The underlying question, as with travel to Mars, is whether the cost will, in the end, be worth the effort. In this case, the frontierism of the "red planet" metaphor establishes China as both betting high stakes on success and paying a high price for a possible future. Yet, like all agricultural adventures into unknown lands, the media representations examined here suggest that the market itself may be dictating ventures that stand at odds with the resource availability and, perhaps, the longer-term desires for a top-notch international viticulture reputation.

Terroir as Conceptual Critique

In each case examined above—the gold rush, the stampede, and the red planet— the land and its infertility converge with local economic history to forge a critique of culture, society, or nation. Rather than dismiss this complex articulation as a flawed discourse motivated solely by Western avarice striving to maintain hegemony, understanding the discourse as *also* tied to Western histories and practices surrounding wine can place value on the material life of articulations. In other words, if depictions offered in news texts are "rhetorical articulations," then they arise within complex sociocultural milieus establishing "relationships that enable diverse modes of rhetoric to function."[57] Seen this way, a rhetoric of "rushing" in a "stampede"—even a rhetoric of "space wine" able to survive harsh winters—arises not exclusively from within geopolitical anxieties but also from concrete practices and other economic and agricultural abstract ideals in the West.

This is not to suggest that multiple intertwining factors forging cultural critiques do not come together to function politically to suppress national agendas. Indeed, they can, and they prove persuasive precisely because they have broader import. Many of the critiques in the aforementioned texts may well become potent to Western readers on the basis that "rushing" and "stampeding" ignore the carefulness of terroir as organizing principle in viticulture, thereby positioning Chinese winemakers (and Chinese governments) as completely missing the point of wine cultivation. The rhetorical maneuver, in this way, props up a second kind of criticism: that CPC economics ignores the agricultural needs of farmers and pushes adoption of Western lifestyles without knowledge of how those lifestyles connect to deep-seated concerns about the survival of a wine industry and the prosperousness of farmers. Frontier metaphors, like so much political communication, enable subtle and subsequent meanings that cut deep into nationalistic aspirations, well beyond the strictly literal.

Relatively banal appeals to terroir also work to support critiques of China. For instance, an article from *The Telegraph* describes terroir in a way that implies thoughtless viticulture development in China. The text reads: "It's the right terroir that is the pot of gold at the end of the wine rainbow. Without it, you can make decent wine but it will always be generic, just-another-wine, never special, always missing something. You have to be very lucky to alight on the right grape for the right place straight away. Or you have to have a lot of people in a lot of places toiling away very hard to identify it."[58] In context of an article about Chinese wines, the comment borders between instruction and ridicule. Because red wine is associated with good luck in China, the note about being "very lucky" to plant a varietal that succeeds straightaway implies both that Chinese farmers should keep trying and that the high levels of investment in making a fine red wine in China may be wasted and unrealistic. Tying the comment specifically to the Irish myth about a "pot of gold" at the end of a rainbow produces a subtle, yet potent, critique, positioning fine wine in China as a contemporary mythology and imagining Chinese farmers as so silly that fine wine might as well be a pot of gold waiting to be plucked up and magically uncovered, calling attention to an illusive mirage or impossible dream. The reality, so the trope communicates, is the opposite of the myth—fine wine requires hard work and long periods of time in fitting the right grape to the right plot of soil.

An article from the *New York Times* raises a similar critique in a discussion of terroir, stating: "When I mentioned to a colleague that I was going to try a few Chinese wines, he looked at me sadly and said, 'I'm sorry.'" The author concludes the opening section by saying, "What they [the wines] lack is any sense of distinctiveness, or, to use a bit of wine jargon, terroir." The author then remarks that Chinese winemakers look to Bordeaux "as a model" but do so "without a singular terroir," which means that Chinese winemakers lack consistent testing of soils, thorough understanding of the practices of vine cultivation, and knowledge about the sustainability principles of winemaking used in Bordeaux. Consequently, the article recognizes some Chinese "ambition" yet remains thoroughly dampened with skepticism about the Chinese wine industry. Reviews of several Chinese wines end the article, and they describe wines in a range from the "simple" to those with "a hint of nuance and complexity."[59]

Appeals to terroir in these cases operate either within a struggle over "cultural capital" as a pathetic attempt to "defend [dominant geopolitical] status positions" or as an expression of capitalist cynicism rooted in historical agricultural experiences, or as a watery attempt to encourage sustainable viticulture processes in China.[60] The fullest view is surely from amid all three, within the overarching propensity to maintain largely dominant Western discourses about why fine wine is *fine* in the first place and within a recognition of material conditions that cause wines to taste bland or to smell different from famous French, Italian, or Californian ones. Politics and economics, visions of terrible histories and visions of wealthy futures, converge with taste or are swigged in a sip of wine, or are swilled in glass of wine, or ferment like the yeasts inside barrels of wine that transform from sugars to ethanol and carbon dioxide. The financial trouble of the family farmer, the unpredictability of the weather, the dullness of the big corporate wine all swirl among charged geopolitical dynamics. A complex view of motivations embedded in rhetorical productions seems a reasonable way to comprehend the sampled texts; the culture of independence for a free press in the United States and United Kingdom rebalances the tendency to completely write off criticisms of China as fully politically motivated, even as Western writers may sometimes find themselves engulfed or circumscribed by their own colonialist legacies. Accordingly, articles like the ones examined in this chapter, expressing degrees of negativity about China's wine regions, must be evaluated as motivationally intricate and textually dense, multiple in view and interpretation.

Conclusion: Reconfiguring Metaphor

Because metaphors "have material consequences," metaphoric criticism might be said to hold a particular role, not just to describe, but to "replace dysfunctional metaphors," seeking ones that encourage better social interactions.[61] In this set of sampled texts from US and UK media reports, the "gold rush," the "stampede," and the "red planet" all depict Chinese wine growers, and the CPC itself, as often foolhardy or equivalent to those nomadic treasure hunters of the nineteenth century while still noting, on occasion, Chinese determination and inventiveness. The capitalist enterprise in China is therein praised for entrepreneurial competitiveness but derided for its agricultural incompatibilities with viticulture processes, which remain slanted, so the texts indicate, toward corporate profiteering and which keep the local farmer unable to grow fine wine. The history of Western agricultural busts may well operate here as a subterranean "terministic screen"[62] at a time when the East booms and a struggle for dominance rages across multiple levels of geopolitics. Thus, given such complexity, suggesting alternative metaphors is no simple matter. Dualisms and multiple interpretations embedded in frontier metaphors raise a question about what exactly is a "functional" versus "dysfunctional" metaphor in the first place.

There is no easy answer. But what can be said is that frontierism, instead of being viewed as a simple framework for a news text, might better be conceptualized as a way of looking. If the rugged individualistic risk-and-reward structure inherent in American frontierism is a way of understanding Chinese viticulture development, then what becomes apparent are several key disjunctions and misalignments of the metaphor.[63] For instance, an individualistic metaphor risks overlooking strong-handed economic intervention. What disappears is a top-down strategy, hierarchical pecking orders of profit embedded in state-run agencies that appoint provincial governors, choose policies, delegate funding, and generate propaganda. Party governance itself converges in ways unfamiliar to many Western contexts and is, accordingly, not always illuminated by familiar frontierism metaphors.

Here, the "red planet" perhaps better communicates structural dependencies that otherwise evaporate in the Wild West of the "gold rush" and the "stampede." Yet, the "red planet" metaphor, too, has multiple shortcomings. It emphasizes the state's financial backing for red wine development at the expense of the individual farmer's ability to make good wine and the possibility that white wines may well prove more palatable in China than anticipated; going to space to produce viable red wine varietals risks making Chinese people appear intractable in their superstitions and seem increasingly silly to some Western readers. Conversely, the "red planet" also positions Chinese state power as active in a "space race" that America and Russia have long dominated, and in that way, the metaphor positions the Chinese nation as a competitive global superpower, albeit far behind, but one aligning economic strength with new cultural investment in the material and symbolic race for elite status represented by fine red wine.

The communicative complexities of adopting any particular metaphor should now be evident. Consequently, instead of forging new creative metaphors to feed to a voracious Western media, understanding the entailments of recurrent metaphors and then negotiating them—or reclaiming them—while considering the lessons that they teach proves a more pragmatic strategy. In this case, Chinese winemakers and the governing bodies that fund wine development in China might look beyond the view that criticisms are purely geopolitical machinations and, rather, study the economic shortcomings and the resulting stances that have emerged with respect to wine growing. Indeed, the development of terroir as a form of personal economic self-guarantee for the individual farmer living with a delicate crop and an unpredictable climate highlights a paradox in capitalism when applied to wine. Namely, some agricultural development flourishes when resisting fast expansion and quick profit. Winemakers adhering to the lifestyle principles embedded in terroir increase selectivity and generate heightened interest and intrigue around their product, pumping up demand and improving prices. Resisting speed and immediate profit in exchange for land management can result in stronger profits over the long term. Embracing this paradoxical dynamic not only fosters a more sustainable industry but undermines Western criticisms about China's unbridled development.

Adopting terroir not as a means to comply with stuffy Western ideals that dominate a global wine industry but as a means to extend the reach and appeal of Chinese wine has double benefit. First, expressing affective investment in the land of China frames Chinese wine development around the love of China itself. Any speedy development is repositioned, then, as the need to discover previously unknown potentials latent in the land before China's fast-expanding cities sweep away the opportunity in a well-oiled economy. Expressions of love for what the land can do, in this regard, authorize the development of vineyards and seem to support the individual farmer's quest and, indeed, passion for farming as a central driving force behind the development; this rhetorical position stands opposed to dehumanized state power as the driver of development. Creatively repositioning hundreds of new vineyards as a material creation of the human "capacity to act," indeed, situates the people's own disposition or affect in the same way that rhetorical scholars do—a bodily force stirring up "the horizon of potentiality" and unable to be denied as a driver of change.[64] In this case, aligning the capacity of the land with the affective intensity of Chinese farmers' functions as an attempt to reconfigure—or forge a convergence of—Western rhetorics with/in China's agricultural and cultural advantage. Getting Western media outlets to write about the heart of China's farmer is, however, another matter.

Moreover, embracing the economic concern, that is, the sustainability of farming, inherent in the celebration of terroir has an opportunity to reconfigure existing media discourses about China's wine industry. Terroir offers the chance to express special attention to Western economic suspicions about capitalism's inability to absorb agricultural arenas and benefit those on the ground level, especially those working at the social bottom, that is, "the people." If cultivation of red varietals, for example, matches local preferences and if the land yields a wine that tastes good with local foods, then terroir in this conception is composed as something uniquely Chinese, reconfigured with "Chinese characteristics" just as with capitalism itself. Put another way, to reclaim terroir to its fullest extent requires presenting an original combination of Chinese soil and the Chinese palate as the basis for economic oversight, propelling a new rhetoric about limiting corporate dominance to discover what makes a fine wine "fine" *in China*.

Following this path means learning from others, such as French elites in Burgundy, who have successfully used terroir as a way of "confirming their own individual economic and social status and selling their uniqueness at global level." Because terroir emphasizes "artisanship" and the local preferences of the farmer, the term becomes a powerful rhetorical mechanism, a way "by which societies are able to use globalization and modernity to suit their own purpose."[65]

As with linguistic reclamations of derogatory terms, building on rhetorics of terroir functions to revise media representations and simultaneously "own" previous criticisms.[66] But if this is to be achieved successfully, then the attendant economic implications must also be "owned." Limitations on overdevelopment and corporate profiteering on a global scale—where the wine is clearly not being produced for Chinese palates—must not undercut the presentation of a special Chinese terroir wherein the wine tastes the way that Chinese people want their wine being produced from their own unique land to taste. The challenge here is allowing Chinese farmers and consumers to have a say in the production of Chinese wine, to find a healthy cooperation between state and Party agendas, business leaders, and industry experts, among other voices in order to attract interest in China while also, and through, demonstrating care for Chinese people and the specific needs of viticulture.

Overall, if US and UK media reports are going to introduce old frontier metaphors into discussions of China's new wine industry, then managing the implications by positioning state control as a benefactor of Chinese affective investment over and above pure financial investment may effectively harness underlying ideals to China's advantage. However, persuasion demands tangible material action that needs to take seriously the historical lessons living beneath both the practices and the Western rhetoric of terroir—that is, persuasion is not discursive only but also material and, thus, demands careful guidance of convergences, including legal protections over land, sustainable agricultural practices, and sensitivity to local preferences. If these tasks are tackled together, China's wine industry may be able to resist the pitfalls of massive profit-driven production and allow the people of the wine region and their distinctiveness to dominate what wine can become, not only in the eyes of Western readers, but in the mouths and hearts of those who will surely enjoy it.

NOTES

1. Michael E. Brown, Owen R. Coté Jr., Sean M. Lynn-Jones, and Steven E. Miller, *The Rise of China* (Cambridge: MIT Press 2000); G. John Ikenberry, "The Rise of China and the Future of the West," *Foreign Affairs*, January–February 2008, https://www.foreignaffairs.com/articles/asia/2008-01-01/rise-china-and-future-west; Edward N. Luttwak, *The Rise of China vs. the Logic of Strategy* (Cambridge: Harvard University Press, 2012); Gideon Rachman, "The Rising Power of China Will Create New Political Fissures in the West," *The*

Guardian, August 14, 2016.

2. Patrick Dodge, "Imagining Dissent: Contesting the Façade of Harmony through Art and the Internet in China," in *Imagining China: Rhetorics of Nationalism in an Age of Globalization*, ed. Stephen J. Hartnett, Lisa B. Kernänen, and Donovan Conley (East Lansing: Michigan State University Press, 2017), 311–338; David R. Gruber, "The (Digital) Majesty of All under Heaven: Affective Constitutive Rhetoric at the Hong Kong Museum of History's Terracotta Warrior Exhibit," *Rhetoric Society Quarterly* 44, no. 2 (2014): 148–167; Stephen J. Hartnett, "'Tibet Is Burning': Competing Rhetorics of Liberation, Occupation, Resistance, and Paralysis on the Roof of the World," *Quarterly Journal of Speech* 99, no. 3 (2013): 283–316; Shui-yin S. Yam, "Affective Economies and Alienizing Discourse: Citizenship and Maternity Tourism in Hong Kong," *Rhetoric Society Quarterly* 46, no. 5 (2016): 410–433. Huling Ding and Jing Zhang, "Social Media and Participatory Risk Communication during the H1N1 Flu Epidemic: A Comparative Study of the United States and China," *China Media Research* 6 (2010): 80–90; Anjali Vats and LeiLani Nichime, "Containment as Neocolonial Visual Rhetoric: Fashion, Yellowface, and Karl Lagerfeld's 'Idea of China,'" *Quarterly Journal of Speech* 99, no. 4 (2013): 423–437; Chris Paterson and Toussaint Nothias, "Representations of China and the United States in Africa in Online Global News," *Communication, Culture and Critique* 9, no. 1 (2016): 107–125.

3. Tania Branigan, "China's Taste for High-End Fashion and Luxury Brands Reaches New Heights," *The Guardian*, April 26, 2011; Emma Gonzales, "Cheese Finding Its Special Niche in China," *China Daily*, September 7, 2015, http://usa.chinadaily.com.cn/epaper/2015-09/07/content_21810935.htm. Peter Neville-Hadley, "Quenching China's Wine Market," *Wall Street Journal*, December 9, 2015.

4. Henry Samuel, "Chinese Now Own 100 Bordeaux Chateaux, as Wine Mania Grows," *The Telegraph*, January 30, 2015.

5. Nic Cavell, "How China Conquered France's Wine Country," *New Republic*, November 24, 2015.

6. Michelle FlorCruz, "China's Wine Industry Explodes, but Not Yet on the World Stage," *International Business Times*, May 3, 2015, http://www.ibtimes.com/chinas-wine-industry-explodes-not-yet-world-stage-1902284. Corey Young, "China Has Become a Large Wine Consumption country," *GBTimes*, March 5, 2015, http://gbtimes.com/business/china-has-become-large-wine-consumption-country. Erich Follath and Wieland Wagner, "China Seeks Role as Second Superpower," *Spiegel Online*, November 2, 2012, http://www.spiegel.de/international/world/global-ambitions-china-seeks-role-in-world-as-second-superpower-a-864358-2.html.

7. Jennifer Smith Maguire and Ming Lim, "Lafite in China: Media Representations of 'Wine Culture' in New Markets," *Journal of Macromarketing* 35, no. 2 (2015): 239.

8. Emma Mawdsley, "Fu Manchu versus Dr. Livingston in the Dark Continent? Representing China, Africa and the West in British Broadsheet Newspapers," *Political Geography* 27, no. 5 (2008): 523.

9. Tatiana Suspitsyna, "Cultural Hierarchies in the Discursive Representations of China in the *Chronicle of Higher Education*," *Critical Studies in Education* 56, no. 1 (2014): 21–22.

10. Jaibal Naduvath, "Examining Representation of the Non-local: China in the UK Media in the Run-Up to the Beijing Olympics," *China Report* 50, no. 2 (2014): 110–115.

11. Quian Gong and Philippe Le Billon, "Feeding (on) Geopolitical Anxieties: Asian Appetites, News Media Framing and the 2007–2008 Food Crisis," *Geopolitics* 19 (2014): 29 4.10.1080/14650045.2014.896789.

12. Paterson and Nothias, "Representations of China," 108.

13. See Alain Deloire, T. Prévost, and Mary T. Kelly, "Unravelling the Terroir Mystique—an Agro-socio-economic Perspective," *CAB Reviews Perspectives in Agriculture Veterinary Science Nutrition and Natural Resources* 3, no. 32 (2008): 3, 10.1079/PAVSNNR20083032; Robert E. White, *Soils for Fine Wines* (New York: Oxford University Press, 2003); Cornelis Van Leeuwen and Gerard Seguin, "The Concept of Terroir in Viticulture," *Journal of Wine Research* 17, no. 1 (2006): 1–10.

14. Yasheng Huang, *Capitalism with Chinese Characteristics: Entrepreneurship and the State* (Cambridge: Cambridge University Press, 2008).

15. Marion Demossier, "Beyond *Terroir:* Territorial Construction, Hegemonic Discourses, and French Wine Culture," *Journal of the Royal Anthropological Institute* 17, no. 4 (2011): 700–702.

16. Tom Phillips, "China's Bordeaux: Winemakers in 'Gold Rush' to Turn Desert into Vineyards," *The Guardian*, June 13, 2016, https://www.theguardian.com/world/2016/jun/14/china-bordeaux-wine-region-desert-ningxia-vineyards-gold-rush.

17. Dodge, "Imagining Dissent," 311; Stephen Hartnett, "Alternative Modernities, Post-colonial Colonialism, and Contested Imaginings in and of Tibet," in Hartnett, Keränen, and Conley, *Imagining China*, 91–138; Lisa Keränen, Patrick Dodge, and Donovan Conley, "Modernizing Traditions on the Roof of the World: Displaying 'Liberation' and 'Occupation' in Three Tibet Museums," *Journal of Curatorial Studies* 4, no. 1 (2015): 78–106. Max Black, *Models and Metaphors* (Ithaca, NY: Cornell University Press, 1962); Celest M. Condit, "Pathos in Criticism: Edwin Black's Communism as Cancer Metaphor," *Quarterly Journal of Speech* 99, no. 1 (2013): 1–26; Leah Ceccarelli, *On the Frontier of Science: An American Rhetoric of Exploration and Exploitation* (East Lansing: Michigan

State University Press, 2013); Robert L. Ivie, "Metaphor and the Rhetorical Invention of Cold War 'Idealists,'" *Communication Monographs* 54, no. 2 (1987): 165–182; George Lakoff and Mark Johnson, *Metaphors We Live By* (Chicago: University of Chicago Press, 1980).

18. Marita Gronnvoll and Jamie Landau, "From Viruses to Russian Roulette to Dance: A Rhetorical Critique and Creation of Genetic Metaphors," *Rhetoric Society Quarterly* 40, no. 1 (2010): 46–70.

19. Maguire and Lim, "Lafite."

20. Sharan B. Merriam, *Qualitative Research and Case Study Applications in Education* (San Francisco: Jossey-Bass, 1998).

21. Carl R. Burgchardt, "Metaphoric Criticism," in *Readings in Rhetorical Criticism*, ed. Carl R. Burgchardt (State College, PA: Strata Publishing, 1995), 335. Josef Stern, *Metaphor in Context* (Cambridge: MIT Press, 2000). Celeste M. Condit, Benjamin R. Bates, Ryan Galloway, Sonja Brown Givens, Caroline K. Haynie, John W. Jordan, Gordon Stables, and Hollis Marshall West, "Recipes or Blueprints for Our Genes? How Contexts Selectively Activate the Multiple Meanings of Metaphors," *Quarterly Journal of Speech* 88, no. 3 (2002): 303–325.

22. Ivor A. Richards, *The Philosophy of Rhetoric* (Oxford: Oxford University Press, 1936), 96. Black, *Models and Metaphors*, 38.

23. Stern, *Metaphor in Context*, 92–93.

24. Condit, "Pathos in Criticism," 1.

25. Sara J. Newman, "Aristotle's Definition of Rhetoric in *The Rhetoric*," *Written Communication* 18, no. 1 (2001): 8.

26. Gronnvoll and Landau, "Viruses to Russian Roulette," 46.

27. Lakoff and Johnson, *Metaphors We Live By*, 158.

28. Condit et al., "Recipes or Blueprints," 303.

29. Paul Beaudry, Fabrice Collard, and Franck Portier, "Gold Rush Fever in Business Cycles," *Journal of Monetary Economics* 58, no. 2 (2011): 84–97; George Henderson, *California and the Fictions of Capital* (Oxford: Oxford University Press, 1999).

30. Stern's approach is effectively outlined in a book review written by Camp; see Elisabeth Camp, "Joseph Stern, 'Metaphor in Context [book review],'" *Noûs* 39, no. 4 (2005): 715–731.

31. Reuters, "China Overtakes France and Italy for Red Wine," *The Telegraph*, July 29, 2014, http://www.telegraph.co.uk/foodanddrink/wine/10603892/China-overtakes-France-and-Italy-for-red-wine.html. Victoria Moore, "Red Dawn for Chinese Wine," *The Telegraph*, September 17, 2016, https://www.telegraph.co.uk/food-and-drink/wine/victoria-moore-red-dawn-for-chinese-wine/.

32. Palash Ghosh, "Why Is the Color Red Associated with Communism?," *Ibtimes*, June 30, 2011, http://www.ibtimes.com/why-color-red-associated-communism-295185.

33. Maguire and Lim, "Lafite," 231.

34. Phillips, "China's Bordeaux."

35. Ibid.

36. Beaudry, Collard, and Portier, "Gold Rush Fever," 85.

37. Sam P. Ho and Ralph W. Heunemann, *China's Open Door Policy: The Quest for Foreign Technology and Capital; A Study of China's Special Trade* (Vancouver: University of British Columbia Press, 1984), 27–28.

38. Ibid. Phillips, "China's Bordeaux."

39. Maguire and Lim, "Lafite," 239.

40. Henderson, *California*, xi, x–xvii, xvi.

41. Phillips, "China's Bordeaux."

42. For discussion of the overarching concept, see Henderson, *California*.

43. Jane Sasseen, "China's Winemakers Seek Their Own Napa Valley," *New York Times*, November 7, 2015, https://www.nytimes.com/2015/11/08/business/international/chinas-winemakers-seek-to-grow-their-own-napa-valley.html.

44. Ibid.

45. Kristine Lu Stout, "From Zero to Lafite: China Misses Its 'Gateway Wine,'" *CNN*, September 27, 2014, https://www.cnn.com/2014/09/27/world/asia/china-wine-kristie-lu-stout/index.html.

46. Nicola Davison, "China's Wine Boom of Little Profit to Giant Pandas and Small Farmers," *The Guardian*, July 26, 2013, https://www.theguardian.com/environment/2013/jul/26/china-wine-panda-farmer-tibet-aba.

47. Ceccarelli, *Frontier of Science*, 4.

48. Michael Shudson, "The Objectivity Norm in American Journalism," *Journalism* 2, no. 2 (2001): 149–170.

49. See Sekh Rahim Mondal, "Interrogating Globalization and Culture in Anthropological Perspective—the Indian Experience," *Journal of Globalization Studies* 3, no. 1 (2012): 152–160.

50. See Mawdsley, "Fu Manchu," 523.

51. Tom Phillips, "The Red Planet: China Sends Vines into Space in Quest for Perfect Wine," *The Guardian*, September 22, 2016, https://www.theguardian.com/world/2016/sep/22/the-red-planet-china-sends-vines-into-space-in-quest-for-perfect-wine.

52. Ibid.

53. See Carola Traverso Saibante, "China's Red Wine Record: A Lucky Challenge,"

Finedininglovers.com, April 16, 2014, https://www.finedininglovers.com/stories/red-wine-consumer-china/; Reuters, "China Overtakes France.".

54. Victoria Moore, "A Bottle of Beijing Please. Is China Wine Any Good?," *The Telegraph*, April 28, 2015, http://www.telegraph.co.uk/foodanddrink/wine/11568849/A-bottle-of-Beijing-please-is-Chinese-wine-any-good.html.

55. Phillips, "Red Planet."

56. Hartnett, "Tibet Is Burning," 284.

57. Nathan Stormer, "A Working Paper on Rhetoric and Taxis," *Quarterly Journal of Speech* 90, no. 3 (2004): 257.

58. Moore, "Red Dawn."

59. Eric Asimov, "A Tasting of Chinese Wines," *New York Times*, November 7, 2015, https://www.nytimes.com/2015/11/08/business/international/a-tasting-of-chinese-wines.html.

60. McGuire and Lim, "Lafite," 230.

61. Gronnvoll and Landau, "Viruses to Russian Roulette," 47.

62. Burke, 1966, 45.

63. Ceccarelli, *Frontier of Science*, 4–6.

64. Eric Rand, "Bad Feelings in Public: Rhetoric, Affect and Emotion," *Rhetoric & Public Affairs* 18, no. 1 (2015): 161.

65. Demossier, "Beyond *Terroir*," 702.

66. Adam Galinski, Kurt Hugenberg, Karla Groom, and Galen Bodenhausen, "The Reappropriation of Stigmatizing Labels: Implications for Social Identity," *Identity Issues in Groups: Research on Managing Groups and Teams* 5 (2003): 221–253.

US–China Communication and a New Type of Great Power Relations

F our months after his inauguration as president of the United States, Donald Trump hosted Chinese president Xi Jinping at Mar-a-Lago, Trump's unofficial seaside headquarters in Florida. Following the summit, Trump tweeted that the meetings had "created tremendous goodwill and friendship."[1] Likewise, Xi's response similarly acknowledged the positive rapport the two had established, saying, "We had a long and in-depth communication and more importantly, we have further built up understanding and established a kind of trust, and we have initially built up a working relationship and friendship."[2] Trump echoed the sentiment, claiming, "The relationship developed by President Xi and myself, I think, is outstanding. I believe lots of very potentially bad problems will be going away."[3] Chinese and Western media sources alike reported that the meeting was a positive first step in relationship-building. As Chinese foreign minister Wang Yi summarized, "Both sides agreed that the meeting . . . was positive and fruitful."[4]

Still on the highs of friendship, trust, and rapport, seven months later President Xi hosted President Trump at their first Beijing-based summit in November 2017. China, rolling out the red carpet, called the second summit between leaders a "state-visit plus," something the *Global Times* explained China had not done "since the CPC took power in 1949."[5] The state-visit plus, as portrayed in Chinese state media, "shows China's sincerity in laying down a long-term development plan for Sino-US ties through more effective and flexible diplomacy."[6] An iconic summit photograph was disseminated through international channels and blanketed the front pages of Chinese newspapers.[7] The image, showcasing Trump and Xi with the first ladies in front of the Hall of Supreme Harmony signified the importance China placed on the summit and on the positive relationship between the two leaders.[8] The image represented the notion that China had reached a new status, that the China–US relationship had entered a new era, and that here together in the "Forbidden City" Trump and Xi—and the United States and China—now shared a new type of respect, a blossoming international relationship, and a new understanding. Further, the world's two superpowers were now united, standing shoulder to shoulder in Beijing, where, historically, Chinese emperors held ceremonies and met visiting officials.[9] Indeed, standing as an iconic representation laced with authoritative undertones magnifying China's confidence and new standing, Xi observed that "the ongoing state visit is of great significance—it is a focus of attention from both countries, as well as globally, and it will yield positive outcomes."[10] The state-visit plus signaled a key moment in the Sino–US relationship, showcasing the beginnings of what Xi has called a "new type of great power relations."[11]

Each leader encoded political purposes in the joint press statement released at the formal closing of the summit. Trump's comments reiterated the need for a "fair and reciprocal" relationship, thus echoing his comments about building "free, fair, and reciprocal trade," made earlier on his five-nation tour of Asia. He also alluded to what would later drive US–China tensions over trade and technology. Critics worried that Trump was fawning over his newfound friendship with Xi, yet the president responded to his critics, saying, "Right now, unfortunately, it is a very one-sided and unfair [relationship]. But—but—I don't blame China. After all, who can blame a country for taking advantage of another country for the benefit of its own citizens? I give China great credit."[12] As was becoming a habit, the US president was publicly siding with the leader of a foreign nation, pinning any troubles in the relationship on poor prior leadership on the part of America.

Whereas Trump's comments shifted the focus from criticizing China to blaming the Obama administration for the US–China trade imbalance, Xi's comments highlighted the notion that a new type of great-power relations had commenced. Repeating claims that populate his writings and speeches, Xi intoned, "I conveyed China's firm commitment to deeper reform, greater opening up, and a path of peaceful development, and China's desire to expand converging interests with other countries and promoting coordination and cooperation among major countries."[13] Xi's remarks on converging Chinese interests with the United States and other countries built upon a United Nations speech delivered earlier that year, in January 2017, at the UN office in Geneva. In the speech Xi proclaimed,

> Actions hold the key to building a community of shared future for mankind. To achieve this goal, the international community should promote partnership, security, growth, inter-civilization exchanges and the building of sound ecosystems. [Xi outlined four of] China's commitments: 1) China's commitment to world peace, 2) China's commitment to pursuing common development, 3) China's commitment to fostering partnerships, and 4) China's commitment to upholding the international system "with the UN at its core," the UN Charter, and its core role in international affairs.[14]

Xi thus detailed the notion of a "community of shared future for mankind," which encompasses his call for a new type of great-power relations between China, the United States, and the world, wherein "China and the United States should share global leadership as equals and break a historical pattern of conflict between rising and established powers."[15] After the summit *China Daily* reported that "both sides appeared equally enthusiastic about the constructive relationship they have promised to cultivate."[16] In both his UN and state-visit-plus comments, Xi was seeking to reset the international balance of power, positioning China as an equal partner to the United States, no longer a rising or developing nation so much as a new global power.

But the majestic soft power-play from the Forbidden City, the trust and rapport built in the first two Trump-Xi summits, and Xi's vision for a new type of great-power relations with the United States and China together leading a community of shared interest—the entire vision, as Xi imagined it—was "Trumped" by the first shots of the US–China trade war. Just months after the Beijing summit, Trump and the United States signaled the start of the trade war by imposing 30 percent tariffs on solar panels and washing machines.[17] Tensions escalated throughout 2018, with the United States implementing tariffs on $250 billion of Chinese goods, and China retaliating with $130 billion of its own tariffs, setting the rivalry for the unforeseeable future, with even more tariffs and retaliations ongoing through 2019.[18]

After several failed talks and a general breakdown of communication between US and Chinese negotiators, Trump and Xi called for a third meeting, on December 1,

2018, at the close of the G20 Summit in Buenos Aires. Over dinner, Presidents Trump and Xi managed to settle on a ninety-day "cease fire," agreeing to suspend new trade tariffs in the trade war while resuming negotiation talks.[19] But then, four days later, on December 5, 2018, multiple media outlets confirmed the Canadian detention of a high-profile Chinese citizen, who was apprehended the same evening (December 1) that Trump and Xi met during the G20 in Buenos Aires.[20] Huawei's chief financial officer, Meng Wanzhou, was detained by Canadian officials in Vancouver en route to Mexico from Hong Kong, at the request of the US authorities. Whether intentional or not, Trump was in Latin America calling for a trade war "truce" while his agents, working with Canadian colleagues, were arresting a key Chinese entrepreneur, hence signaling that Trump's words and actions did not align and that the United States would not shy away from using police force to try to stop what was believed to be unfair Chinese trade practices.

Complicating matters, Trump stated that Meng's detention was not connected to the trade war, yet he would consider using the case if it would give the United States a better trade deal.[21] On January 28, 2019, the United States formally filed for Meng's extradition on charges that Huawei violated US sanctions by selling US equipment to companies in Iran. As discussed in Jufei Wan and Bryan R. Reckard's chapter in this volume, the US indictment targets Huawei's use of an unofficial subsidiary company in Hong Kong under the name of Skycom Technology Company Limited. The charge was that Skycom served as Huawei's Iran-based subsidiary, a move the US Justice Department argued violated US sanctions against doing business with Iran.[22] Meng was accused of fraud and of having "direct involvement" with Huawei's false reporting to HSBC Bank; in this way, the charges against Meng are "similar to ones that the United States government made in 2016 against ZTE . . . in which executives had described 'cutoff companies' that would do business with Iran, North Korea and other nations placed under sanctions under the American government."[23] The fact that Meng and Huawei were charged with international business crimes parallel to those previously leveled against ZTE is significant, for in the eyes of American intelligence officials, these combined efforts on the part of two of China's mega-tech leaders pointed to the conclusion that the CPC was intentionally undermining the US sanctions regime against Iran. In short, so the thinking went in America, Xi must have known that his leading tech giants were playing dirty, even while he was talking nice in his meetings with Trump.

On December 10, 2018, Chinese vice foreign minister Le Yucheng summoned John McCallum, the Canadian ambassador to China, issuing the warning "Immediately release our citizen or bear the consequences," followed by the summoning of Terry Branstad, US ambassador to China, protesting Meng's detention at the request of US authorities.[24] On December 11 and 12 two Canadians, Michael Spavor and Michael Kovrig, were detained in Beijing on charges of "engaging in activities that harm China's national security.[25] A third imprisoned Canadian, Robert Lloyd Schellenberg, was retried and resentenced from fifteen years in prison to the death penalty. Canadian president Justin Trudeau accused Beijing of arbitrarily detaining the two Canadians and using the resentencing (Canada has outlawed the death penalty) as a move to pressure Canada for Meng's release.[26] Lashing back, a *Global Times* editorial criticized Trudeau, stating, "Westerncentrism has been very obvious in recent disputes between China and Canada. Whatever Canada does is rule of law, but whatever China does is not."[27] Along with Canada and other cases in Poland, Russia, and Iran, Steve LeVine has explained that these "tit-for-tat jailings, in part, suggest a new stage in hostility in the US–China race for technological and economic dominance in the coming decades," and it involves the global community.[28]

And so, from the initial Trump-Xi summit, the building up of friendship, rapport, and trust, and the orchestration of a community of countries with shared future backed by a new type of great-power relations—to the trade war shots fired and exchanged, to the charges against Huawei CFO Meng Wanzhou, and the detention and resentencing of Canadians ushering in this new era of "hostage diplomacy"—this flurry of tit-for-tat US–China jabs, hooks, and crosses mixed with geopolitical struggle and economic-cyber-military warfare has sent ripples throughout the international community, signaling what Noah Feldman has described as the "Cool War."[29] As Feldman posits, "The practical question for United States–China geopolitical relations is much simpler: Can either side accommodate itself to the geopolitical vision of the other? And if not, how will the conflict proceed?"[30] Ian Bremmer has noted, "It's the first time to my knowledge that tariffs and a trade war have led to arrests/de facto hostage taking."[31] Thus, the storyline includes clashes, crashes, and fragmentation that continue to play out in the tangled spheres of geopolitics and trade, connecting accusations of forced technology transfer and intellectual property theft with security threats and a new era of hostage diplomacy.

As China's story of communication convergence has gone international, it has also brought media platforms together with politics, ideology, and information flow and containment. The battle over Huawei has placed the building of 5G infrastructure at the forefront of a global national security debate. The threat, as the United States perceives it, is that Huawei is intertwined with the Chinese government, the Party, and the military, and if it provides the foundations for a global infrastructure, its authoritarian regime will have the ability to monitor, surveil, and collect information that economies, governments and societies depend on.[32] The United States has gone on the offensive, warning countries of the risk that Huawei would pose if in control of the infrastructure, where the most powerful weapons are cyber-controlled, thereby gaining an "economic, intelligence, and military advantage." [33] For the United States and its close network of allies, the intelligence-sharing partnership "Five Eyes," Huawei, hostages, and a new type of great-power relations are the stakes in a new arms race, in a world more globally connected than ever, where information and infrastructure are the weaponry.[34]

China has countered with questions about whether America's anti-Huawei global pressure campaign is really about threats to national security or American ambition to maintain hegemony and prevent China from gaining a competitive advantage.[35] With neither side foreseeably accommodating the other, these examples are the latest of forces testing the balance of international competition and global rivalry, where increased convergence has also led to clashes over international suspicion on issues of military and geopolitical power, ideology, nationalism, security, fairness, trade, and technology.

We have witnessed the recent "New Era" accumulation of Chinese power around the core and changes along the central axis hardwiring Party politics with state media infrastructure.[36] As China continues its rejuvenation, the paradox of simultaneous convergence and fragmentation continues apace in the struggle for a "new type of great-power relations" within China's borders (i.e., current Hong Kong protests and Xinjiang re-education camps), in the region (i.e., cross-strait relations or lack thereof; militarization and rebalancing in the South China Sea), and on the world stage (i.e., US–China relations and China's One Belt, One Road initiative). The changes are transforming China not only domestically, but also internationally in its relations with the world. And so this book has been about transformation and communication convergence, about politics, platforms, and participation in the age of convergence. Together the chapters of this book have chronicled some of the monumental changes and constant (re)forming and (re)shaping of communication along the supply chain taking place in contemporary China; how changes to the configuration of communication networks and platforms are altering inter(national) mechanisms for controlling participation, funneling the flows and filtering of information, and the ongoing processes of what Guobin Yang has explained as the fluid and multifaceted nature of China's constantly evolving internet-control regime, which also serves the regulation of Chinese society."[37]

Never before have so many netizens had such access to the community of connections and diverse tools of participation on and between communication platforms. Simultaneously, never before have Chinese citizens been met with such sweeping changes of reform and regulation since, arguably, the Cultural Revolution.[38] These contrasting notions of Chinese citizenship (*gongmin*), what netizens have termed *pimin*, or "shitizenship," have surfaced in the "widely shared sense of powerlessness and disenfranchisement felt by ordinary Chinese citizens" under state regulations that continue to tighten their grip on Chinese civil society.[39]

As convergence around the core in China continues apace, and as China and the United States continue to come crashing together, we will no doubt continue to witness the interplay manifesting in the politics, platforms, participation, and flows and control of information along the global communication supply chain. The authors of this book have tried to show a range of perspectives, many critical of the ongoing changes playing out in the new era. As the United States continues to advocate for "internet freedom" and as the Party continues to push for "internet sovereignty," both have called for an increased (cyber)security in the name of (inter) national security. Strikingly, China has turned its technological infrastructure inward on its northwestern Xinjiang region, raising red flags about the implementation of a "Social Credit System," the "Police Cloud," and "Integrated Joint Operations Platform" that detects deviations from "normalcy," connecting behaviors to political untrustworthiness.[40] This and other cases raised in this collection are just some of the latest examples of the competing tensions where value systems collide and global rivalries continue to escalate tensions surrounding fair practice, intellectual property, geopolitics, human rights, and fundamental values. The ongoing clashes and escalatory tensions illuminate our pressing need to further (re)consider US–China relations, to renew our commitment to engaging in communication for justice, and to together hope for future global imaginings of peace.

NOTES

1. The first Trump-Xi summit was held in the United States at Mar-a-Lago on April 6,–7, 2017. See Trump Twitter archive and tweets containing the word "China" at http://www. trumptwitterarchive.com/archive/China/ttff. For the tweet on "tremendous goodwill and friendship" see https://twitter.com/realdonaldtrump/status/850722648883638272.

2. "Trump-Xi Summit: Top Accomplishment Is Getting to Know Each Other," *Straits Times*, April 8, 2017, https://www.straitstimes.com/world/united-states/trump-xi-summit-top-accomplishment-is-getting-to-know-each-other.

3. "U.S. and China Forge New Paths," *Australian Review*, April 10, 2017, https://www. theaustralian.com.au/nation/inquirer/us-and-china-forge-new-paths/news-story/3f322 c950a1a82add10030e980de3844. Trump's and Xi's statements post-Mar-a-Lago summit were represented in various news sources including the *New York Times*, the *Washington Post*, *Xinhua News*, the *Global Times*, and *China Daily*.

4. "'Fruitful' Xi-Trump Meeting Charts Course of U.S.-China Ties under Global Gaze," *Xinhua Net*, April 8, 2017, http://www.xinhuanet.com//english/2017-04/08/c_136192708.htm.

5. Isaac Stone Fish, "Was the Trump-Xi Summit in Beijing a Hit or a Miss?," *China File*, November 14, 2017, http://www.chinafile.com/conversation/was-trump-xi-summit-beijing-hit-or-miss.

6. Zhang Hui, "Trump to Get State-Visit Plus Experience in China," *Global Times*, October 31, 2017, http://www.globaltimes.cn/content/1072911.shtml.

7. For instance, see "Xi Offers Hand of Friendship to Trump," *China Daily*, November 9, 2017, and the accompanying front-page picture, http://www.chinadaily.com.cn/world/2017-11/09/content_34298816.htm.

8. Images of Trump and Xi with the First Ladies in front of the Hall of Supreme Harmony can be found with a Google Images search using the terms "Trump and Xi 2017 Hall of Supreme Harmony."

9. Li Jingjing and Li Shengnan, "Opera, Tea and Other Highlights of Xi and Trumps Visit to the Forbidden City," *China Global Television Network* (*CGTN*), November 8, 2017, https://news.cgtn.com/news/326b7a4e34597a6333566d54/share_p.html.

10. Xi's comment as noted in "Xi Offers Hand of Friendship."

11. Jane Perlez and Mark Lander, "Wooing Trump, Xi Jinping Seeks Great Power Status for China," *New York Times*, November 6, 2017, https://www.nytimes.com/2017/11/06/world/asia/trump-xi-jinping-visit-china.html.

12. Trump's quotation comes from Tom Phillips, "Trump Praises China and Blames U.S. for Trade Deficit," *The Guardian*, November 9, 2019, https://www.theguardian.com/world/2017/nov/09/donald-trump-china-act-faster-north-korea-threat.

13. "Remarks by President Trump and President Xi of China in Joint Press Statement at the Great Hall of the People: Beijing, China," *U.S. Embassy and Consulates in China*, November 9, 2017. Full text remarks are accessible at the US Embassy and Consulates in China website, https://china.usembassy-china.org.cn/selected-quotes-press-statement-president-trump-joint-press-conference-president-xi/.

14. Xi Jinping, "Towards a Community of Shared Future for Mankind," *The Governance of China*, vol. 2 (Beijing: Foreign Languages Press, 2017), 588–601. Speech delivered on January 18, 2017, at the United Nations Office at Geneva.

15. Perlez and Landler, "Wooing Trump." For more on Xi's reference to breaking the pattern of conflict between rising and established powers, see Allison Graham, *Destined for War: Can America and China Escape Thucydides's Trap?* (New York: Houghton Mifflin Harcourt, 2017).

16. Brenda Goh and Michael Martina, "Chinese State Media Cheer Xi-Trump Meeting, Say Confrontation Not Inevitable," *Reuters*, April 8, 2017, https://www.reuters.com/article/us-usa-china-media/chinese-state-media-cheer-xi-trump-meeting-say-confrontation-not-inevitable-idUSKBN17A06Y.

17. "U.S.–China Trade War: A Timeline from First Tariffs to the 90-Day Truce," *South China Morning Post*, December 26, 2018, https://www.scmp.com/news/china/diplomacy/article/2179505/us-china-trade-war-timeline-first-tariffs-90-day-truce.

18. The $250 billion figure in tariffs on Chinese goods comes from ibid. The $160 billion figure in tariffs on American goods comes from "U.S.-China Trade War: Deal Agreed to Suspend New Trade Tariffs," *BBC News*, December 2, 2018, https://www.bbc.com/news/world-latin-america-46413196.

19. Mark Landler, "U.S. and China Call Trade Truce in Trade War," *New York Times*, December 1, 2019, https://www.nytimes.com/2018/12/01/world/trump-xi-g20-merkel.html. The initial truce set March 1, 2019, as the deadline to reach an agreement. Since then the truce was extended for another two ninety-day periods, as negotiations continued. For more on the round of shots fired in August 2019, see Jeff Stein, Taylor Telford, Gerry Shih, and Rachel Siegel, "Trump Retaliates in Trade War by Escalating Tariffs on Chinese Imports and Demanding Companies Cut Ties with China," *Washington Post*, August 23, 2019. In January 2020, the United States and China negotiated a "phase one" trade deal easing trade tensions and ceasing indefinitely any further tariffs. See Ana Swanson and Alan Rappeport, "Trump Signs China Trade Deal, Putting Economic Conflict on Pause," *New York Times*, January 15, 2020, https://www.nytimes.com/2020/01/15/business/economy/china-trade-deal.html.

20. Daisuke Wakabayashi and Alan Rappeport, "Huawei C.F.O. Is Arrested in Canada for Extradition to the U.S.," *New York Times*, December 5, 2018, https://www.nytimes.com/2018/12/05/business/huawei-cfo-arrest-canada-extradition.html.

21. "Donald Trump Says He Would Intervene in Arrest of Huawei CFO Sabrina if It Helped Secure Trade Deal with China," *South China Morning Post*, December 12, 2018, https://www.scmp.com/news/china/diplomacy/article/2177540/

donald-trump-says-would-intervene-arrest-huawei-cfo-sabrina.

22. See "US v. Huawei Technologies Co., Ltd., Huawei Device USA Inc., Skycom Tech Co. Ltd., Wanzhou Meng," at US Department of Justice: https://www.justice.gov/usao-edny/press-release/file/1125036/download, filed January 24, 2019. See also Kate Conger, "Huawei Executive Took Part in Sanctions Fraud, Prosecutors Say," *New York Times*, December 7, 2018. For earlier stories on the US tracking of Huawei, see Steve Stecklow, "Huawei Partner Offered Embargoed HP Gear to Iran," *Reuters*, December 31, 2012, https://www.reuters.com/article/us-iran-huawei-hp/exclusive-huawei-partner-offered-embargoed-hp-gear-to-iran-idUSBRE8BT0BF20121230; and Steve Stecklow, "Huawei CFO Linked to Firm That Offered HP Gear to Iran," *Reuters*, January 31, 2013, https://www.reuters.com/article/us-huawei-skycom/exclusive-huawei-cfo-linked-to-firm-that-offered-hp-gear-to-iran-idUSBRE90U0CC20130131.

23. Conger, "Huawei Executive Took Part."

24. Curtis Stone, "China to Canada: Trampling on the Rights of Chinese Citizens Comes with a High Cost," *People's Daily Online*, December 10, 2018, http://en.people.cn/n3/2018/1210/c90000-9526941.html. For the warning/advice issued in Chinese state media, "Canada should not be wrong-headed any longer but immediately release the senior executive and effectively protect her legitimate rights and interests, otherwise there will be serious consequences and Canada is to take all responsibility," see "Chinese Citizens' Legitimate Rights, Interests, Inviolable," *China Daily*, December 9, 2018, http://www.chinadaily.com.cn/a/201812/09/WS5c0c70f1a310eff30328feaf.html. A similar warning appeared in a *Global Times* op-ed, "Canada Will Pay for Its Bad Behavior," December 23, 2018, http://www.globaltimes.cn/content/1133305.shtml.

25. See "Foreign Ministry Spokesperson Lu Kang's Regular Press Conference on December 13, 2018," http://www.china-embassy.org/eng/fyrth/t1621651.htm. See also "China's Canadian Hostages: Is the Use of Pawns the Bad New Normal in Trade and Diplomatic Disputes?," *New York Times*, December 23, 2018, https://www.nytimes.com/2018/12/23/opinion/editorials/china-canada-huawei-trump.html.

26. See Lily Kuo, "'Hostage Diplomacy': Canadian's Death Sentence in China Sets Worrying Tone, Experts Say," *The Guardian*, January 15, 2019, https://www.theguardian.com/world/2019/jan/15/hostage-diplomacy-canadians-death-sentence-in-china-sets-worrying-tone-experts-say. See also "Trudeau Expresses 'Extreme Concern' after Canadian Sentenced to Death on Drug Charges in China," *Washington Post*, January 14, 2019, https://www.washingtonpost.com/world/asia_pacific/china-sentences-canadian-man-to-death-in-drug-case-linked-to-huawei-row/2019/01/14/058306a0-17fb-11e9-a804-c35766b9f234_story.html?utm_term=.25ec7d7099ba.

27. "Schellenberg Trial Shows Canada's Arbitrary View of Rule of Law," *Global Times*, January 14, 2019, http://www.globaltimes.cn/content/1135762.shtml.

28. See Steve LeVine, "The New Age of Hostage Diplomacy," *Axios*, January 12, 2019, https://www.axios.com/international-arrests-poland-china-hostage-diplomacy-e1f249f0-6a45-430d-88e2-aed7ce4ecfc3.html, and Erica Pandey and Steve LeVine, "A New Era of Hostility in the U.S.-China Fight," *Axios*, December 16, 2018, https://www.axios.com/us-china-canada-huawei-arrests-engagement-aee65f5c-9071-4bfd-a8d0-65cb7995a618.html?utm_source=newsletter&utm_medium=email&utm_campaign=newsletter_axiosfutureofwork&stream=future.

29. Noah Feldman, "Overview: The Cool War Continues," *Democracy* 52 (2019), https://democracyjournal.org/magazine/52/overview-the-cool-war-continues/.

30. Ibid.

31. The quote from Ian Bremmer appears in Steve LeVine's report "New Age of Hostage Diplomacy."

32. "Could Huawei Signal the End of the 'Five Eyes,'" *Cipher Brief*, March 28, 2019.

33. For example, see David E. Sanger, Julian E. Barnes, Raymond Zhong, and Marc Santora, "In 5G Race with China, U.S. Pushes Allies to Fight Huawei," *New York Times*, January 26, 2019, https://www.nytimes.com/2019/01/26/us/politics/huawei-china-us-5g-technology.html.

34. The Five Eyes network consists of Australia, Canada, New Zealand, the United States, and the United Kingdom. As explained in "Could Huawei Signal the End," the Five Eyes share "a vast scope of intelligence, including highly sensitive signals intelligence and communications intelligence at a level of detail not typical in international intelligence cooperation. There is also a tacit understanding that these nations would refrain from spying on each other."

35. See Chen Qingqing, "U.S. Led Geopolitical Campaign against Huawei Won't Affect Its Future: Rotating Chairman," *Global Times*, February 24, 2019, http://www.globaltimes.cn/content/1139980.shtml; Chen Qingqing, "U.S. Attack on Huawei Makes It Stronger: Well Organized Geopolitical Campaign Led by Washington Set to Fail," *Global Times*, March 7, 2019, http://www.globaltimes.cn/content/1141368.shtml; Shen Yi, "U.S. Crackdown on Huawei Driven by Selfishness, Wrong Perception," *Global Times*, March 22, 2019, http://www.globaltimes.cn/content/1143095.shtml.

36. See "Xi Calls for Building World-Class New Mainstream Media," *Xinhua*, September 26, 2018.

37. Guobin Yang, *The Power of the Internet in China: Citizen Activism Online* (New York: Columbia University Press, 2009), 47–51. As Yang explains on page 49, the framework

"encompasses 1) institutional building, 2) legal instruments, 3) ethical self-discipline, 4) technical instruments, and 5) proactive discursive production."

38. For more on this, see Guobin Yang, "China's Long Revolution," in *Power of the Internet*, 209–226.

39. Peidong Yang, Lijun Tang, and Xuan Wang, "Diaosi as Infrapolitics: Scatological Tropes, Identity Making and Cultural Intimacy on China's Internet," *Media, Culture and Society* 37, no. 2 (2015): 207. See also Bingjuan Xiong, "Communication Citizenship in China's Digital Society," *Journal of International and Intercultural Communication* 12, no. 2 (2019): 128–145.

40. On the sanitization of China's social media platforms, see Qian Zhecheng, "For China's Web Platforms, the Future Is Sanitized," *Sixth Tone*, December 26, 2018, http://www.sixthtone.com. See also Maya Wang, "Cambridge Analytica, Big Data and China," *Human Rights Watch*, April 18, 2018. For more on "Police Cloud," see "China: Police 'Big Data' Systems Violate Privacy, Target Dissent"; for "Joint Operations Platform," see "China: Big Data Fuels Crackdown in Minority Region: Predictive Policing Program Flags Individuals for Investigations, Detentions." The Human Rights Watch articles are accessible at https://www.hrw.org.

Acknowledgments

This book has been the production of over five years of hard work and collaboration. It would not have been possible without the chapter authors' patience, passion, and persistence. Thank you for sticking with me and seeing this project to completion.

At Michigan State University Press, I am indebted to series editor Stephen Hartnett. Stephen, your energy, leadership, guidance, mentorship—and mojo—is the stuff of legends. Thank you for championing this US–China series, for paving the way for so many of us, and for fighting so hard for open platforms where we can engage the challenging and needed issues and conversations of our day.

I am grateful to MSU Press editor in chief Catherine Cocks for her support and guidance throughout the process—thank you for helping make this a reality. Thanks go to the MSU Press team for their tireless help with all the moving parts behind the scenes—Anastasia Wraight, Kristine Blakeslee, Elise Jajuga, and Terika Hernandez. I also want to thank the anonymous reviewers for their invaluable suggestions that helped make this book stronger.

Acknowledgment goes to the National Communication Association's NCA-CUC Visiting Fellows Program team: Stephen Hartnett, Qingwen Dong, and Trevor Parry-Giles for their support of this project and for the opportunity to work on this manuscript as a fellow-in-residence during the fall 2018 semester. Thank you to both parties at the NCA and Communication University of China for believing in the vision and for all that you are doing to build a communication platform for US–China relations in the age of globalization. When we look back at the last five years, it is truly remarkable how much we have accomplished in working together.

Special thanks go to the CUC team, especially Professor Zhi Li, President Hu Zhengrong, and Dean Gao Xiaohong for their friendship and support from day one in all our collaborations and partnerships, for their hospitality throughout my time as a Visiting Fellow, and for being such supportive and gracious colleagues whether we are meeting at your campus or in the United States. Your dedication to China–US collaboration, friendship, and partnership has been visionary.

At the University of Colorado Denver (CU Denver), I am grateful to the Office of Research Services and the Department of Communication, for their funding support of this project. I am also grateful for the support of ICB Professional Development Funds from the CU Denver College of Liberal Arts and Sciences. There are also many CU Denver, and International College Beijing folks that deserve acknowledgment for their conversations, support, and friendship throughout the years: Stephen Hartnett, Lisa Keränen, Hamilton Bean, Sonja Foss, Barbara Walcosz, "The Tonys," Andrew Gilmore, Soumia Bardhan and Saurav, Donovan Conley, Jeffrey Golub, E.j. Yoder, John Sunnygard, the best program assistant in the world—Michelle Médal, Dongjing Kang, Mia Fischer, Tony Smith, Clay Harmon, Payton Wu, Jared Woolly, Kirsten Lindholm, Xiyuan Liu, Moana De Almeida, Lu Wu, James McNeil, Amy Hasinoff, Sarah Fields, Yvette Bueno-Olson, Sarah Burke Odland, Kristy Frie, Lisa Dicksteen, Jeremy Make, Alana Jones, Jessica Tharp, Chris Doxtator, Chris Bodden, Don Hatcher, Matthew Klein, Shauna Musser, Jason Hostutler, Chris Willford, Yi-Chia Chen, James Hu, Marcy Morris, Nicholas Golding, Ernest Boffy-Ramirez, Soojae Moon, Enoch Cheng, Larry Hamelin, Rob Rostermundt, Gary Larson, Leslie Bai, Vivian Shyu, Pam Laird, and the University of Colorado Denver's Association for Lecturers and Instructors (UCDALI) team. Thanks also go to the administrative leaders who have been supportive through the years: Pamela Jansma, Laura Argys, JoAnn Porter, Payton Wu, Chris Bodden, Winnie Shen, Joanne Wambeke, Huang Guanghua, Xu Tingwu, Meng Fanxi, James Wu, Wang Ning, Megan Qi Yan, Liu Chang, Yang Chenfei, Chris Liu, Bai Jing, Yan Fang, and Song Yue.

To all the folks who were involved with the 2016 NCA-CUC conference, where the idea for this book originated, thank you. Thanks to those from the NCA's Task Force for Fostering International Collaboration in the Age of Globalization who helped us set the tone: Stephen Hartnett, Qingwen Dong, Zhi Li, Esther Lee Yook, Paaige Turner, Stephen Croucher, Todd Sandel, Soumia Bardhan, Eddah Mutah, Lisa Keränen, Carolyn Calloway-Thomas, Tiffany Bell, Jasmine Phillips, and Janet Colvin. Thanks to those who kept the conversations going and helped make the 2018 NCA-CUC conference a success: Phaedra Pezzullo, Guobin Yang, Mohan Dutta, Nicholas Zoffel, Shaunak Sastry, Zhuo Ban, Michelle Murray Yang, Ted Striphas, Gary Kreps, Ron Shields, Jeremy Morris, Stephen McConnell, Zhang Rudong, Jingfang Liu, Marwan Kraidy, Pauline Hope Cheong, Leah Sprain, Jiang Fei, Viola Huang, Xinhgua Li, G. Thomas Goodnight, Janice Hua Xu, Wenjie Yan, Vincent Lei Huang, Susan Parrish-Sprowl and John Parrish-Sprowl, Zimu Zhang, Stephanie Kelly, Li Mengsheng, and Sophie Wade. Your good work has made the bridges wider for so many of us doing interdisciplinary work in US–China Communication Studies.

For your continued collaboration, optimism, and your positive outlook throughout the years, thanks to our friends in Shenzhen: Dean Wang, Professor Pan, Dean Chao, and the 2019 Shenzhen Forum planning team. A special acknowledgment here to the 2019 Hong Kong Communication Workshop team: your work is inspirational.

I also want to acknowledge my colleagues and friends at the Association for Chinese Communication Studies (ACCS) for their support—Chiaoning Su, Rya Butterfield, Meina Liu, Joyce Chen, Julie Lin Zhu, Hairong Feng, Jiang Shaohai, Jasmine Wang Yi, and all the other ACCS leaders before us who made what we have today possible—thank you.

I would have gone mad long ago if not for my ICB family and friends. Thanks for helping me keep the balance: Matt O'Brien, Raphael Smith, Jeff Golub, Richard Webster, Ben Walters, Sunnia Ko, Peter Krasnolpolsky, Mark and Caroline Henderson, James Eyre, Erik Nilson, Carol Richman, Mike Fuchsman, Alberto Mendoza, Frank D., Derek, Stanley, Alphonso Buie, Chris Kelly, Tom Newell, Sam Whitaker, Griffin Denay Keedy, and Chaz Hager.

To all the students I have had the pleasure of getting to know throughout the years—Chinese and international—who ask questions, who answer mine, who have taken up the critical approach in considering multiple perspectives and engaging them before making up their minds: "Good good study, day day up."

Finally, to my to my family outside the academy—my wife, mother, brother, father, uncles, aunties, and cousins on both sides of the Pacific—thanks for helping me keep my feet on the ground while my head was exploring the clouds, for bringing the good cheer as I bounced ideas back and forth with you, and for reminding me that life is good.

About the Contributors

Patrick Shaou-Whea Dodge is an associate professor Clinical Teaching Track at the University of Colorado Denver's International College in Beijing, where he has lived and worked since 2007. He was the 2018 inaugural fellow for the NCA-CUC Visiting Fellows Program for Communication and Media Research, and is serving as the vice president of the Association for Chinese Communication Studies, assuming the presidency in 2021. His work has appeared in journals such as the *Chinese Journal of Communication*, *Journal of International and Intercultural Communication*, and *Intercultural Communication Studies*.

Qingwen Dong is a professor and the director of the graduate program in the Department of Communication at the University of the Pacific. He is a recipient of the university's highest teaching and research honor, the Award for Eberhardt Teacher/Scholar; its highest honor for scholarship, the Award for Faculty Research Lecturer; and its highest honor for service, the Award for Excellence in Undergraduate Research Mentoring. He serves two distinguished professorships and has served multiple visiting professorships in China. His research focuses on the relationship between socialization and various media. Over the past seven years, he has directed seven Pacific summer institutes, training a number of professors and students from the top Chinese universities, including the Communication University of China, Tongji University, and Shenzhen University.

Andrew Gilmore received his PhD from the Department of Communication Studies at Colorado State University. His research interests lie in rhetorical theory and criticism, with a particular focus on Hong Kong's complex relationship with mainland China. Andrew's work addresses issues surrounding national identity, cultural preservation, censorship, governmentality, and questions of democracy. His recent work on the Umbrella Revolution explores the use of buildings, transportation, and other everyday items as tools of protest that, in some cases, can also be utilized to maintain hegemonic structures of inequality and power.

David R. Gruber is an assistant professor in the Department of Media, Cognition, and Communication at the University of Copenhagen. His work focuses on the rhetoric of bodies, science, and technology. He is a coeditor of the *Routledge Handbook of Language and Science*. He has published in *Rhetoric Society Quarterly*, *Public Understanding of Science*, *Journal of Technical Communication*, and other journals.

Stephen J. Hartnett is a professor in the Department of Communication at the University of Colorado Denver, and served as the 2017 president of the National Communication Association. He coedited *Imagining China: Rhetorics of Nationalism in an Age of Globalization*. His scholarship on US–China relations has also appeared in the *Quarterly Journal of Speech*, *Rhetoric & Public Affairs*, the *Journal of International and Intercultural Communication*, *Public Seminar*, and *SupChina*.

Zhengrong Hu is editor in chief at China Education Television. He was president of the Communication University of China (2016–2018), president of the China Communication Association (2006–2010), and board member at the Asian Media Information and Communication Center and the Beijing Journalists Association. His research areas include new media, international communication, media policy, and the political economy of communication. He was a research fellow in the Kennedy School of Government at Harvard University (2005) and a Leverhulme Visiting Professor at the University of Westminster (2006). He has published widely in both English and Chinese, including the *Annual Report of China's International Communication* (2014–2016), *Global Media Industries* (2011–2016), *Thirty Years of Chinese Media: 1978–2008* (2008), and in a number of refereed journals.

Lisa B. Keränen is an associate professor and Chair of the Department of Communication at the University of Colorado Denver, where she is an associate of the Program for Arts & Humanities in Health Care of the Center for Bioethics and Humanities. Her most recent book is the coedited *Imagining China: Rhetorics of Nationalism in an Age of Globalization*; her other publications in this area appear in the *Journal of International and Intercultural Communication, Journal of Curatorial Studies*, and the *Chinese Journal of Communication*. She is a past president of the Association for the Rhetoric of Science, Technology, and Medicine.

Yimeng Li is a graduate student at the Communication University of China majoring in international journalism and communication. She received her BA in German language and literature. Her research interests focus on national image, mass media, social network, framing, and the Belt and Road Initiative. Her thesis, "National Image of China Constructed by German Media: A Case Study on the Related Reports of the 'One Belt, One Road' Initiative," was recognized by her university as an Outstanding Master's Thesis. Yimeng now lives in Beijing. She enjoys playing badminton (poorly) and reading science fiction novels.

Zhi Li is a professor in the School of Television at the Communication University of China, a member of the National Communication Association, and a member of the Association for Education in Journalism and Mass Communication. His scholarly and teaching interests include media criticism, rhetoric, documentaries, and broadcast journalism. His research has examined narratives and the rhetoric of media, Chinese documentaries in cross-cultural communication, and critical discourse methodologies. He is working on a short video project that aims to produce Chinese stories from foreign perspectives and is also exploring creative ways of storytelling through new media technologies.

Jack Kangjie Liu is a professor in the School of Journalism and Communication at the Guangdong University of Foreign Studies. He was formerly a print journalist in both China and Australia. He has published over thirty journal articles, book chapters, and international papers, completing a Chinese National Social Sciences Funding Project on contemporary Chinese migration and diasporic social media. His research areas intersect at social media, global communication, and diasporic communication. He is the lead researcher of a Chinese National Social Sciences Funding Project and has participated in the annual conferences of the International

Communication Association (ICA) and the International Association of Media and Communication Research (IAMCR).

Michelle Murray Yang is an assistant professor at the University of Maryland. Her research examines portrayals of China and US–Sino relations in US media and political discourse. She is the author of *American Political Discourse on China*.

Peimin Qiu received her MA in communication and new media at the University of Macau in 2015. She currently works in Guangzhou, China, for ByteDance, a creative media marketer for the government and the tourism industry.

Bryan R. Reckard is a PhD student at the University of Illinois, where he is writing about US foreign policy in the Pacific and Asia with an emphasis on the rhetoric surrounding international conflicts and war. He explores how rhetoric produced by and about the military plays a role in achieving the US military's regional and global objectives, how military and foreign policy rhetoric encourages and discourages international conflict, and how military power is communicated in media.

Todd L. Sandel received his PhD at the University of Illinois and is an associate professor of communication at the University of Macau, China. He is past editor in chief of the *Journal of International and Intercultural Communication*, associate editor of *The International Encyclopedia of Language and Social Interaction*, and author of *Brides on Sale: Taiwanese Cross Border Marriages in a Globalizing Asia*, for which he received the 2016 Outstanding Book Award from the International & Intercultural Division of the National Communication Association. His research has appeared in *Language in Society, Research on Language & Social Interaction, Journal of Intercultural Communication Research, Journal of Contemporary China, China Media Research, Journal of Pragmatics*, and elsewhere.

Jufei Wan received her MA from the Department of Communication at the University of Colorado Denver, where she studied US–China relations with a focus on rhetoric and strategic communication. Jufei received her BA degree in English at the Wuchang University of Technology, China. Her research interests include political rhetoric surrounding technology and international conflicts, strategic public relations in organizations, critical media studies, and gender and sexuality.

Da Wang is a dual-degree MA candidate at the Communication University of China and National Taiwan University. In 2016 he received his BA degree in broadcast journalism from the Television School at the Communication University of China. His current research interests include international journalism and communication, cultural studies, media criticism, and documentary studies.

Dan Wang is a research associate and lecturer in the School of Communication at Hong Kong Baptist University. Wang received her MA in international journalism from the University of Leeds and her PhD in communication studies from Hong Kong Baptist University. Her main research interest lies in reconciling political economy with micro-sociological details. Wang's doctoral dissertation is about how a Communist Party newspaper organization responded to the impact of digital media. She has published in *Journalism Studies*, *Global Media and China*, and the *Sage Handbook of Game Studies*.

Xi Wang earned her bachelor's degree at the Communication University of China. During her undergraduate studies she majored in broadcast journalism and researched documentaries and cross-cultural communication. She is a graduate student in the Master of Arts Program in Social Sciences at the University of Chicago. Her current research interests are urban and political sociology, migration, and media analysis.

Index

Dubuc, Nancy, 54, 55–56

E

Economic Espionage Act, 74

Economist, The (publication), xxv, 31, 114

education: of ethical standards, 9, 10; language program, 177; Leung and, 38; in Macao, 181; mainlandization of, 21, 23, 27–28, 30. *See also* language

Eighteenth Party Congress (CPC), x, xxvi (n. 9)

elections: in Hong Kong, 19, 21, 26, 37, 41; in United States, xv, 109, 110

emojis, 192–195, 200

Entman, Richard, 90 (n. 10)

epideictic rhetoric, 100, 150, 153. *See also* blame discourse; crisis communication

espionage. *See* cyber intrusion

Estes, Adam Clark, 79

ethical standards, 9, 10, 141–142

ethical violations, 128–139. *See also* cyber intrusion

exclusion and populist rhetoric, 13–14. *See also* class divisions

F

Facebook, xv, xvii, 5, 77, 184

Falun Gong, xvii

Fang Wu, 150

fangyan, 175–179, 194, 199–201, 201 (n. 3). *See also* language

FBI Most Wanted, 76–78, 81

Feldman, Noah, 239

film. *See* documentary films and national imaginaries

Fink, Steve, 131

Five Eyes network, 240, 245 (n. 34)

5G networks, 88, 103, 104–105, 108, 114, 239–240. *See also* cybersecurity

five stages of crisis management system, 131

folklore, 61

Forbes (publication), 31

four stages theory of crisis communication, 131

fragmentation, xv–xxi, 6–8, 13, 33–36, 53, 240–241. *See also* communication; convergence

frames, as structures, 62–63, 71–73, 81–82, 90 (n. 10), 91 (n. 17)

freedom, 10–11, 34, 52, 85, 99. *See also* censorship; "internet freedom"; mainlandization

G

gentrification, 32–33. *See also* class divisions

Germany, 83, 114, 115

Global Times (publication), xviii, 113, 235–236, 239

gold rush metaphor, 215–218

Google, xvii, xviii, 117, 136

Great Britain, 13, 20, 115, 154, 245 (n. 34)

Great Firewall, xvii, 10–11. *See also* censorship

Greenberg, Andy, 80

Gruber, David R., 22, 36

Guangdong province, 29, 179

Guangming Daily (publication), 135

Guardian, The (publication), 209, 212–221

Guidebook for Civilised Tourism, 25

Guo Cheng Ma, 135

Guo Ping, 105, 108

Journalism and Communication Disciplinary
Supervisory Committee of China (JCDS),
3, 11
Jyutping system, 186

K

Karolinska Institute, 36
Kim Soo-hyun, 197–199
King, Eric, 80
King-wa Fu, 151
Kong Qingdong, 24–25
Kovrig, Michael, 239
Kuomintang (KMT), 177. *See also* China
Kwan-choi Tse, Thomas, 27

L

Lai, Alex, 20
language: Cangjie system, 186; code
mixing and code switching, 178–179,
185–190, 195–199, 204 (n. 40); diversity
of verbal and unity of written forms,
175–178, 199–201; *fangyan*, 175–179, 194,
199–201, 201 (n. 3); Jyutping system,
186; national program of, 24–25, 28–29,
177–178; Pinyin system, 176, 177–178, 186;
putonghua, 176, 177–178; through emojis
and stickers, 192–195, 200; violence
using, 7–8. *See also* Cantonese language;
crisis communication; education;
Mandarin language
Lantos, Tom, xvii
Lau Chaak-ming, 28
Law, Nathan, 26
Lei Yang, 127
Leng Song, 63
Leung, CY ("689"), xxii, 21–22, 23–24, 36–40,

41. *See also* Hong Kong
LeVine, Steve, 239
Le Yucheng, 238
Li, Parker, 98
Li Cheng, 99
Lieberthal, Kenneth, 72
Li Helin, xiv
Li Keqiang, 158, 162, 163

London 7/7 bombings, 154
Lu Xing, 100
Lynch, Loretta, 78

M

Ma, Jack, 29
Macao, 176–179
Macao Association for Internet Research, 184
Macau TDM, 181
"Made in China 2025" program, 88, 102–103,
117, 119 (n. 31)
mainlandization, 19–24, 40–41; as culture
clash, 24–25; of education, 23, 27–28,
38; of Hong Kong's media, 23, 29–30; of
Hong Kong's political system, 25–26; as
term, 20, 22
Man, Joyce, 33
Mandarin language, 176; code mixing and
code switching, xxiv, 178–179, 185–190,
195–199, 204 (n. 40); Leung's speech in,
34; national program and, 24–25, 28–29,
177–178; syntax of, 180. *See also* language
Mandiant, 73, 80
Mao Zedong, v, x, xxvii (n. 17), 38, 98, 102,
178. *See also* Communist Party of China
(CPC)
Marriott, 110